CALCULATED BETS
Computers, Gambling, and Mathematical Modeling to Win

This is a book about a gambling system that works. It tells how the author used computer simulations and mathematical-modeling techniques to predict the outcome of jai alai matches and bet on them successfully, thus increasing his initial stake by over 500 percent in one year! His methods can work for anyone; at the end of the book he tells the best way to watch jai alai and how to bet on it.

With humor and enthusiasm, Skiena details a life-long fascination with the computer prediction of sporting events. Along the way, he discusses other gambling systems, both successful and unsuccessful, for such games as lotto, roulette, blackjack, and the stock market. Indeed, he shows how his jai alai system functions like a miniature stock-trading system.

Do you want to learn about program trading systems, the future of Internet gambling, and the real reason brokerage houses do not offer mutual funds that invest at racetracks and frontons? How mathematical models are used in political polling? The difference between correlation and causation? If you are interested in gambling and mathematics, odds are this is the book for you!

Steven Skiena is Professor of Computer Science at the State University of New York, Stony Brook. He is the author of two popular books, *The Algorithm Design Manual* and the award-winning *Computational Discrete Mathematics*, a new edition of which is being published by Cambridge University Press. He is the recipient of the Office of Naval Research (ONR) Young Investigator's Award and the Chancellor's Award for Excellence in Teaching at Stony Brook.

OUTLOOKS
PUBLISHED BY CAMBRIDGE UNIVERSITY PRESS AND
THE MATHEMATICAL ASSOCIATION OF AMERICA

Mathematical content is not confined to mathematics. Eugene Wigner noted the unreasonable effectiveness of mathematics in the physical sciences. Deep mathematical structures also exist in areas as diverse as genetics and art, finance and music. The discovery of these mathematical structures has in turn inspired new questions within pure mathematics.

In the Outlooks series, the interplay between mathematics and other disciplines is explored. Authors reveal mathematical content, limitations, and new questions arising from this interplay, providing a provocative and novel view for mathematicians, and for others an advertisement for the mathematical outlook.

CALCULATED BETS

COMPUTERS, GAMBLING, AND
MATHEMATICAL MODELING **TO WIN**

STEVEN SKIENA

State University of New York at Stony Brook

Mathematical Association of America

CAMBRIDGE
UNIVERSITY PRESS

PUBLISHED BY THE PRESS SYNDICATE OF THE UNIVERSITY OF CAMBRIDGE
The Pitt Building, Trumpington Street, Cambridge, United Kingdom
MATHEMATICAL ASSOCIATION OF AMERICA
1529 Eighteenth Street, NW Washington, DC 20036

CAMBRIDGE UNIVERSITY PRESS
The Edinburgh Building, Cambridge CB2 2RU, UK
40 West 20th Street, New York, NY 10011-4211, USA
10 Stamford Road, Oakleigh, VIC 3166, Australia
Ruiz de Alarcón 13, 28014 Madrid, Spain
Dock House, The Waterfront, Cape Town 8001, South Africa

http://www.cambridge.org

First published 2001

Printed in the United States of America

Typefaces Utopia 9.5/13.5 pt. and ITC Kabel   *System* LaTeX 2$_\varepsilon$ [TB]

A catalog record for this book is available from the British Library.

Library of Congress Cataloging in Publication Data
Skiena, Steven S.
    Calculated bets : computers, gambling, and mathematical modeling to win /
Steven S. Skiena.
        p.   cm. – (Outlooks)
    Includes bibliographical references and index.
    ISBN 0-521-80426-4 – ISBN 0-521-00962-6 (pb.)
    1. Mathematical models.   2. Gambling – Mathematical models.
3. Jai alai – Betting.   I. Title.   II. Series.
    QA401 .S474   2001
    511'.8 – dc21   2001025483

ISBN 0 521 80426 4 hardback
ISBN 0 521 00962 6 paperback

To my parents, Morris and Ria Skiena, for introducing me to jai alai.
Children look to their parents to teach them values, and you taught
us the value of a good quiniela at an early age.

And to our new daughter Bonnie;
We look forward to teaching you the best of what our parents taught us.

CONTENTS

CONTENTS

PREFACE

This is a book about predicting the future. It describes my attempt to master a small enough corner of the universe to glimpse the events of tomorrow, today. The degree to which one can do this in my tiny toy domain tells us something about our potential to foresee larger and more interesting futures.

Considered less prosaically, this is the story of my 25-year obsession with predicting the results of jai alai matches in order to bet on them successfully. As obsessions go, it probably does not rank with yearning for the love of one you will never have or questing for the freedom of an oppressed and downtrodden people. But it is *my* obsession – one that has led me down paths that were unimaginable at the beginning of the journey.

This book marks the successful completion of my long quest and gives me a chance to share what I have learned and experienced. I think the attentive reader will come to understand the worlds of mathematics, computers, gambling, and sports quite differently after reading this book.

I tell this tale to introduce several things that have long interested me to a larger audience:

- *The joys of jai alai* – Jai alai is a spectator sport and gambling forum that is underappreciated and misunderstood by the public. I'd like to acquaint a new audience with this fun and exciting game and whet the interest of current fans by making them more aware of what determines the outcome of each match. If you stick with me, you will learn the best way to watch jai alai and bet on it.

■ *The power of mathematical modeling* – Mathematical models govern our economy and help forecast our weather. They predict who will win the election and decide whether your mortgage should be granted. However, the man on the street knows little about what mathematical models are and how they work. In this book, I use our jai alai system to explain how mathematical models are designed, built, and validated.

■ *The mathematics of money* – Gambling and mathematics have a long and interesting history together. I'll discuss other gambling systems, both successful and unsuccessful, for such games as lotto, roulette, blackjack, and the stock market. Indeed, my jai alai system functions very much as a stock-trading system in miniature. You will learn how program-trading systems work, the future of Internet gambling, and the real reason brokerage houses don't offer mutual funds that invest at racetracks and frontons.

■ *The craft of computer programming* – For most nonprogrammers, the ideas behind modern computing systems lie shrouded beneath a thick mist of buzzwords and technology. These buzzwords give no hint of the process by which computer programs are made to work or of the elegance and beauty that underlie the best software. In this book, you will discover how my students and I built a particularly interesting computer program. I use our jai alai system to explain to the layperson such computer science concepts as parsing and random number generation, why real programmers hate Microsoft, and the true glories of the Internet.

■ *The aesthetics of data* – Many people don't like the looks of charts, graphs, and tables, no matter how many colors they are printed in. But done right, such data representations can be a thing of beauty – vehicles driving us to understand the story that the numbers are trying to tell. In this book, you will get to see a variety of data sets presented in several different ways. You will get a first-hand look at how to interrogate numbers and make them talk.

Finally, this is the story of a mild-mannered professor who places money on the line to test whether his system really works. Do I hit it rich or end up a tragic, bankrupt figure? You will have to read to the end to see how I make out.

My goal has been to produce a book that will be interesting and understandable even to those with little background in each of our three main topics: jai alai, mathematics, and computing. I explain all the jai alai lingo that I use, and thus you will be able to appreciate what we are doing even if you have never been to a fronton. If you can understand how mortgage interest is calculated, you have all of the mathematical background you need to follow what we are doing. Even if you have never programmed a computer, you will be able to understand the ideas underlying our system. Either way, after reading this book you will have a better understanding of how and why computers are programmed.

Maybe you will even be inspired to try some mathematical modeling of your own! At the end of this book I suggest some possible projects to get you started.

I have tried to make this book as fun to read as it was to write. In particular, I have striven to be in the spirit of Bill James, the popular writer whose books on baseball go deeply into the essence of the game. He uses advanced statistical analysis and historical research to unearth hidden trends and overturn conventional wisdom. One perceptive review notes that part of the fun in reading his work comes from the spectacle of a first-rate mind wasting itself on baseball. Part of the fun of this book, I hope, is the spectacle of a second-rate mind wasting itself on jai alai.

ACKNOWLEDGMENTS

First and foremost, I thank Dario Vlah, Meena Nagarajan, and Roger Mailler, the three students who labored to build the system described in this book. Without the efforts of these three musketeers the project could never have been completed. I hope they enjoyed working with me half as much as I did with them. I would also like to thank our system administrators Brian Tria and Anne Kilarjian, who patiently kept our computer systems up and running, and Gene Stark, who kept the phones ringing.

I would like to thank the management of the following frontons: Dania Jai-Alai, Milford Jai-Alai, Berenson's Hartford Jai-Alai, and World Jai-Alai for providing me with records of games played at their frontons over the years. I particularly thank Bob Heussler for permission to use his jai alai action photographs as well as for his time during our field trip to Milford. Thanks are also due to Dr. Simona Rusnak Schmid, Carl Banks, *The New Brunswick Home News*, the Institute for Operations Research, and the Management Sciences (INFORMS) for permission to use copyrighted materials.

I am grateful to the people at Cambridge University Press, particularly Lauren Cowles, Caitlin Doggart, and Cathy Siddiqi, for taking a flier on this gambler's tale. Eleanor Umali of TechBooks did a great job with production. Finally, Persi Diaconis worked his magic in helping me find a publisher, and I thank him for his interest and enthusiasm.

CHAPTER ONE

THE MAKING OF A GAMBLER

My interest in jai alai began during my parents' annual escape from the cold of a New Jersey winter to the promised land of Florida. They stuffed the kids into a Ford station wagon and drove a thousand miles in 2 days each way. Florida held many attractions for a kid: the sun and the beach, Disney World, Grampa, Aunt Fanny, and Uncle Sam. But the biggest draw came to be the one night each trip when we went to a fronton, or jai alai stadium, and watched them play.

Mom was the biggest jai alai fan in the family and the real motivation behind our excursions. We loaded up the station wagon and drove to the Dania Jai-Alai fronton located midway between Miami and Fort Lauderdale. In the interests of preserving capital for later investment, my father carefully avoided the valet parking in favor of the do-it-yourself lot. We followed a trail of palm trees past the cashiers' windows into the fronton.

Walking into the fronton was an exciting experience. The playing court sat in a vast open space, three stories tall, surrounded by several tiers of stadium seating. To my eyes, at least, this was big-league, big-time sport. Particularly "cool" was the sign saying that no minors would be admitted without a parent. This was a very big deal when I was only 12 years old.

1

We followed the usher who led us to our seats. The first game had already started. We watched as the server spun like a top and hurled the goathide sphere to the green granite wall, where it rocketed off with a satisfying thunk. His opponent climbed up the sidewall to catch the ball in his basket, or cesta, and then – with one smooth motion – slung it back to whence it came. The crowd alternated between ooh and ah as the players caught and released the ball. The players barked orders to their partners in a foreign tongue, positioning each other across the almost football–field-sized court. Thunk, thunk, thunk went the volley until a well-placed ball finally eluded its defender.

After each point, the losing side would creep off the court in shame replaced by another team from the queue. The action would then resume . . . thunk, thunk, thunk . . . .

You have to visit a jai alai fronton to really appreciate the sights and sounds of the crowd. Most of the spectators, at least the most vocal ones, don't seem terribly knowledgeable about the players or game. Indeed, many are tourists or retired people who wouldn't recognize a *pelotari*, or jai alai player, if they woke up in bed with one. There is only one player they are interested in: themselves. The spectators have money riding on each and every point and are primarily concerned about the performance of their investment:

> "You stink, red."
> "Drop it, number 5."
> "Just one more point, Laxi – uh, whatever your name is."

Occasionally a more knowledgeable voice, usually with a Spanish accent, would salute a subtle play: "*Chula! Chula!*".

The really neat thing about jai alai is that events happen in discrete steps instead of as a continuous flow, and thus the game is more like tennis than basketball or horse racing. After watching a few games, I began to get the hang of the scoring system. The pause between each point gives you time to think about how the game is shaping up and what the prospects for your bet currently are. Sometimes you can look ahead and figure out an exact sequence of events that will take you to victory. "Look, if 1 beats 5 on this point, then loses to 7, and then 4 wins its next two points, the game ends 4–2–1 and I win!"

With each point, the loyalties of the crowd change rapidly. A wonderful aspect of the jai alai scoring system is that the dynamics of the game can change almost instantaneously. In baseball, you can be 12 runs ahead, and thus giving up one run costs you absolutely nothing. This is not so in jai alai. No matter how far ahead you are, the loss of a single point can kill by forcing you to sit down to watch your opponent win the match. Suddenly a team given up for dead trots back on the court, and then it becomes a whole new game.

Fan loyalty is particularly fleeting because it is often the case that a bettor now needs to defeat the same player he or she was rooting for on the previous point.

"You stink, blue."
"Drop it, number 6."
"You're my main man, Sourball. I mean Sor-ze-ball."

After we got settled into our seats, my father gave me, the oldest of the three kids, a pair of rumpled one-dollar bills. It was enough for one bet over the course of the evening. "Use it wisely," he said.

But what did wisely mean? On his way into the fronton, my father had invested 50 cents on a *Pepe's Green Card*. *Pepe's Green Card* was a one-page tout sheet printed on green cardboard. I was much too young to catch any allusion to Pepe's immigration status in the title. For each of the games played that evening, Pepe predicted who would finish first, second, and third alongside a cryptic comment about each player such as "wants to win," "tough under pressure," or "in the money."

On the top of the card, in a box on the right-hand side, Pepe listed his single "best bet" for the evening. That night, Pepe liked a 4–2–1 trifecta in the sixth match.

My brothers and I studied this strange document carefully. We liked the idea of a tout sheet. It would help us spend our money wisely. As kids, we were used to being told what to do. Why should it be any different when we were gambling?

"Boy, this is great. Pepe must really know his stuff," I said.

My brother Len agreed. "You bet! We've got nothing but winners here."

"Dad, why do other people pick their own numbers when Pepe has all the winners here?" asked Rob, the youngest.

"Pepe, my *pupik!*" came my parental voice of authority. "Pepe wouldn't know a winner if he stepped on one."

"Look, Pepe gives a best bet. A 4–2–1 trifecta in the sixth match. It can't possibly lose."

3

My father shook his head sadly. "Trifectas are the longest shots of all, the toughest bet one can make in jai alai. You have almost no chance of winning. Why don't you bet on something that gives you a better chance to win?"

In retrospect, it is clear that my father was right. To win a trifecta, you must identify the players who will come in first, second, and third – all in the correct order. There are $8 \times 7 \times 6 = 336$ possible trifectas to bet on, only one of which can occur in any given game.

But we trusted Pepe. And besides, it was now *our* money. Eventually, we convinced our father to trade in our 2 dollars for a 4–2–1 trifecta ticket on Game 6.

We waited patiently for our chosen moment.

At last the public address announcer informed us it was one minute to post time for Game 6. Last-minute bettors scrambled to the cashiers to the accompaniment of the betting clock: tick, tick, tick, tick.

The chosen game proved to be a doubles match. Eight pairs of men, each pair wearing a numbered jersey of a prescribed color, marched out to ceremonial bull-fighting music: the "March of the Toreadors." They gave the crowd a synchronized, if half-hearted, wave of the cesta, and all but the first two teams straggled back to the bench.

The betting clock completed its countdown, which was terminated by a loud buzzer announcing that betting was now closed. The referee whistled, and the first player bounced the ball and served. The game was on.

We cheered for team 2, at least until they played team 4. We switched our allegiance to team 4 up until the moment it looked like they would get too many points and win without 2 and 1 in their designated positions. We booed any other team with a high score because their success would interfere with the chances of our favorites.

We watched in fascination as player 2 held onto first place, while player 1 slid into a distant but perfectly satisfactory second-place position. When player 4 marched on the court for the second time, my mother noticed what was happening. "My G-d, only two more points and the kids win!"

This revelation only made us cheer louder. "Green! Green! Green!," I yelled.

"Four! Four! Four!," my brothers chimed in.

Player 4 got the point, leaving us only one point shy of the big payoff.

The designated representative from team 4 served the ball.

We followed up with the play-by-play: "Miss it, ooh. No, catch it! Ah! Miss it, ooh. No, catch it! Ah! Miss it . . . ."

He missed it!

Family pandemonium broke out as we waited the few moments it took for the game to become official. Our trifecta paid us $124.60 for a 2-dollar bet – an incomprehensibly large amount of money to a bunch of kids. The public address announcer, in shock, informed all in the house that *Pepe's Green Card* had picked the winning trifecta in the previous game. Mom told all in earshot that her kids had won the big one. Dad sauntered up to the cashier to collect our winnings for us, kids being forbidden from entering the betting area by state law.

We kids took the family out to dinner the next night. We experienced the thrill of being the breadwinner, hunters returning from the kill. It was indeed fun being a winner – so much fun that I starting wondering how Pepe did it. It was clear that most people in the crowd didn't understand what was going on at the fronton, but Pepe did. Maybe I could figure it out, too.

An old gambling axiom states that luck is good, but brains are better. Indeed, it took me almost 25 years, but finally I have figured it out. Let me tell you how I did it . . . .

CHAPTER TWO

WHAT IS JAI ALAI?

Jai alai is a sport of Basque origin in which opposing players or teams alternate hurling a ball against the wall and catching it until one of them finally misses and loses the point. The throwing and catching are done with an enlarged basket or cesta. The ball or pelota is made of goatskin and hard rubber, and the wall is of granite or concrete – which is a combination that leads to fast and exciting action. Jai alai is a popular spectator sport in Europe and the Americas. In the United States, it is most associated with the states of Florida, Connecticut, and Rhode Island, which permit pari-mutuel wagering on the sport.

In this chapter, we will delve deeper into the history and culture of jai alai. From the standpoint purely crass of winning money through gambling, much of this material is not strictly necessary, but a little history and culture never hurt anybody. Be my guest if you want to skip ahead to the more mercenary or technical parts of the book, but don't neglect to review the basic types of bets in jai alai and the Spectacular Seven scoring system. Understanding the implications of the scoring system is perhaps the single most important factor in successful jai alai wagering.

Much of this background material has been lifted from the fronton Websites described later in this chapter and earlier books on jai alai. I

A pelotari in action at Milford.

particularly urge readers interested in more background to explore Websites such as www.jaialai.com or my own www.jai-tech.com.

How the Game Is Played

The term *jai alai* comes from the Basque word meaning "merry festival." In the English vernacular this is sometimes spelled as it sounds, that is, "hi-li," although the use of the corrupted spelling seems to be fading.

In the Basque provinces of Spain and France, where jai alai began, the sport is known as *cesta punta. Cesta punta* is a traditional part of Basque festivals, which accounts for the connection. The Spanish call the game *pelota vasca* (Basque ball). Whatever the game itself is called, jai alai has a lingo associated with its equipment and strategy that we detail below.

EQUIPMENT

Jai alai is best viewed as a variant of handball in which two sets of players (or pelotaris) alternate throwing the ball against the wall and catching the rebound. The most important pieces of equipment, therefore, are the hand, the ball, and the wall:

7

A return from backcourt.

■ *The cesta* – Basques played early forms of jai alai with bare hands and then with leather gloves and wooden paddles until the cesta was introduced. Some credit Melchoir Curachaque with inventing the cesta after breaking his wrist in Buenos Aires in 1888. Another story gives the patent to a young French Basque who tried hurling the ball with his mother's curved wicker basket.

Either way, the word *cesta* is Spanish for basket. Every cesta is handmade to the player's specific requirements and constructed by interweaving thin reeds found exclusively in the Pyrenees Mountains through a frame of Spanish chestnut. The life of a typical cesta is only about 3 weeks. Cestas cost about $300 each, and a professional player goes through about 15 of them per year. Like cigars, cestas are stored in humidors to prevent them from getting too dry and brittle.

■ *The pelota* – Named after the Spanish word for ball, the pelota is slightly smaller than a baseball and harder than a rock. The ball's liveliness comes from its virgin rubber core, which is significantly larger than the equivalent core of a baseball. This core is covered by one layer of nylon and two outer layers of goat skin. The stitches on the pelota are embedded so as to minimize damage when it slams into the cesta.

Each pelota has a court life of only 20 minutes or so before the cover splits owing to the punishment it takes hitting the wall during play. These pelotas, which are made by hand at a cost of about $150, are then recycled by sewing on new covers and subsequently aged or "rested" for at least one month in order to regain full liveliness.

Pelotas in play have been clocked at over 180 miles per hour, which is twice the speed of a major league fast ball. The combination of hard mass and high velocity makes it a very bad idea to get in the way of a moving pelota.

Pelota is also used as the name for a sport with religious overtones played by the ancient Aztecs. Those guys took their games very seriously, for the losing team was often put up as a human sacrifice. Such policies presumably induced greater effort from the players than is seen today even at the best frontons, although modern jai alai players are able to accumulate more experience than their Aztec forebears.

■ *The Court* – The most interesting part of the playing court is the granite front wall, which makes a very satisfying clicking sound whenever a pelota hits it at high speed. At Milford Jai-Alai in Connecticut, this front wall is 34-feet high and 35-feet wide and is made of 8-inch-thick granite blocks.

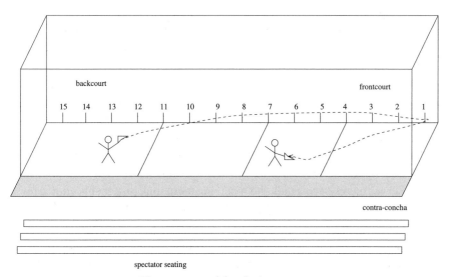

The geometry of the playing court.

9

The court (or cancha) can be thought of as a concrete box with one of the long sides of the box removed. A wooden border (the contra-cancha) extends out 15 feet on the floor outside this box. The pelota makes an unsatisfying thwack sound whenever it hits the wood, signaling that the ball is out of bounds. A wire screen prevents pelotas from leaving the court and killing the spectators, thus significantly reducing the liability insurance frontons need to carry. At Milford, the court is 178 feet long, 50 feet wide, and 46 feet tall. Although courts come in different sizes, players stick to one fronton for an entire season, which gives them time to adjust to local conditions.

The numbers from 1 to 15 are painted along the back walls of the court. The *front court* is the region near the small numbers, and the *back court* is near the big numbers. The lines marked 4, 7, and 11 designate the underserve, overserve, and serve lines, respectively. The rest of the numbers function, like pin markers in bowling, that is, only as reference points to help the players find where they are on the court.

STRATEGY

The rules of jai alai are quite similar to those of tennis and racquetball. In all of these sports, the goal is to accumulate points by making the other side misplay the ball.

All games begin with a serve that must land between the 4 and 7 lines of the court. The receiving player must catch the pelota in the air or on the first bounce and then return it to the front wall in one continuous motion. It is illegal for the player to stop the pelota's motion or to juggle it. The players continue to volley until the pelota is missed or goes out of bounds. Three judges, or referees, enforce the rules of play.

An aspect of strategy peculiar to jai alai is that the server gets to choose which ball is to be used. At each point, he may select either a lively ball, average ball, or a dead ball – all of which are available when he serves. Once the server has chosen a ball, the receiving team may inspect his choice for rips or tears and has the right to refuse the ball should they find it to be damaged in any way.

Jai alai matches are either singles or doubles matches. Doubles are more common and, in my opinion, far more interesting. The court is simply too long for any single person to chase down fast-moving balls. One key to being an effective player is correctly judging whether it will be easier to catch the ball as it flies directly off the frontwall or to wait for the rebound off the back wall. Doubles players specialize as either frontcourters or backcourters, depending upon where they are stationed. Frontcourters must be faster than the backcourters because they have more ground to cover and less time to react, whereas backcourtsmen require stronger arms to heave the pelota the full length of the court.

Understanding the court geometry is essential to appreciate the importance of shot placement. Although the ball does spin and curve, jai alai players rely more on raw power and placement than English[1] to beat their opponents. The following are the most interesting shots :

- *Chic-chac* – In this shot, the ball first hits the floor of the court close to where the floor meets the back wall and then bounces up, hits the back wall, and comes out with little or no bounce. If one is placed close enough to the crack in the wall, it becomes a . . .

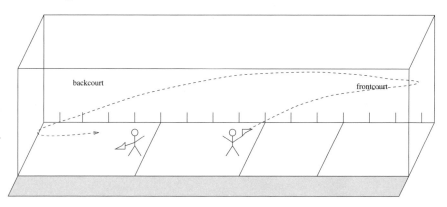

- *Chula* – Pronounced *choo-la,* this is everybody's favorite thing to yell at a jai alai match. You will hear cries of *chula* every time it looks like the ball will get wedged into the crack between the back wall and floor. The ESPN SportsCenter anchor Kenny Mayne shouts *chula* whenever a baseball batter bounces a line drive low off the outfield wall.
- *Rebote* – An attempted return after the ball bounces off the backwall. The proper technique is to dive head first towards the wall, scoop up the ball, and then fling it forward from the prone position. The

---

[1] Traditional Basque players don't rely on English much to speak, either.

rebote is considered the hardest single shot to master in jai alai.

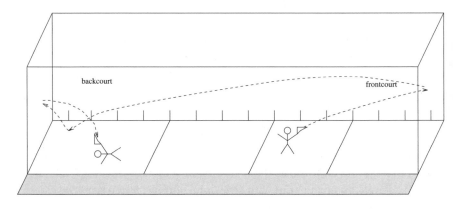

■ *Carom* – A thrown ball that hits the side wall, the front wall, and the floor, before going into the screen. This kill shot usually ends the point.

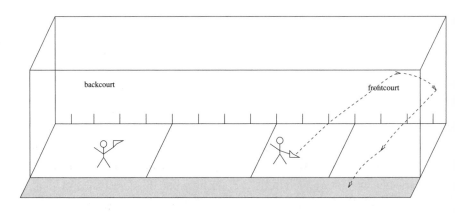

■ *Dejada* – A short lob that hits the front wall just above the foul line and drops in with a small bounce. This is the kind of shot that makes singles games boring, although it is trickier than it looks because of the spin of the ball.

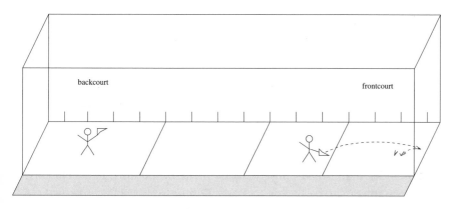

■ *Arrimada* – A ball that is returned to hug the side wall, which gives the opposition limited room to maneuver.

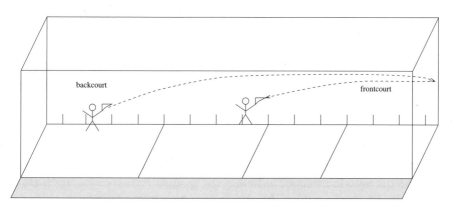

Although each point is contested by two teams of either one or two players per team, eight teams are involved in any given match. As governed by the Spectacular Seven scoring system (to be described later in this chapter in greater detail), the first two teams play, and the losing team goes to the end of the line as the winner keeps playing. Having eight teams in any given match greatly enlivens the space of betting possibilities. The composition of the teams and post (starting) positions assigned to each player changes in each match. To help the fans (and possibly the players) keep everything straight, regulations require that the shirt colors for each post position be the same at all frontons. In Florida, the shirt colors for each post position are as follows:

Post Position	1	2	3	4	5	6	7	8
Shirt Color	Red	Blue	White	Green	Black	Yellow	Brown	Purple

Because each player needs jerseys with his uniform number in each of these eight colors, laundry (and, as we will see, fairness) considerations dictate that no player appear in a particular position too often each night.

History of the Game

Tracking down definitive information on the history of jai alai posed more difficulties than I might have imagined. The best book on jai alai's early history appears to be Blazy's *La Pelote Basque* from 1929, whose neat old photos and line drawings lose none of their charm even though the book was written in French. Similarly, the definitive *Historia de la Pelota Vasca en Las Americas* is written in Spanish.

Unfortunately, if I were a pelotari, my nickname would be Monolingual. Therefore, most of the history reported below comes from less authoritative sources. Some cite legends that jai alai was invented by Saint Ignatius of Loyola, a Basque. Others sources trace the origins of the game even earlier to Adam and Eve. These same legends assure us that they spoke to each other in Basque.

THE BASQUES

About three million Basques live in their green and beautiful homeland in the Pyrenees Mountains. The land of the Basques (called *Eskual Herria* in the Basque language) straddles the border of France and Spain, comprising three French and four Spanish provinces. The Basques are a distinctive people with several unique characteristics:

- *Language* – Basque is apparently the only Western European language that does not belong to the Indo–European family of languages. Written Basque is as strange-looking as the language is strange-sounding, featuring an extraordinary number of *x*'s and an apparent disregard for vowels. The Basques refer to themselves as *Euskaldunak* or "speakers of the Euzkara." Contemporary theories suggest that Basques may have descended from early Iberian tribes, and this language presumably came with them.

  Legend states the Devil tried to learn Basque by listening behind the door of a Basque farmhouse. After 7 years, he mastered only two words: "Yes, Ma'am." This, say the Basques, is a tribute to their women as well as the difficulty of their tongue.

■ *Blood* – Blood-type frequencies cement the Basque's claims of ethnic uniqueness. They have the world's highest frequency of type O and RH negative blood. The Basques clearly are a people who did not mingle with outsiders.

■ *Toughness* – The Basques are a tough people with a strong determination to preserve their national character. They defended themselves against the Phoenicians, the Greeks, the Romans, and the Visigoths. The Basques wiped out half of Emperor Charlemagne's rear guard at the battle of the Pass of Roncesvalles. Guernica was a Basque village leveled in the Spanish Civil War and made famous by Picasso's painting; now it is the home of the largest fronton on Europe.

The Basque love of freedom continues today. For over 30 years, the terrorist group ETA (*Euskadi ta Askatasuna,* which is translated as "Basque Homeland and Liberty") has been fighting Spain to win the independence of the Basque region, killing some 800 people in the process. More recently, the spectacular new Guggenheim Museum in Bilbao has put the Basque region on the map for something other than jai alai or terrorist activities.

Indeed, the Basque region of Spain and France is a terrific place to spend a vacation. A one-week trip could combine the unique architecture of Bilbao with the spectacular beaches of San Sebastian. You can drive winding cliff roads along an unspoiled rocky coast, stopping to eat fresh seafood and *tapas,* the little plates of savory appetizers that have spread throughout Spain but originated in the Basque country. You can stop in nearby Pamplona to see the running of the bulls made famous by Hemingway. And, of course, you can watch the finest jai alai in the world.

JAI ALAI IN THE BASQUE COUNTRY

The first thing to know is that at least four types of pelota are played professionally in the Basque country, and you will see all of them if you spend enough time watching Basque television. They differ primarily in the implement used to hit the ball:

■ *Cesta punta* – This is the variation of pelota that has come to the United States as jai alai and uses a long, curved basket (cesta) for catching and throwing the ball.

- *Remonte* – This is the most challenging variation of the sport and uses a smaller, shallower basket than the cesta. Players are not permitted to catch the ball but must hit it back immediately. The result is an even quicker game than cesta punta that is a lot of fun to watch.
- *Mano* – Spanish for "hand," *mano* is just that – handball. Played on a smaller court than *cesta punta*, it remains a fast-moving game with serves that can reach speeds of over 60 miles per hour.
- *Pala* – The players whack the ball with small, flat-sided wooden clubs. *Pala* is more popular among amateur players because these clubs are considerably cheaper than baskets. Still, it amazes me that anyone succeeds in hitting a fast-moving ball with these foot-long clubs.

The Spectacular Seven scoring system is in use primarily in the United States. Much more common in France and Spain are *partidos*, in which two teams (red and blue) play to a designated number of points, usually 35 or 40. The first player to get, say, 35 points wins the match. All championship matches are partidos. Such matches can take hours to play, just like tennis matches.

In partido betting, spectators are encouraged to bet even after the game has begun. This system is quite interesting. A bookmaker sits in the center of the room, updating the odds in a computer after each point is played. The latest odds are immediately displayed on the scoreboard. The cashiers face the spectators with their own computer screens and a load of tennis balls. Any fan interested in placing a bet yells (in Basque) for the cashier to throw him or her a tennis ball, which contains a slot in which to deposit money. The fan touches his or her cheek to bet on red, or arm to bet on blue. The cashier processes this signal and the enclosed cash and returns a tennis ball with a ticket indicating the bet amount and current odds.

Setting the right odds at each point in the match presents a considerable challenge for the bookmaker. To make its money, the house shaves 16% off of all bets. The system is sufficiently complicated that I was discouraged from betting when I attended a match in Pamplona, which is a friendly gesture towards inexperience you won't see in any casino.

The first indoor fronton was built in 1798 in Markina, Spain. Not long after this, the great Spanish painter Goya designed a tapestry called the "Game of Pelota" that now hangs in the Escorial Palace near Madrid. Today, professional jai alai can be watched in Spain at frontons in Pamplona (Huarte), San Sebastian, and Guernica. In France, the premier fronton is in Saint-Jean-de-Luz, a lovely village near the sea.

Basque players dominate world jai alai. Of the 48 players on the 1998 Milford Jai-Alai roster, 30 list their nationality as Spanish Basque and 4 more as French Basque. The close-knit Basque player's association has been credited with helping to preserve the integrity of the sport by rigorously policing itself. This association eventually evolved into the International Jai-Alai Players Association (www.ijapa.com), which is a union affiliated with the United Auto Workers.

Jai alai has been played whereever Basques have lived. Before World War II, jai alai was played in Havana and such exotic places as Shanghai and Tientsin, China. The Havana fronton was one of the best in the world before Castro outlawed the sport in the late 1950s. At least until recently, jai alai was played professionally in Italy, the Philippines, Macao, and Indonesia.

Jai alai achieved international recognition when it was played in the 1992 Barcelona Olympic Games as a demonstration sport.

JAI ALAI IN THE UNITED STATES

Jai alai was introduced in the United States in 1904 at the Saint Louis World's Fair, which, if I recall correctly, was also where the ice-cream cone was first unveiled to a hungry populace. The sport caught on to such an extent that America's first permanent jai alai fronton was built in 1924 on what is now the parking lot of Hialeah racetrack in Miami, Florida. It was almost immediately destroyed in a hurricane but then quickly rebuilt. Ten years later, in 1934, wagering on jai alai was legalized in Florida. Today, jai alai contributes an estimated $200 million per year in total economic revenues to the Florida economy.

After the Basques, Americans constitute the largest population of professional jai alai players. Many of these players learned the sport at a long-standing amateur facility in North Miami or the more recent amateur fronton at Milford, Connecticut. Jai alai underwent a big boom in the mid-1970s. At its peak in 1978, there were 10 frontons in Florida, 3 in Connecticut, 2 in Nevada, and 1 in Rhode Island. Referenda to expand the sport to New Jersey and California failed by narrow margins, but further growth seemed inevitable.

However, the jai alai industry today is not what it used to be. The first problem was the long and nasty players strike, which lasted 3 years starting in 1988 and left serious wounds behind. Proclaimed "one of the biggest messes in U.S. labor history" (Balfour 1990), it directly involved

> the International Jai Alai Players Association, eight different employers in three different states, the National Labor Relations Board, two other federal agencies, three state agencies, federal courts, state courts, immigration restrictions and threatened deportations, state licensing procedures, yellow dog contracts, a secondary boycott by *employers* in Spain, Basque machismo, the governor of Florida, and the United Automobile Workers.

The strike poisoned relationships between the players and the frontons, significantly lowered the quality of play through the use of underskilled scab players, and greatly disenchanted the fans. It was a lose–lose situation for all concerned.

But even more damaging has been the competition from other forms of gambling that has been cutting heavily into the fronton's business. Since 1988, when the Florida Lottery started, the number of operating frontons there has dwindled to five (Miami, Dania, Orlando, Fort Pierce, and Ocala), the last two of which are open only part of the year. Connecticut's Hartford and Bridgeport frontons closed in the face of competition with the Mashantucket Pequot's Foxwoods Resort Casino, leaving Milford Jai-Alai as the sport's only outpost in the state.

Several prominent frontons skate on thin financial ice and are in danger of suffering the fate of Tampa Jai-Alai, which closed down on July 4, 1998. The primary hopes of the industry now rest on embracing casino gambling, and owners have been lobbying the governments of Connecticut and Florida to permit frontons to operate slot machines on the side. Besides competition, fronton owners complain about the amount of taxation they must pay. In the year before it closed, Tampa Jai-Alai paid $1.76 million to the state in taxes while reporting operating losses of over $1 million.

NORTH AMERICAN FRONTONS

In North America, professional jai alai is now played only in Florida, Connecticut, Rhode Island, and Mexico. Each fronton is owned and operated by private businessmen but licensed by the state. Frontons are good-sized businesses, like baseball teams, which, counting players, coaches, betting clerks, vendors, and support staff, can each employ several hundred people. The following are the major frontons in the United States:

- *Dania Jai-Alai* – Dania opened in 1953 as the second jai alai fronton in the United States. The fronton seats 5600 people and claims an annual attendance of over 650,000. Dania's fortunes have risen recently when the state of Florida permitted this fronton to add a poker room that operates concurrently with the jai alai matches. *Address:* 301 East Dania Beach Baleverd, Dania, Florida 33004. *Phone:* 305–949–2424. *URL:* http://www.dania-jai-alai.com/.
- *Milford Jai-Alai* – The only remaining fronton in Connecticut, it is my favorite place to see a match. Proclaimed "the Tiffany of frontons," the $9.2 million building has been written about in the *Architectural Record*. Their Worldwide Web site is updated daily, which will prove crucial for the system described in this book. *Address:* 311 Old Gate Lane, Milford, Connecticut 06460. *Phone:* 203–877–4242. *URL:* http://www.jaialai.com/.
- *Orlando–Seminole Jai-Alai* – Yes, you can combine a visit to jai alai with Disney World! Open since 1962, the Orlando–Seminole fronton seats 3163. Its new Worldwide Web site is quite slick. *Address:* 6405 South U.S. Highway 17–92, Casselberry, Florida 32730. *Phone:* 407–339–6221. *URL:* http://www.orlandojaialai.com/.
- *Miami Jai-Alai* – Opened in 1925 as the Biscayne Fronton, it has held as many as 15,000 jai alai fans for a single match. Desi Arnaz's band played the opening march here in his post-Cuba, pre-Lucy days. Miami is part of the Florida Gaming chain (formerly World Jai-Alai), which also operates Ocala Jai-Alai, Fort Pierce, and what is left of Tampa. They aggressively promote amateur jai alai, through several schools in Spain and France and one in Miami. *Address:* 3500 N. W. 37th Avenue, Miami, Florida 33142. *Phone:* 305–633–6400. *URL:* http://www.fla-gaming. com/miami/.
- *Newport Jai-Alai Sports Theater* – Open since 1976 and the only fronton in Rhode Island, Newport's Website now posts schedules and results regularly. I've never been there, but I've heard complaints from jai alai aficianados that the quality of play at this facility is substandard and that it seems to function largely as an adjunct to a casino gambling operation. One of these days I'll have to check it out. *Address:* 150

Admiral Kalibfus Road, Newport, RI 20840. *Phone:* 401–849–5000. *URL:* http://bermuda.newtonline.com/nja/.

■ *Ocala Jai-Alai* – Located near Gainesville, Florida, it offers live jai alai May through October. Ocala serves as somewhat of a farm team for American players, and thus it is a good place to see up-and-coming domestic talent. *Address:* 4601 N.W. Highway 318, Orange Lake, Florida 32686. *Phone:* 352–591–2345. *URL:* http://www.ocalajaialai.com.

■ *Fort Pierce Jai-Alai* – Part of the World Jai-Alai empire, it has been located in Port Saint Lucie County since 1974. Fort Pierce currently operates from January through April, presumably to coincide with baseball's spring training season. *Address:* 1750 South Kings Highway (at Pico's Road), Fort Pierce, Florida 34945–3099. *Phone:* 407–464–7500. *URL:* http://www.jaialai.net/.

Mexico's most prominent fronton is the Tijuana Jai-Alai Palace, which opened in 1947. More recently, frontons have opened and closed in Acapulco and Cancun.

The jai alai palace is the classiest structure on Revolucion Avenue in the tourist part of Tijuana. In front of the fronton, a statue of a pelotari with his cesta aloft strides the world. Alas, no gambling is allowed at the matches played Friday and Saturday nights in the Jai-Alai Palace, although there is a betting parlor next door that simulcasts games from Miami. There are much easier ways to lose your money in Tijuana – easier but ultimately less satisfying than jai alai. *Address:* 1100 Revolucion Ave., Tijuana, B.C. Mexico. *URL:* http://www.geocities.com/Colosseum/Sideline/7480/.

Amateur play in the United States focuses at Milford and the North Miami Jai-Alai School. All told, there are about 500 active players in the United States.

THE PLAYERS

Like all athletes, no matter how strong, no matter how talented, jai alai players are people with feelings and passions motivated by the same forces that affect us all. The rest of this book will consistently ignore the fact that players are people. Our system for predicting the outcome of jai alai matches treats players as machines that generate points according to a

TABLE 2.1. The 1998 Milford Jai-Alai Player Roster

No.	Player	Pos.	Height	Wgt.	Age	Nat.	Hometown
10	Altuna	F	6'1"	185	26	Basque	Tolosa, Sp.
11	Tino	F	5'10"	165	36	American	Milford, CT
12	Aitor	F	5'10"	165	21	Basque	Markina, Sp.
13	Aja	F	5'6"	150	32	Basque	Getxo, Sp.
14	Douglas	F	5'11"	155	29	American	Cheshire, CT
18	Sorozabal	F	5'11"	170	31	Fr/Basque	Biarritz, Fr.
19	Xabat	F	5'11"	175	26	Basque	Bolivar, Sp.
21	Olate	F	5'10"	180	23	Basque	Bolivar, Sp.
22	Eggy	F	5'10"	195	32	American	Agawam, MA
23	Zarandona	F	6'2"	190	25	Basque	Durango, Sp.
24	Urquidi	F	5'10"	175	23	Basque	Markina, Sp.
25	Tevin	F	6'1"	160	25	American	Bridgeport, CT
26	Goixarri	F	5'11"	160	27	Basque	Mutriku, Sp.
31	Jandro	F	5'6"	140	39	Span	Barcelona, Sp.
32	Beitia	F	5'10"	170	27	Basque	Mutriku, Sp.
35	Alfonso	B	5'10"	175	38	Basque	Murelaga, Sp.
36	Aragues	F	6'1"	155	25	Fr/Basque	Biarritz, Fr.
38	Liam	F	6'	165	38	American	Fairfield, CT
40	Lander	F	6'2"	185	23	Basque	Berriatua, Sp.
41	Iruta	F	6'	180	23	Basque	Markina, Sp.
42	Ara	F	5'10"	180	30	Basque	Markina, Sp.
44	Jon	F	5'9"	155	24	Basque	Berriatua, Sp.
45	Borja	F	6'	170	26	Basque	Egloibar, Sp.
46	Iker	F	5'11"	180	22	Basque	Markina, Sp.
51	Arrieta	B	5'10"	180	25	Basque	Markina, Sp.
54	Retolaza	B	6'	185	33	Basque	Markina, Sp.
55	Lasa	B	6'1"	200	36	American	East Granby CT
60	Brett	B	6'2"	190	31	American	Agawam, MA
63	Alberto	B	6'1"	180	27	Basque	Benidorm, Sp.
65	Aritz	B	5'11"	180	20	Basque	Berriatua, Sp.
66	Sergio	B	6'3"	220	25	Basque	Vitoria, Sp.
67	Ibar	B	5'8"	175	30	Basque	Markina, Sp.
68	Zabala	F	6'	175	40	Chile	Guernica, Sp.
70	Capozzo	B	6'1"	205	31	Italy	East Haven, CT
72	Azpiri	B	6'3"	175	24	Basque	Ondarroa, Sp.
73	Fitz	B	5'11"	185	29	American	Bridgeport, CT
74	Acin	B	6'1"	200	39	Fr/Basque	St. Jean De Luz, Fr.
75	Matera	B	6'	170	30	American	Milford, CT
77	Alvarez	B	5'11"	175	31	Basque	Markina, Sp.
80	Guisasola	B	6'0"	190	27	Basque	Echebarria, Sp.
81	Wayne	B	6'0"	185	24	American	Portsmouth, RI
84	Arruti	B	6'0"	175	28	Basque	Mutriku, Sp.
85	Edward	B	6'6"	195	28	American	Trumbull, CT
86	Richard	B	6'	165	30	Basque	Milford, CT
88	Raul	B	5'10"	180	31	Basque	Mutriku, Sp.
89	Baronio	B	5'10"	170	25	Fr/Basque	Anglet, Fr.
91	Jorge	B	5'9"	190	32	Basque	Markina, Sp.
92	Badiola	B	5'11"	210	38	Basque	Ondarroa, Sp.

Alfonso with the rebote at Milford.

given probability distribution. This section is the only portion of this book in which we will ignore the numbers and look at the people who have stories to tell.

Just as with soccer players, it is traditional for jai alai players (or pelotaris) to adopt a one-word player name such as Pele. Many players use their actual first or last name. The Basques often use shortened versions of their last names, which can approach 20 letters in their full glory. Other players choose their mother's maiden name, while some take the name of their home town. Brothers or children of established players often append a number to their mentor's name becoming, say, Javier II. Naturally, players prefer the fans to call them by name rather than uniform color or number.

There are stars in jai alai as there are in every sport. Many old timers consider Erdorza Menor to be the best player of all time. Perhaps the best American player was Joey Cornblit, known as Joey, who was a star for many years beginning in the early 1970s. Capturing the international essence of

Heaving the pelota the full length of the court. Can you find it?
Hint: Look in a corner of the photo.

the sport, Joey was born in Montreal of Israeli parents, grew up in Miami, and learned to speak Basque. He honed his game playing summers in Spain after turning professional at age 16.

As in baseball, many of the best players throw hard. The *Guinness Book of World Records* credits Jose Ramon Areitio with throwing the fastest ball ever. His pelota was clocked at 188 mph on Friday, August 3, 1979, at Newport Jai-Alai. This is almost twice the speed of a top-notch fast ball. Numbers like these support the claim that jai alai is the world's fastest ball game. Fortunately, the playing court is long enough to enable players and fans to follow the action.

Still the game is fast and dangerous. Since the 1920s at least four players have been killed by a jai alai ball. The only U.S. fatality occurred during the early 1930s at the old Biscayne fronton when the frontcourter Ramos was struck in the back of the head by his partner. He died a few days later. In 1967, a champion player named Orbea was hit in the head, and he lay in a coma for weeks. Ultimately he recovered, eventually becoming the player-manager at Dania and Milford jai alai. Still, this incident forced the introduction of helmets because the traditional Basque head gear (red or blue berets) didn't do much to stop a pelota. Fortunately, there have been few instances of serious head injuries ever since.

Legend recounts at least one instance of the pelota being used for self-defense. Perkain was a champion player who fled to Spain to escape the guillotine during the French Revolution. Still, he could not resist returning to France to defend his title against a French challenger. When threatened with arrest, he succeeded in making his escape by beaning the law enforcement official with the ball. Chula!

Jai alai players come in all shapes and sizes. The players on the 1998 Milford roster ranged in height from 5 feet 6 inches to 6 feet 3 inches and in weight from 140 to 220 pounds. Frontcourt players are typically shorter and quicker, for they must react to balls coming at them directly off the frontwall. Backcourt players must be stronger and more acrobatic to enable them to dive for odd bounces yet recover to toss the ball the length of a football field in one smooth motion. It is not that unusual to see players sporting substantial bellies, but appearances can be deceiving. These are highly skilled, conditioned athletes. According to pedometer studies, each player runs about one mile per game, and each player typically appears in four to six games per night, five nights per week. As in tennis, the players must be versatile enough to play both offense and defense. The sport is not as easy as it looks. Babe Ruth once tried a few shots, failing even to hit the frontwall before he concluded that the cesta was "not my racket."

Pelotaris can have long careers. Three of the members of the 1998 Milford roster (including Alfonso, shown in the figure on the page 22) have played at Milford since at least 1982. As in baseball, professional players range in age from less than 20 to over 40. Both youth and experience have their advantages on the court.

Not all players have such long careers, of course. I recently read an article in *The Jewish Week* about the Barry sisters, famous stars of the Yiddish stage. The granddaughter of Claire Barry, one of the sisters, recently married a professional jai alai player named Bryan Robbins. This newspaper account identifies Bryan as a "nice Jewish boy" and notes approvingly that he has ended his jai alai career to become a medical student.

The open wall of the court results in an asymmetry that makes it very undesirable to have the cesta on the left hand. Therefore, all professionals today are right-handed, or at least use that hand for playing jai alai. There have been exceptions, however. Marco de Villabona managed to be a competitive player after losing his right arm. A nineteenth-century player named Chiquito de Eibar was such a dominant player that he was sometimes required to play with the basket on his left hand as a handicap.

Jai alai is a male sport, although a few women have played the game on an amateur level. Perhaps the best-known amateur player was Katherine Herrington back in the 1940s, who went on to write a book on the sport after playing her last exhibition at Saint-Jean-de-Luz, France, in 1971. The legendary Tita of Cambo, a French Basque, was reputedly so strong that her serves damaged stone walls.

BETTING ON JAI ALAI

Much of the excitement of attending a jai alai match comes from being able to bet on your favorite player or outcome. Indeed, jai alai has been called "a lottery with seats." Each fronton supports a variety of different types of bets, some of which are fairly exotic, but the most popular bets are listed below. These terms should be familiar to anyone acquainted with horse racing, and we will use them throughout the rest of the book.

- *Win* – You bet that your team (or player) will win the game. There are eight possible win bets at a standard fronton.
- *Place* – You bet that your team (or player) will finish either first or second in the game. You will receive the same payoff regardless of whether your team is first or second. This is a less risky bet than picking a team to win, but the payoff is usually less as well. There are eight possible place bets at a standard fronton.
- *Show* – You bet that your team (or player) will finish either first, second, or third. This is the least risky and hence lowest-paying wager

available at most frontons. There are eight possible show bets at a standard fronton.

- *Quiniela* – You pick two teams to finish first and second. The order in which your two teams finish is irrelevant – so long as they finish 1 and 2 you receive the *quiniela* price. *Quiniela* comes from the Basque word for 'twin,' but this type of bet has spread beyond jai alai to other pari-mutuel sports as well. Personally, I find the quiniela bet to be the single most exciting choice for the spectator because it seems one always has a chance to win at some point in the match. There are $(8 \times 7)/2 = 28$ possible quiniela bets at a standard fronton.

- *Exacta* or *Perfecta* – You pick two teams to finish first and second in that given order. If you pick a 2–6 exacta, it means that 2 must win and 6 must come in second. In olden times, this used to be called a "correcta" bet. There are $(8 \times 7) = 56$ possible exacta bets at a standard fronton, which is twice that of the quiniela.

- *Trifecta* – You pick the three teams (or players) that finish first, second, and third in that exact order. If you play a 2–5–3 trifecta, then 2 must win, 5 must finish second (place), and 3 must come in third (show). There are $8 \times 7 \times 6 = 336$ possible trifecta bets at a standard fronton. Trifectas are the riskiest conventional bet, but the one that typically pays the highest returns.

Different frontons operate under slightly different betting rules. One aspect that varies is the size of the minimum bet allowed. Dania Jai-Alai currently has a $2.00 minimum bet, whereas Milford has a $3.00 minimum bet. Frontons tend not to have maximum bet limits because those are imposed by common sense. As will be discussed in Chapter 6, jai alai is a pari-mutuel sport, and thus you are trying to win money from other people, not from the house. No matter how much you invest, you can't win more money than other people have bet. We will discuss this issue more deeply later on, but as a rule of thumb there is probably from $5,000 to $15,000 bet on any given jai alai match.

Any bettor is free to make any combination of these types of bets on any given match. Indeed, frontons provide certain types of aggregate bets as a convenience to their customers.

- *Boxing* – Betting all possible combinations of a given subset of numbers. For example, a 1–2–3 trifecta box bets on all six possible trifectas, which can be built using those three numbers: 1–2–3, 1–3–2, 2–1–3, 2–3–1, 3–1–2, and 3–2–1. Ordering a box can simply be a convenience, but certain frontons allow one to bet a trifecta box at a cost that works out to less than the minimum bet per combination. Indeed, we will exploit this freedom with our own betting strategy.

■ *Wheeling* – Betting a fixed set of numbers with all other numbers used for the remaining slots. For example, a 1–2 trifecta wheel defines bets on the following six trifectas: 1–2–3, 1–2–4, 1–2–5, 1–2–6, 1–2–7, and 1–2–8. Certain venues presumably allow one to bet a trifecta wheel at a cost that works out to less than the minimum bet per combination.

Even more exotic bets, such as the Daily Double or Pick-6 (select the winners of two or six given matches), are becoming more popular because of their potentially enormous payoffs, but we won't discuss them any further.

The Spectacular Seven Scoring System

This book reports our attempt to model the outcome of jai alai matches, not horse racing or football or any other sport. The critical aspect of jai alai that makes it suitable for our kind of attack is its unique scoring system, which is unlike that of any other sport I am aware of. This scoring system has interesting mathematical properties that just beg the techno-geek to try to exploit it. For this reason, it is important to explain exactly how scoring in jai alai works.

As a pari-mutuel sport, jai alai has evolved to permit more than two players in a match. Typically, eight players participate in any given match. Let's name them 1, 2, 3, ..., 8 to reflect their position in the original order of play. Every point is a battle between only two players, with the active by pair determine by their positions in a first-in, first-out (FIFO) queue. Initially, player 1 goes up against player 2. The loser of the point goes to the end of the queue, and the winner stays on to play the fellow at the front of the line. The first player to total (typically) seven points is declared the winner of the match. Because seven is exactly one point less than the number of players, this ensures that everyone gets at least one chance in every match. Various tiebreaking strategies are used to determine the place and show positions.

Let's see some examples of how particular games might unfold. We start with Example 1, a game destined to end in a 5–1–3 trifecta. The left side of each line of the example shows the queue of players waiting their turn to compete. The two players not on this queue play the next point. As always, player 1 starts against player 2, and everybody begins with 0 points. Suppose player 1 beats player 2 (the event reported on the center of the first line). After this event, each player's updated score is shown on the right side of the table. Player 1 collects his first point and continues playing against the next player in line, player 3. The loser, player 2, sulks his way back to the bench and to the end of the player queue.

Continuing on with this example, player 1 wins his first three points before falling to player 5. For the next three points nobody can hold service, with 6 beating 5, 7 beating 6, and 8 beating 7. The survivor, 8, now faces the player sitting at the top of the queue, player 2, the loser of the opening point.

Here, the scoring system gets slightly more complicated. If you stop to think about it, a problem with any queue-based scoring system is that

EXAMPLE 1. A Simulated 5–1–3 Trifecta Illustrating Spectacular Seven Scoring

Queue						Point	Score							
1	2	3	4	5	6	winner	1	2	3	4	5	6	7	8
3	4	5	6	7	8	1–beats–2	1	0	0	0	0	0	0	0
4	5	6	7	8	2	1–beats–3	2	0	0	0	0	0	0	0
5	6	7	8	2	3	1–beats–4	3	0	0	0	0	0	0	0
6	7	8	2	3	4	5–beats–1	3	0	0	0	1	0	0	0
7	8	2	3	4	1	6–beats–5	3	0	0	0	1	1	0	0
8	2	3	4	1	5	7–beats–6	3	0	0	0	1	1	1	0
2	3	4	1	5	6	8–beats–7	3	0	0	0	1	1	1	1
3	4	1	5	6	7	8–beats–2	3	0	0	0	1	1	1	3
4	1	5	6	7	2	3–beats–8	3	0	2	0	1	1	1	3
1	5	6	7	2	8	3–beats–4	3	0	4	0	1	1	1	3
5	6	7·	2	8	4	1–beats–3	5	0	4	0	1	1	1	3
6	7	2	8	4	3	5–beats–1	5	0	4	0	3	1	1	3
7	2	8	4	3	1	5–beats–6	5	0	4	0	5	1	1	3
2	8	4	3	1	6	5–beats–7	5	0	4	0	7	1	1	3
–	–	–	–	–	–	5–1–3	5	0	4	0	7	1	1	3

the players whose initial post positions are at the bottom of the queue start out at a serious disadvantage because the earlier players have more opportunities to collect points. In order to reduce the disadvantage of late post positions, the Spectacular Seven scoring system increases the reward for each winning volley after the seventh physical point from one to two points.

Our illustrative game is now at the midgame division line. Player 8 goes against player 2 and scores on a well-placed *chic-chac*. After winning the previous point, player 8 had a score of 1. Because the contest against 2 was the eighth physical point, it counts twice as much as before, and thus the total score for player 8 goes from 1 to 3. Player 3 comes off the queue to win the next two points, giving him a score of $2 \times 2 = 4$. Player 1, the winner of the first three points, now steps forward and dethrones the current leader, giving him a total score of five points. Because the first player to get to seven points is the winner, player 1 needs only the next point for victory (remember it counts for 2). But number 5 is alive and knocks player 1 to the end of the line. Now with a total of three points, player 5 continues on to beat his next two opponents, giving him a total of seven points and the match. Player 1 (with five points) and player 3 (with four points) stand alone for place and show, resulting in a 5–1–3 trifecta.

We have now seen two aspects of the Spectacular Seven scoring system. First, it is ruthless. By losing a single volley, the leading player can be sent to the end of the line and may never get another chance to play. Second, point doubling improves the chances for players at the bottom of the queue, particularly player 8. Players 1 or 2 would have to beat their first seven opponents to win without ever going back to the queue, whereas player 8 only has to win his first four volleys (the first of which counts for 1 and the last three of which count for two points each). Because it is rare for any player to win seven in a row, the early players are penalized, and the system is *supposed* to even out.

The Spectacular Seven scoring system was introduced in the United States in the 1970s to speed up the game and add more excitement for bettors. Most games last from 8 to 14 minutes, allowing for 15 matches a night with enough time to wager in between matches. The ratio of action-to-waiting is much better in jai alai than horse racing because each race lasts only 2 or 3 minutes. The Spectacular Seven scoring system apparently emerged from a research project at the University of Miami, meaning that I have not been the first academic to be seduced by the game.

EXAMPLE 2. A Simulated 1–2–7 Trifecta Illustrating Tiebreaking for Show

Queue						Point	Score							
1	2	3	4	5	6	winner	1	2	3	4	5	6	7	8
3	4	5	6	7	8	1–beats–2	1	0	0	0	0	0	0	0
4	5	6	7	8	2	1–beats–3	2	0	0	0	0	0	0	0
5	6	7	8	2	3	1–beats–4	3	0	0	0	0	0	0	0
6	7	8	2	3	4	5–beats–1	3	0	0	0	1	0	0	0
7	8	2	3	4	1	6–beats–5	3	0	0	0	1	1	0	0
8	2	3	4	1	5	7–beats–6	3	0	0	0	1	1	1	0
2	3	4	1	5	6	7–beats–8	3	0	0	0	1	1	2	0
3	4	1	5	6	8	2–beats–7	3	2	0	0	1	1	2	0
4	1	5	6	8	7	2–beats–3	3	4	0	0	1	1	2	0
1	5	6	8	7	3	4–beats–2	3	4	0	2	1	1	2	0
5	6	8	7	3	2	1–beats–4	5	4	0	2	1	1	2	0
6	8	7	3	2	4	1–beats–5	7	4	0	2	1	1	2	0
		tiebreaker				7–beats–4	7	4	0	2	1	1	4	0
–	–	–	–	–	–	1–2–7	7	4	0	2	1	1	4	0

In Example 1, place and show were easily determined because the second and third highest point totals were unique. This is not always the case. Our second example shows a match in which two players are tied for second at the moment player 1 has won the match. In this case, a one-point tiebreaker suffices to determine place and show. In general, tiebreaking can be a complicated matter. Consider the final example in which *four* players simultaneously tie for third place. The complete rules of the Spectacular Seven describe how to resolve such complicated scenarios. Sometimes higher point totals are required in Spectacular Seven matches; for example, the target is often nine points in superfecta games, allowing win-place-show-fourth wagering. The system naturally extends to doubles play by treating each two-man team as a single two-headed player.

But Isn't It Fixed?

Bookies and bettors alike are not interested in wagering on professional wrestling, which is a situation unique among nationally televised sports. The reason is not that fans don't care about who is going to win a given

EXAMPLE 3. A Simulated 1–8–5 Trifecta Illustrating More Complex Tiebreaking

Queue						Point	Score							
1	2	3	4	5	6	winner	1	2	3	4	5	6	7	8
3	4	5	6	7	8	1–beats–2	1	0	0	0	0	0	0	0
4	5	6	7	8	2	1–beats–3	2	0	0	0	0	0	0	0
5	6	7	8	2	3	1–beats–4	3	0	0	0	0	0	0	0
6	7	8	2	3	4	1–beats–5	4	0	0	0	0	0	0	0
7	8	2	3	4	5	1–beats–6	5	0	0	0	0	0	0	0
8	2	3	4	5	6	1–beats–7	6	0	0	0	0	0	0	0
2	3	4	5	6	7	8–beats–1	6	0	0	0	0	0	0	1
3	4	5	6	7	1	8–beats–2	6	0	0	0	0	0	0	3
4	5	6	7	1	2	8–beats–3	6	0	0	0	0	0	0	5
5	6	7	1	2	3	4–beats–8	6	0	0	2	0	0	0	5
6	7	1	2	3	8	5–beats–4	6	0	0	2	2	0	0	5
7	1	2	3	8	4	6–beats–5	6	0	0	2	2	2	0	5
1	2	3	8	4	5	7–beats–6	6	0	0	2	2	2	2	5
2	3	8	4	5	6	1–beats–7	8	0	0	2	2	2	2	5
6	7	–	–	–	–	5–beats–4	8	0	0	2	4	2	2	5
5	–	–	–	–	–	7–beats–6	8	0	0	2	4	2	4	5
–	–	–	–	–	–	5–beats–7	8	0	0	2	6	2	4	5
–	–	–	–	–	–	1–8–5	8	0	0	2	6	2	4	5

match – they cheer madly for Stone Cold Steven Austin and their favorite stars. The problem isn't market size because more people watch professional wrestling than professional hockey games and hence are potential bettors. The problem *certainly* isn't that people have ceased looking for new opportunities to gamble, for you can now get odds on anything from the presidential election to the pregame coin toss at the Super Bowl.

Professional wrestling has no chance to succeed as a gambling venue because the betting public understands that the results of wrestling matches are choreographed in advance. Hence, to someone in the know, there is no uncertainty at all about who will win. I wouldn't accept a bet from anyone who might really know the outcome beforehand, and neither would you.

Many people are afraid to bet on jai alai because they are betting on players who happen to be people. Professional players want to win. But give them sufficient financial incentive to lose, and they will lose. In horse racing, you can be pretty sure that the horse did not bet on the race, but such confidence seems misplaced in jai alai.[2]

Obviously, the frontons themselves have a strong incentive to avoid betting scandals. Anything that scares away potential bettors is a fundamental threat to their business. Every fronton pays players both a fixed salary and a bonus for each game they win, and thus they have incentive to play hard and win. The frontons have strong rules against match fixing, and any player not on the up-and-up will become persona non grata at every fronton in the world. Players at a top fronton like Milford earn in the ballpark of $50,000 over the course of an 8-month season (for stars the earnings go into six figures), and thus they do have incentive to play fairly.

In the course of my research for this book, I have uncovered only limited discussions of crooked jai alai betting. Nasty things apparently occurred in the United States in the late 1970s, which no one likes to talk about today, but several Florida and California state documents from the 1950s and 1960s I studied stress that the sport had no whiff of scandal up to that point. They credited this to a strong players union and the close-knit structure of the Basque community, which polices its own. It is hard for an outsider to fix a game with a player who speaks only Basque.

The one game-fixing scandal I have seen documented occurred in Florida, apparently during the strike years, when underskilled and undedicated scab players roamed the court. Groups of three or four players per match were bribed by the fixer to play dead, who then bought multiple quiniela boxes covering all pairs of honest players. The betting volume required to turn a profit on the deal was also high enough to catch the attention of the fronton. Eventually, it was used to help convict the head fixer in criminal court.

The nature of jai alai particularly lends itself to suspicions of fixing. Players have to catch a rock-hard ball hurled at 150 miles per hour using an outsized basket strapped to their arm. Often, a seemingly catchable ball will dribble out of a player's cesta, and immediately cries of "fix" will come from bettors who have invested on this player's behalf. But let's be fair. The width of the cesta in the area where the ball enters is only 3 to 3.5 inches,

---

[2] Of course, one may be concerned about the jockey's possible investment strategy.

whereas the diameter of the ball is almost 2 inches. This leaves only an inch or so as the margin of error, which is not much – especially when the ball is curving or wobbling.

The fan's fear of cheating has some interesting consequences. The published program listing the schedule for each match always includes each player's birthdate, even though some of the players are quite long in the tooth. Why? I've heard that suspicious fans think that Joey's fellow players will, as a present, let him win matches on his birthday, and these bettors want to share in the celebration.

All this said, we don't worry about fixes in our betting system and won't concern ourselves with them any more in this book. Why? That our system predicts the outcome of jai alai matches much better than chance tells us that most games are not fixed. Even the most cynical bettor will admit that performing a successful fix requires a certain amount of energy, investment, and risk. These considerations dictate that only a small fraction of games will be fixed. For a system like ours, which relies on making lots of small bets instead of a few big ones, fixes can be written off as a cost of doing business. Spend too much time worrying about fixes and you turn into a conspiracy theorist and then a nut case. I have the serenity to accept the things I cannot change.

Other Betting Systems

Betting systems have existed for as long as gambling has. A betting system is either bogus or clever, depending upon whether it is based on a sufficiently deep understanding of the given game so that there is some method to the madness.

Gambling systems, even bogus ones, are always interesting to hear about because they say something about how people perceive (or misperceive) probability. My favorite bogus systems include the following:

- *Doubling up in casino gambling* – Consider the following strategy for gambling in roulette. Walk into the casino and bet a dollar on black. If it wins, boldly pocket your earnings. If not, bet $1 again on black. If it wins, you are back to where you started. If it loses, bet $2 on black to recoup your losses. After each loss, keep doubling up. Inevitably, you are going to win sometime, and at that point you are all caught up. Now you can start again from the beginning. You can't ever lose money with this scheme, can you?

What's the problem? Nothing really, so long as you have an infinitely deep pocket and are playing on a table without a betting limit. If your table *has* a betting limit or you are not able to print money, you will eventually reach a point at which the house will not let you bet as much as you need in order to play by this system. At this point you will have been completely wiped out.

This doubling or Martingale system offers you a high probability of small returns in exchange for a small possibility of becoming homeless. Casinos are more than happy to let you take this chance. After all, Donald Trump has a much deeper pocket than either you or I have.

■ *The O'Hare straddle* – An alternate doubling scheme is as follows: Borrow a large amount of cash on a short-term basis. Set aside enough money for a ticket on the next plane to South America. Bet the rest on one spin of the roulette wheel at even money. If you win, return the principal and retire on the rest. Otherwise, use the plane ticket.

Mathematically, the key to making this work is being bold enough to wager all the money on a single bet rather than making multiple smaller bets. The casino extracts a tax on each "even-money" wager via the 0 and 00 slots on the wheel. You pay more tax each time you re-bet the winnings, thus lowering your chances of a big killing. However, the most likely result of playing the O'Hare straddle will be a sudden need to increase your fluency in Spanish.

■ *Collecting statistics on lottery numbers* – Some people carefully chart the frequency with which lottery numbers have come in recently and then play the numbers that are either "due" or "hot." Unfortunately, the notion of a number "being due" or "being hot" violates all laws of probability (technically the assumption that the numbers arise from independent Bernoulli trials). Lottery numbers are selected by drawing numbered balls from a jar, or some equivalent method. Provided that the balls have been thoroughly mixed up, there is no way a ball can "know" that it has not been selected for a while and hence is due. Similarly, the notion of a number's "being hot" makes sense only when the numbers have been drawn according to a nonuniform random number generator.

As we will see, poor random number generators certainly exist; I will talk more about this in Chapter 3. There is also historical precedent for poorly mixed-up balls. During the Vietnam War, the U.S. military draft selected soldiers by lottery according to birthday. A total of 365 balls, each bearing one possible birthdate, were tossed into a jar, and unlucky 19-year-olds were mustered into the army if their birthdate was selected. In 1970, several newspapers observed that December's children had a startlingly high chance of being drafted, and indeed, the lottery selection procedure turned out to be flawed. It was fixed for the next year, which was presumably small consolation to those left marching in the rice paddies.

Although each lottery combination is just as likely to come in as any other, there is one formally justifiable criterion you can use in picking lottery numbers. It makes a great deal of sense to try to pick a set of numbers nobody else has selected because, if your ticket is a winner, you won't have to share the prize with anybody else who is a winner. For this reason, playing any ticket with a simple pattern of numbers is likely to be a mistake, for someone else might stumble across the same simple pattern. I would avoid such patterns as 2–4–6–8–10–12 and even such numerical sequences as the primes 2–3–5–7–11–13 or the Fibonacci numbers 1–2–3–5–8–13 because there are just too many mathematicians out there for you to keep the prize to yourself.

There are probably too many of whatever-you-are-interested-in as well; thus, stick to truly random sequences of numbers unless you like to share. Indeed, my favorite idea for a movie would be to have one of the very simple and popular patterns of lottery numbers come up a winner; say, the numbers resulting from filling in the entire top row on the ticket form. As a result, several hundred people will honestly think they won the big prize only later to discover it is not really so long (only $5,000 or so). This will not be enough to get members of the star-studded ensemble cast out of the trouble they got into the instant they thought they became millionaires.

On the other hand, well-founded betting systems are available for certain games *if* you know what your are doing:

■ *Card counting in blackjack* – Blackjack is unique among casino games in that a sufficiently clever player can indeed have an advantage over the house. In blackjack, each player starts with two cards, and the goal is to collect a set of cards whose total points are as close to 21 as possible without going over. The key decision for any player is whether to accept an additional unknown card from the house. This card will increase your point total, which is good, unless it takes you over 21, which is bad. You win money if your total is closer to 21 than the dealer's, who must play according to a well-defined strategy.

If you know nothing about the cards you are to be dealt, the dealer's strategy is sufficient to guarantee the house a nice advantage. However, a sufficiently clever player *does* know something about the hand he or she will be dealt. Why? Suppose in the previous hand the player saw that all four aces had been dealt out. If the cards had not been reshuffled, all of those aces would have been sitting in the discard pile. If it is assumed that only one deck of cards is being dealt from, there is no possibility of seeing an ace in the next hand, and a clever player can bet accordingly. By keeping track of what cards he or she has seen (*card counting*) and properly interpreting the results, the player knows the true odds that each card will show up and thus can adjust strategy accordingly. Card counters theoretically have an inherent advantage of up to 1.5% against the casino, depending upon which system they use.

Edward Thorp's book *Beat the Dealer* started the card-counting craze in 1962. Equipped with computer-generated counting charts and a fair amount of chutzpah, Thorp took on the casinos. Once it became clear (1) that he was winning, and (2) it wasn't just luck, the casinos became quite unfriendly. Most states permit casinos to expel any player they want, and it is usually fairly easy for a casino to detect and expel a successful card counter. Even without expulsion, casinos have made things more difficult for card counters by increasing the number of decks in play at one time. If 10 decks are in play, seeing 4 aces means that there are still 36 aces to go, greatly decreasing the potential advantage of counting.

For these reasons, the most successful card counters are the ones who write books that less successful players buy. Thorp himself was driven out of casino gambling in Wall Street, where he was reduced to running a hedge fund worth hundreds of millions of dollars. Still, almost every mathematically oriented gambler has been intrigued by card counting at one point or another. Gene Stark, a colleague of mine about whom you'll read more later, devised his own card-counting system and used it successfully a few times in Atlantic City. However, he discovered that making significant money off a 1.5% advantage over the house requires a large investment of either time or money. It isn't any more fun making $5.50 an hour counting cards than it is tending a cash register.

■ *The eudaemonic pie* – Physicists tend to be good at mathematics. A few years ago, the American Physical Society had its annual convention in Las Vegas, during which the combination conference hotel and casino took a serious financial hit. The hotel rented out rooms to the conference at below cost, planning to make the difference back and more from the gambling losses of conference goers. However, the physicists just would not gamble. They knew that the only way to win was not to play the game.

But another group of physicists did once develop a sound way to beat the game of roulette. A roulette wheel consists of two parts, a moving inner wheel and a stationary outer wheel. To determine the next "random" number, the inner wheel is set spinning, and then the ball is sent rolling along the rim of the outer wheel. Things rattle around for several seconds before the ball drops down into its slot, and people are allowed to bet over this interval. However, in theory, the winning number is preordained from the speed of the ball, the speed of the wheel, and the starting position of each. All you have to do is measure these quantities to sufficient accuracy and work through the physics.

As reported in Thomas Bass's entertaining book *The Eudaemonic Pie*, this team built a computer small enough to fit in the heel of a shoe and programmed in the necessary equations. Finger or toe presses at reference points on the wheel were used to enter the observed speed of the ball. It was necessary to conceal this computer carefully; otherwise, casinos would have been certain to ban the players the moment they started winning.

Did it work? Yes, although they never quite made the big score in roulette. Like Thorp, the principals behind this scheme were eventually driven to Wall Street, building systems to bet on stocks and commodities instead of following the bouncing ball. Their later adventures are reported in the sequel, *The Predictors*.

■ *Flooding large lottery pools* – Lotteries in the United States keep getting bigger. The bigger a jackpot, the more that people want to play.

Many states have switched to systems of accumulated pools in which, if no grand prize winner emerges in a given week, the money rolls over to supplement next week's prize. The pool grows very large whenever a few weeks go by without a winner. Whenever the pool gets large enough (say $100 million), it starts a betting frenzy that draws national attention.

The interesting aspect of large pools is that any wager, no matter how small the probability of success, can yield positive expected returns given a sufficiently high payoff. Most state lotteries are obligated to pay some fraction (say 50%) of all betting receipts back to the bettors. If nobody guesses right for a sufficiently long time, the potential payoff for a winning ticket can overcome the vanishingly small odds of winning. For any lottery, there exists a pool size sufficient to ensure a positive expected return if only a given number of tickets are sold.

But once it pays to buy one lottery ticket, then it pays to buy *all* of them. This has not escaped the attention of large syndicates that place bets totaling millions of dollars on all possible combinations, thus ensuring themselves a winning ticket.

State lottery agents frown on such betting syndicates, not because they lose money (the cost of the large pool has been paid by the lack of winners over the previous few weeks) but because printing millions of tickets ties up agents throughout the state and discourages the rest of the betting public. Still, these syndicates like a discouraged public. The only danger they face is other bettors who also pick the winning numbers, for the pool must be shared with these other parties. Given an estimate of how many tickets will be bought by the public, this risk can be accurately measured by the syndicate to determine whether to go for it.

Syndicate betting has also occurred in jai alai in a big way. Palm Beach Jai-Alai ran an accumulated Pick-6 pool that paid off only if a bettor correctly picked the winners of six designated matches. This was quite a challenge because each two-dollar bet was an $8^6 = 262,144$-to-1 shot for the jackpot.

On March 1, 1983, the pool stood at $551,332 after accumulating over 147 nights. This amount was more than it would have cost to buy one of every possible ticket. That day, an anonymous syndicate invested an additional $524,288 to guarantee itself a large profit, but only if it didn't have to share. Only $21,956 was wagered on Pick 6 that night by other bettors, giving the syndicate an almost 96% chance of keeping the entire pot to itself, which were terrific odds in its favor. Indeed, only the syndicate held the winning combo of 4–7–7–6–2–1, a ticket worth $790,662.20.

CHAPTER THREE

MONTE CARLO ON THE TUNDRA

Several years passed from that carefree winter day when *Pepe's Green Card* led me to my first trifecta. I found myself in high school taking a course in computer programming and got myself hooked. It was very empowering to be able tell a machine what to do and have it do exactly what I asked. All I had to do was figure out what to ask it.

I Was a High School Bookie

During my sophomore year of high school, I got the idea of writing a program that would predict the outcome of professional football games. Frankly, I wasn't too interested in football as a sport (I remain a baseball fan at heart), but I observed several of my classmates betting their lunch money on the outcome of the weekend football games. It seemed clear to me that writing a program that accurately predicted the outcome of football games could have significant value and would be a very cool thing to do besides.

In retrospect, the program I came up with now seems hopelessly crude. It first read in the statistics for teams x and y; stats such as the total number of points scored this year, the total number of points allowed, and the number of games played so far. My program averaged the points scored by team x and the points allowed by team y to predict the number of points *x* would score against *y*.

$$P_x = \frac{(\text{points scored by team } x) + (\text{points allowed by team } y)}{2 \times (\text{games played})}$$

$$P_y = \frac{[(\text{points scored by team } y) + (\text{points allowed by team } x)]}{2 \times (\text{games played})}$$

For example, suppose the Cowboys were playing the Saints. The champion Cowboys had scored 300 points and given up 200, whereas the perennial doormat Saints had scored 200 and given up 400 points, each team having played 10 games. The formulas above would predict the Cowboys to beat the Saints by a score of $(300 + 400)/(2 \times 10) = 35$ to $(200 + 200)/(2 \times 10) = 20$. I would then adjust these numbers up or down in response to 15 other factors, such as yards for and against and home field advantage, round the numbers appropriately, and call what was left my predicted score for the game.

This computer program, *Clyde*, was my first attempt to build a mathematical model of some aspect of the real world. This model had a certain amount of logic going for it. Good teams score more points than they allow, whereas bad teams allow more points than they score. If team *x* plays a team *y* that has given up a lot of points, then *x* should score more points against *y* than it does against teams with better defenses. Similarly, the more points team *x* has scored against the rest of the league, the more points it is likely to score against *y*.

Of course, this very crude model couldn't capture all aspects of football reality. Suppose team *x* has been playing all stiffs thus far in the season, whereas team *y* has been playing the best teams in the league. Team *y* might be a much better team than *x* even though its record so far is poor. This model also ignores any injuries a team is suffering from, whether the weather is hot or cold, and whether the team is hot or cold. It disregards all the factors that make sports inherently unpredictable.

And yet, even such a simple model can do a reasonable job of predicting the outcome of football games. If you compute the point averages as above and give the home team an additional 3 points as a bonus, you will pick the winner of about 2/3 of all football games, whereas the even cruder model of flipping a coin predicts only half the games correctly.

41

That was the first major lesson *Clyde* taught me:

☞ **Even crude mathematical models can have real predictive power.**

As an audacious 16-year-old, I wrote to our local newspaper, *The New Brunswick Home News*, explaining that I had a computer program to predict football games and offering them the exclusive opportunity to publish my predictions each week. Remember that this was back in 1977, well before personal computers had registered on the public consciousness. In those days, the idea of a high school kid actually *using* a computer had considerable gee-whiz novelty value. To appreciate how much times have changed, check out the article the paper published about *Clyde* and me.

I got the job. *Clyde* predicted the outcome of each game in the 1977 National Football League. It was very cool seeing my name in print each week and monitoring the football scores each Sunday to see how *we* were doing. As I recall, *Clyde* and I finished the season with the seemingly impressive record of 135–70. Each week, my predictions would be compared against those of the newspaper's sportswriters. As I recall, we all finished within a few games of each other, although most of the sportswriters finished with better records than the computer.

The *Home News* was so impressed by my work that they didn't renew me the following season. However, for the 1978 season *Clyde's* picks were published in the *Philadelphia Inquirer*, a much bigger newspaper. I didn't have the column to myself, though. Instead, the *Inquirer* included me among 10 amateur and professional prognosticators. Each week we had to predict the outcomes of four games against the point spread.

The point spread in football is a way of handicapping stronger teams for betting purposes. Think back to the Cowboys and Saints football game described earlier. It would be impossible to find a bookie who would let you bet on the Cowboys to win at even-money odds because any Saints victory required a miracle substantial enough to get canonized in the first place. Instead, the bookies would publish a point spread like *Cowboys by 14 points*. If you bet on the Cowboys, they had to win by at least 14 points for you to win the bet. The Saints could lose the game by 10 points and still leave their betting fans cheering. The point spread is designed to make each game a 50–50 proposition and hence makes predicting the outcome of games much harder.

Clyde and I didn't do very well against the spread during the 1978 National Football League season, and neither did most of the other

Student uses computers to predict football winners

By JEFF LEEBAW
Home News staff writer

EAST BRUNSWICK — A 16-year-old East Brunswick High School student has found a way to combine an interest in football with a fascination for computers.

Steven Skiena says he can determine, with a high degree of accuracy, the outcome of professional football games by feeding a computer pertinent information about competing teams.

"The winners will almost always be correct," said the high school junior who lives at 5 Currier Road off Dunhams Corner Road. "I had an 86 per cent accuracy rate when I started predicting at the end of last season."

He does it by feeding the computer a myriad of statistics that include team records, points scored and allowed, average yards gained and allowed during a game, a breakdown of the yards gained and allowed into rushing and passing categories, performances at home and on the road, and more.

The information is gathered from weekly compilations of football statistics and standings. Skiena puts the facts on index cards and then types them into one of the six computer terminals at the high school or a terminal at The Library where he works part-time after school.

"I get a winning team, a decimal score for each team and a point spread," said the teen-ager who completed a computer programming course last year at the high school.

His first attempt at picking winners involved a Monday night game between the Oakland Raiders, the eventual Super Bowl victors, and the Cincinnati Bengals.

It was a difficult game to analyze because Cincinnati was fighting for a playoff berth while Oakland had already clinched a spot in the post season competition.

"Nobody knew whether Oakland would be giving 100 per cent," Skiena said. "But my calculations indicated they would win by 24-20. The final score was 35-20. They went all out."

Skiena said he went on to pick 12 of the 14 winners the following week and accurately predicted Oakland would defeat Minnesota in the Super Bowl.

The National Football League's 1976 Record Book, which breaks down last year's statistics for each of the league's 28 teams, will supply most of the information for the first few weeks of the 1977 season. He will also use statistics from the final two exhibition games played this year by each of the teams.

Skiena wrote a computer program based on 17 statistical variables that might come into play during a football game.

The computer, in essence, asks him questions and he types the answers.

"It starts out by asking for the names of the teams," he said. "Then it will ask for records, points scored, etc...."

The computer program also attempts to include such intangible variables as injuries.

"The injuries are broken down into offense, defense and quarterback," he explained. "Obviously a quarterback injury is the most serious. It's too difficult to break down injuries for every position. When the computer asks for the number of injuries on defense, I'll type in one, two or whatever the figure is."

Will Skiena use his computer results to enter the variety of football pools and contests that are available during the season?

"No," he said. "I don't like to bet on my own predictions. Last season a friend bet on a game I predicted and it happened to be one of the few that were wrong."

STEVEN SKIENA
...to test his accuracy

Predictions published

Steven Skiena will get a chance to display his skill as a pro football prognosticator each Sunday in The Home News.

The youngster's weekly selections will be an "added ingredient to our football coverage," according to Home News Executive Editor Robert E. Rhodes.

"I think it's interesting enough for us to give it a shot," Rhodes said of the teen-ager's computer method of determining the outcome of games. "He seems like an earnest young man and we'll stand behind him."

Skiena will receive a "modest stipend" for predicting the winners, scores for each team and briefly explaining the reasons for his conclusions.

His column will appear for the first time in Sunday's sports section when the National Football League (NFL) opens its 1977 season with a slate of 13 games. Skiena will also predict the outcome of the league's Monday night games.

The Home News is publishing the column in the sports section to test the youngster's system and to offer football fans an entertaining feature. Its purpose is not to encourage betting.

"We'll be printing his selections close enough to the time of the game to prevent betting," Rhodes said. "There's big interest in pro football and more than anything else we want to test his system. I'll be rooting for him."

My first attempt at mathematical modeling.

43

Philadelphia Inquirer touts. We predicted only 46% of our games correctly against the spread, which was a performance good (or bad) enough to finish 7th out of the 10 published prognosticators. We did somewhat better on the game we selected as our best bet of the week, finishing 12–8 and in second place among the touts. Still, picking against the spread taught me a second major life lesson:

☞ **Crude mathematical models do not have real predictive power when there is real money on the line.**

Clyde finished his career with 4 years of picking the results of University of Virginia football games for our student newspaper, *The Cavalier Daily*. Our results were about the same as with the pros. We went 35–19–1, correct on the easy games and wrong on the hard ones.

Clyde's most memorable moment at the University of Virginia came when I was hired to help tutor a member of the football team. Randy was a linebacker, 6 feet 6 inches and 270 pounds. One day I asked him what he thought of *Clyde* in the newspaper, not letting on that I was the man behind the program. He assured me that the entire team felt *Clyde* didn't know bleep.

This taught me a third major life lesson:

☞ **Never argue with a 6-foot 6-inch 270-pound linebacker.**

Back to Jai Alai

Every other winter or so our family migrated down to Florida for fun in the sun and a night at the fronton. Sometimes *Pepe's Green Card* enabled us to break even for the night; other times it let us down. This mixed record impressed upon me the benefits of finding winners for ourselves.

The more jai alai I watched, the more it became apparent to me that the Spectacular Seven scoring system exerted a profound effect on the outcome of jai alai matches. Even a cursory look at the statistics revealed that certain positions were far easier to win from than others. It was simply not the case that good teams would usually beat bad ones, because the arbitrarily chosen position from which you started in the queue made a big difference in how many chances you had to score the required points. If a good team got a bad starting position, its chances of winning might be less than that of a bad team in a good starting position. A good team in a good starting position had a real advantage; them that has, gets.

The Spectacular Seven scoring system means that life isn't fair. Modern business ethics teach us that, whenever you see an unfair situation, you should exploit it for as much personal gain as possible.

How could I exploit the biases of the Spectacular Seven scoring system? I'd have to start by building a mathematical model of the situation, a simulation of the series of events that unfold during each jai alai match. The simple ideas underlying my football program were simply not sufficient for such a complex reality. However, I could get a handle on the situation using the powerful technique of *Monte Carlo* simulation.

Monte Carlo Simulations

Simulations provide insight into complex problems. Simulation is used in economics, engineering, and the physical sciences because it is often impossible to experiment on the real thing. Economists cannot play with the U.S. budget deficit and see how long it takes for the economy to collapse. Rather, they will make a computer model and study the effects of such spending on it. The significance of the simulation results depends on the accuracy of the model as well as how correctly the model has been turned into a computer program.

There are a wide variety of computer simulation techniques, but we will employ a curious method known as *Monte Carlo simulation.* "Monte Carlo" should conjure up an image of a swank casino on the French Riviera, and hence seem particularly appropriate as a technique to model a form of gambling. However, this connection is even deeper because the whole idea of Monte Carlo simulation is to mimic random games of chance.

Suppose we want to compute the odds of winning a particularly exotic bet in roulette, such as having the ball land in a prime-numbered slot (either 2, 3, 5, 7, 11, 13, 17, 19, 23, 29, or 31) three out of the next four times we spin the wheel. The most naive approach would be to watch a roulette wheel in action for a spell, keeping track of how often we win. If we watched for 1000 trials and won 91 times in this interval, the odds should be about 1 in 10. To get a more accurate estimate, we could simply watch the game for a longer period.

Now suppose instead of watching a real roulette wheel in action we simulate the random behavior of the wheel with a computer. We can conduct the same experiments in a computer program instead of a casino, and the fraction of simulated wins to simulated chances gives us the approximate odds – provided our roulette wheel simulation is accurate.

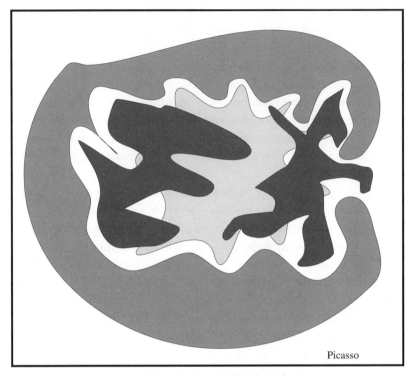

Picasso

A Picasso-like painting of oddly shaped areas.

Monte Carlo simulations are used for far more important applications than just modeling gambling. A classical application of the technique is in mathematical *integration,* which (if you ever took calculus) you may recall is a fancy term for computing the geometric area of a region. Calculus-based methods for integration require fancy mathematical techniques to do the job. Monte Carlo techniques enable you to estimate areas using nothing more than a dart board.

Suppose someone gave you this Picasso-like painting consisting of oddly shaped red, yellow, and blue swirls, and asked you to compute what fraction of the area of the painting is red. Computing the area of the entire picture is easy because it is rectangular and the area of a rectangle is simply its height times its width. But what can we do to figure out the area of the weirdly shaped blobs?

If you throw darts the way I do, it doesn't matter much whether you keep your eyes open or closed. Exactly where the darts land is pretty much a random event. Now suppose that I start blindly throwing darts in the general direction of the painting. Some are going to clang off the wall, but others will occasionally hit the painting and stick there. If I throw the darts randomly at the painting, there will be no particular bias towards hitting a particular part of the painting – red is no more a dart-attractor than yellow is a dart-repeller. Thus, if more darts hit the red region than the yellow region, what can we conclude? There had to be more space for darts to hit the red region that the yellow one, and hence the red area has to be bigger than the yellow area.

Suppose after we have hit the painting with 100 darts, 46 hit red, 12 hit blue, 13 hit yellow, and 29 hit the white area within the frame. We can conclude that roughly half of the painting is red. If we need a more accurate measure, we can keep throwing more darts at the painting until we have sufficient confidence in our results.

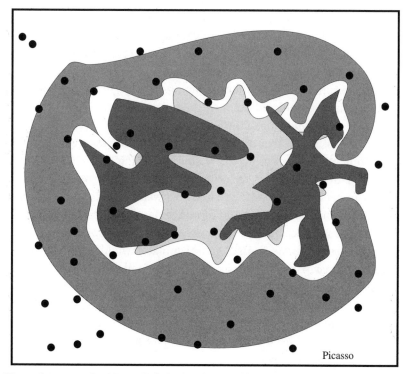

Picasso

Measuring area using Monte Carlo integration. Random points are distributed among the colored regions of the painting roughly according to the fraction of area beneath.

Of course, throwing real darts at a real Picasso painting would be an expensive exercise. It would be much better to perform the entire experiment with a computer. Suppose we scan in an image of the painting and randomly select points from this image. Each random point represents the tip of a virtual dart. By counting the number of selected points of each color, we can estimate the area of each region to as high a degree of accuracy as we are willing to wait for.

I hope these examples have made the idea of Monte Carlo simulation clear. Basically, we must perform enough random trials on a computer to get a good estimate of what is likely to happen in real life. I will explain where the random numbers come from later. But first, I'll show how to build a simulated jai alai match from random numbers.

Building the Simulation

A simulation is a special type of mathematical model – one that aims to replicate some form of real-world phenomenon instead of just predicting it. A simulation of a football game would attempt to "play" the game in question step-by-step to see what might happen. The simulated football game would start with a simulated kickoff and advance through a simulated set of downs, during which the simulated team would either score or give up the simulated ball. After predicting what might happen on every single play in the simulated game, the program could produce a predicted final score as the outcome of the simulated game.

By contrast, my football-picking program *Clyde* was a statistical model, not a simulation. *Clyde* really knew almost nothing that was specific to football. Indeed, the basic technique of averaging the points for-and-against to get a score should work just as well to predict baseball and basketball scores. The key to building an accurate statistical model is picking the right statistical factors and weighing them appropriately.

Building an accurate football-game simulator would be an immensely challenging task. The outcome of each play in football depends on many complicated factors, including the skill matchups between each of the 11 sets of players, how tired or injured each of them are, the offensive and defensive alignments of each team, the coach's strategy, the game situation, and the current field conditions. Jai alai is, by contrast, a much simpler game to simulate.

What events in a jai alai match must we simulate? Each match starts with players 1 and 2 playing and the rest of the players waiting patiently in line. All players start the game with scores of zero points each. Each point in the match involves two players: one who will win and one who will lose. The loser will go to the end of the line, whereas the winner will add to his point total and await the next point unless he has accumulated enough points to claim the match.

This sequence of events can be described by the following program flow structure, or algorithm:

Initialize the current players to 1 and 2.
Initialize the queue of players to {3, 4, 5, 6, 7, 8}.
Initialize the point total for each player to zero.

So long as the current winner has less than 7 points:
Play a simulated point between the two current players.
Add one (or if beyond the seventh point, two) to the
total of the simulated point winner.
Put the simulated point loser at the end of the queue.
Get the next player off the front of the queue.
End *So long as.*
Identify the current point winner as the winner of the match.

The only step in this algorithm that needs more elaboration is that of simulating a point between two players. If the purpose of our simulation is to see how biases in the scoring system affect the outcome of the match, it makes the most sense to consider the case in which all players are equally skillful. To give every player a 50–50 chance of winning each point he is involved in, we can flip a simulated coin to determine who wins and who loses.

Any reasonable computer programmer would be able to take a flow description such as this and turn it into a program in the language of his or her choice. This algorithm describes how to simulate one particular game, but by running it 1,000,000 times and keeping track of how often each possible outcome occurs, we would get a pretty good idea of what happens during a typical jai alai match.

Breaking Ties

The Spectacular Seven scoring system, as thus far described, uniquely determines a winner for every game. However, because of place and show betting, a second- and third-place finisher must also be established.

According to my simulation, ties occur in roughly one-third of all games played, and thus proper handling of these cases is essential.

It is very important to break ties under the same scoring system used by the frontons themselves. To show how complicated these rules are, we present for your amusement the official state of Florida rules governing the elimination games in jai alai:

1. After a winner has been declared, play-off rules to decide place, show and fourth positions vary according to the number of points scored by the participating players or teams, and shall be played according to the players or teams *rotation position* (not post position), i.e., the order in which they were defeated.

2. In the case of a tie after a win position has been officially declared, it shall not be necessary, in order to determine place, show or fourth positions, or all three for the players or teams to score the full game's number of points.

3. When there still remain five or seven players or teams, all of which are tied without a point to their credit, the play-off shall be for a goal of one point less than the number of post positions represented in the play-off.

4. When there still remain five or seven players or teams, all of which are tied without a point to their credit, the play-off shall be continued until the player or team reaches the number of points designated for the game.

5. In case of two ties, after a Winner has been declared official, and there are still two players or teams tied with the same number of points, the place position shall be awarded to the player or team making the next point, and show position goes to the loser of said point.

   In games where a fourth position is required, if:

   (a) Two ties remain after win and place have been determined, the show position shall be awarded to the player or team making the next point, and fourth position shall go to the loser of said point.

   (b) Two ties remain after Win, Place and Show have been determined, the Fourth position shall be awarded to the player or team making the next point.

6. In case of three ties, after a Winner has been declared official, place, show and fourth positions shall be decided among the three players or teams, with the same number of points, through elimination, according to *rotating position*. However, if after playing the first play-off point, any player's or team's score reaches the number of points that the game calls for, said player or team shall immediately

be awarded the place, show or fourth position, as the case may be, and any remaining players or teams shall forfeit the right to play for said position.

7. In case of four or six ties, after a Winner has been declared official and there remain four or six players or teams, tied for place, show or fourth, or all three, play-off shall be through elimination according to their *rotating position*. The first two players or teams will play the first point. The next two players or teams will play for one point, and the remaining (in case of 6) players or teams will also play for one point. Winners of the above points will play additional points to decide place, show and fourth position, as the case may require.

8. In games where a fourth position is required and no place, show or fourth position has been determined and there remain four ties, the losing players or teams of the elimination play-off return and play a final point to determine fourth.

9. If at any time during a play-off a player or team reaches the designated number of points the game calls for, said player, or team, shall immediately be awarded the place, show or fourth position, as the case may be and the remaining players or teams shall forfeit the right to play for said position.

As you can see, the complete tiebreaking rules are insanely complicated. You need a lawyer, not a computer scientist to understand them. The least interesting but most time-consuming part of writing this simulation was making sure that I implemented all of the tiebreaking rules correctly. I wanted the simulation to accurately reflect reality, even those rare realities of seven players ending in a tie (which happens roughly once every 1300 games).

When you are simulating a million games, you must assume that anything that can happen will happen. By including the complete set of tiebreaking rules in the program, I knew my simulation would be ready for anything.

Simulation Results

I implemented the jai alai simulation in my favorite programming language at that time (Pascal) and ran it on 1,000,000 jai alai games. Today, it would take no more than a few minutes of computer time to complete the run; back in the mid-1980s it probably took a few hours.

The simulation produced a table of statistics telling me how often each of the possible win, place, show, and trifecta bets would have paid off

TABLE 3.1. Occurrences of Win-Place and Show in 1,000,000 Random Trials

Position	Win	% Wins	Place	% Places	Show	% Shows
1	162,675	16.27%	179,349	17.93%	151,763	15.18%
2	162,963	16.30%	178,585	17.86%	152,726	15.27%
3	139,128	13.91%	165,681	16.57%	146,561	14.66%
4	124,455	12.45%	133,185	13.32%	137,919	13.79%
5	101,992	10.20%	108,338	10.83%	129,241	12.92%
6	102,703	10.27%	78,227	7.82%	110,686	11.07%
7	88,559	8.86%	82,094	8.21%	88,723	8.87%
8	117,525	11.75%	74,541	7.45%	82,381	8.24%

in 1,000,000 games, on the assumption that all the players were equally skillful. Table 3.1 gives the simulated win, place, and show outcomes for each of the eight post positions. A pioneer in information theory, Richard Hamming, once said that "the purpose of computing is insight, not numbers." Very well. What insights can we draw from this table?

■ Positions 1 and 2 have a substantial advantage over the rest of the field. Either of the initial players is almost twice as likely to be first, second, or third than the poor shlub in position 7.

■ Doubling the value of each point after the seventh point in the match improves player 8's chances to win but does not affect the odds of place or show. The reason is that, for player 8 to do well, he must jump at the first chance he gets. Player 8 can win by winning his first four points, which should happen (if players are assumed to be of equal skill) with probability $(1/2)^4 = 1/16$, or 6.25% of the time. This quick kill thus accounts for over 70% of player 8's wins. The best player 8 can get on a quick run and not win is 5, which often is not enough for a place or show.

■ The real beneficiaries of point doubling are players 1 and 2, who, even if they lose their first point immediately, get the same opportunities as 8 did the second time around. Them as has, gets.

■ Positions 1 and 2 have essentially the same win, place, and show statistics. This is as it should be because 1 and 2 are players of identical skill, both of whom start the game on the court instead of in the queue. Because players 1 and 2 have very similar statistics, our confidence in the correctness of the simulation increases.

■ Positions 1 and 2 do not have *identical* statistics because we simulated "only" 1,000,000 games. If you flip a coin a million times, it almost certainly won't come up exactly half heads and half tails. However, the *ratio* of heads to tails should keep getting closer to 50–50 the more coins we flip.

The simulated gap between players 1 and 2 tells us something about the *limitations* on the accuracy of our simulation. We shouldn't trust any conclusions that depend upon small differences in the observed values. I would be unwilling to state, for example, that player 7 has a better chance of finishing third than first because the observed difference is so very small.

To help judge the correctness of the simulation, I compared its predictions to the outcomes of actual jai alai matches. A complicating factor is that many frontons have their matchmakers take player skill into consideration when assigning post positions. Better players are often assigned to less favorable post positions to create more exciting games.

Table 3.2 shows the winning percentage as a function of post position over a 4-year period at Berenson's Jai-alai, a Hartford, Connecticut, fronton now lamentably out of business.[1] The actual rankings of the post positions roughly agree with the projected order of the simulation, subject to the

TABLE 3.2. Four Years of Actual Winning Post Positions at Berenson's Jai-Alai

Position	1983	1984	1985	1986	Total	%Wins
1	437	387	451	475	1750	14.1%
2	459	403	465	486	1813	14.6%
3	380	403	374	435	1592	12.8%
4	351	345	368	361	1425	11.5%
5	371	370	357	389	1487	12.0%
6	329	414	396	402	1541	12.4%
7	308	371	348	343	1370	11.1%
8	357	366	351	331	1405	11.3%
Totals	2992	3059	3110	3222	12383	100.0%

[1] Their greatest moment of glory came when the fronton hosted a Frank Sinatra concert, pinch-hitting after the roof of the Hartford Civic Center collapsed.

limits of the small sample size. Post positions 1 and 2 won most often at Berenson's, and position 7 least often.

The actual variation in winning percentage by post position is less in practice than suggested by the simulation, and the data shows a little dip for player 4. Thus, we can conclude that the matchmaker's efforts moderate but do not eliminate the post position bias. That matchmakers can influence the outcome of the matches is actually quite encouraging, because it suggests that we can further improve our prediction accuracy by factoring player skills into our model.

Even more interesting phenomena reveal themselves in trifecta betting, where the first three finishers must be picked in order. There are 336 possible trifecta outcomes, and thus the "average" trifecta should have occurred roughly $1,000,000/336 \approx 2976$ times in the course of our simulation. However, as Tables 3.3 and 3.4 show, there is an enormous variation in the frequency of trifecta outcomes. Trifecta 1–4–2 occurs roughly 10 times as often as 1–6–7, which occurs roughly ten times as often as 5–6–8, which occurs roughly 10 times as often as 5–8–7. Certain trifectas are 1,000 times more likely to occur than others! In particular,

■ The best trifectas are 1–3–2, 1–4–2, 1–5–2, 4–1–3, and their symmetrical variants 2–3–1, 2–4–1, 2–5–1, and 4–2–3. Each of these trifectas occurred over 8000 times in the course of the simulation, or more than 2.6 times that of the average trifecta.

The advantages of these favorable trifectas show up in real jai alai results. I compared the simulation's 16 most frequently occurring trifectas with the Berenson's Jai-alai data from 1983 to 1986. These were the eight best trifectas listed above plus 1–2–5, 1–2–6, 4–2–1, 5–1–4, and the four symmetrical variants. My simulation projected each of them should occur between 0.77 and 0.88% of the time, whereas at Berenson's over this period they occurred between 0.49 and 0.86% percent of the time. By contrast, the average trifecta occurs under 0.30% of the time.

This is a significant bias that holds potential for exploitation, although the advantage of favorable trifectas is less pronounced than the disadvantages of unfavorable ones.

■ Several trifectas are *unbelievably* terrible bets, occurring less than 100 times out of 1,000,000 games. That makes them at least a 10,000-to-1 shot, kiddies. The four trifectas appearing least frequently in the simulation were 5–7–8, 5–8–7, 6–7–8, and 6–8–7, which occurred a grand

TABLE 3.3. Occurrences of Trifectas in 1,000,000 Random Trials

Win	Place	Show/Occurrences per Trifecta							
1		1	2	3	4	5	6	7	8
	1	—	—	—	—	—	—	—	—
	2	—	—	2195	5701	7793	7819	7062	2871
	3	—	8065	—	1070	3567	4748	5546	5417
	4	—	8820	3212	—	813	1980	3463	3860
	5	—	8156	6297	2480	—	902	1799	2781
	6	—	5414	5853	4280	1593	—	816	1195
	7	—	2735	5393	5657	3823	1307	—	584
	8	—	580	3932	4886	4508	3096	606	—
2		1	2	3	4	5	6	7	8
	1	—	—	2096	5924	7733	7924	7030	2879
	2	—	—	—	—	—	—	—	—
	3	8033	—	—	1128	3501	451	5472	5548
	4	8841	—	3398	—	797	1928	3519	3783
	5	8025	—	6251	2604	—	898	1824	2717
	6	5387	—	6033	4305	1592	—	743	1214
	7	2788	—	5327	5548	3698	1448	—	603
	8	622	—	3764	4906	4477	3130	701	—
3		1	2	3	4	5	6	7	8
	1	—	6946	—	4761	6106	5956	4833	5629
	2	6800	—	—	4609	6190	5904	4848	5459
	3	—	—	—	—	—	—	—	—
	4	5445	5365	—	—	311	811	1286	2508
	5	4995	4972	—	433	—	308	532	1434
	6	4104	4138	—	1385	299	—	246	566
	7	4059	4147	—	4170	1921	599	—	450
	8	3077	3184	—	4571	3210	2164	397	—
4		1	2	3	4	5	6	7	8
	1	—	7952	8575	—	5277	4031	3268	4173
	2	7731	—	8612	—	5224	4039	3206	4132
	3	6681	6650	—	—	1805	2244	2065	3816
	4	—	—	—	—	—	—	—	
	5	2839	2893	2065	—	—	108	349	463
	6	1888	1947	1600	—	108	—	96	193
	7	2786	2921	3697	—	696	114	—	116
	8	2519	2553	3542	—	1179	270	32	—

TABLE 3.4. Occurrences of Each Trifecta in 1,000,000 Random Trials

Win	Place	Show/Occurrences per Trifecta							
5		**1**	**2**	**3**	**4**	**5**	**6**	**7**	**8**
	1	—	4010	6527	7777	—	2458	1782	2190
	2	4048	—	6616	7738	—	2383	1765	2161
	3	6756	6729	—	2636	—	2178	1839	2707
	4	3809	3847	2082	—	—	657	1174	1456
	5	—	—	—	—	—	—	—	—
	6	1157	1109	1519	993	—	—	42	99
	7	1223	1159	2222	1568	—	41	—	22
	8	842	918	1933	1557	—	255	8	—
6		**1**	**2**	**3**	**4**	**5**	**6**	**7**	**8**
	1	—	2181	2999	6374	6422	—	1514	1345
	2	2228	—	3094	6459	6454	—	1488	1327
	3	6123	6037	—	3611	5020	—	1791	1531
	4	5376	5415	4170	—	1196	—	1454	1337
	5	2048	1978	2392	1309	—	—	305	640
	6	—	—	—	—	—	—	—	—
	7	861	888	1578	1598	750	—	—	6
	8	386	422	977	1051	561	—	7	—
7		**1**	**2**	**3**	**4**	**5**	**6**	**7**	**8**
	1	—	1107	1339	3011	4653	3863	—	851
	2	1097	—	1342	2962	4573	3949	—	796
	3	3635	3579	—	2022	3942	3577	—	1153
	4	4610	4718	4095	—	2035	1890	—	1401
	5	2809	3057	3656	2530	—	320	—	848
	6	1015	990	1405	1260	631	—	—	120
	7	—	—	—	—	—	—	—	—
	8	346	338	775	1089	816	354	—	—
8		**1**	**2**	**3**	**4**	**5**	**6**	**7**	**8**
	1	—	821	829	2425	4403	5658	3744	—
	2	893	—	820	2549	4311	5549	3788	—
	3	3158	3202	—	1278	3311	5874	3785	—
	4	5268	5295	3945	—	1525	3446	2844	—
	5	4397	4492	5590	3010	—	1315	1517	—
	6	2282	2275	3540	3221	1437	—	137	—
	7	776	721	1301	1473	980	340	—	—
	8	—	—	—	—	—	—	—	—

total of 43 times between them. I would like to play poker against any-body who bets such numbers regularly.

The paucity of these trifecta events is not an artifact of our simula-tion but is a phenomenon that really exists. I went back and looked at statistics from 17 seasons at Dania Jai-alai encompassing 29,096 games (Dania's has a significantly longer history than Berenson's). Only 4 of the 336 possible trifectas never occurred over this period: 5–7–8, 5–8–7, 6–7–8, and 6–8–7. These are exactly the four trifectas identified as least likely to occur by the simulation. The model expects them to happen only once every 25,000 games or so, meaning that our results are right on target.

■ A careful study of the tables shows that there is a strong bias against players from neighboring post positions both doing well in a match. For example, the 5–2–4 trifecta occurs almost three times as often as 5–3–4, and 6–3–5 occurs almost five times as often as 6–4–5. This is because neighboring players must play each other early in the game, and the loser is destined to return to the bottom of the queue with at most one point to his name. For both to do well, the point-winner has to go on to earn enough points to lock up second place and then lose to permit his neighbor to accumulate enough points to win.

This bias helps explains the Gang of Four rotten trifectas, because they all have the double whammy of neighboring high-post positions.

Now we know the probability that each possible betting opportunity in jai alai will pay off. Are we now ready to start making money? Unfortunately not. Even though we have established that post position is a major factor in determining the outcome of jai alai matches, perhaps the dominant one, we still have the following hurdles to overcome before we can bet responsibly:

■ *The impact of player skills* – Obviously, the skills of the individual players affect the outcome of the game. A study of season statistics for players over several years reveals that their winning percentage stays relatively constant, like the batting averages of baseball player. Thus, a good player is more likely to win than a bad one, regardless of post position. It is clear that a better model for predicting the outcome of jai alai matches will come from factoring relative skills into the queuing model.

■ *The sophistication of the betting public* – Economic analysis of horse rac-ing has shown that racetracks tend to be fairly efficient markets, meaning that the odds set by the public largely reflect the risk of the situation. Countless other people certainly noticed the impact of post position well before I did, including those who reported on similar simulations such as Goodfriend and Friedman, Grofman and Noviello, and Moser. Indeed, as we will see, the jai alai betting public has largely factored the effect of post position in the odds.

Fortunately for us, however, largely does not mean completely.

■ *The house cut* – Frontons keep about 20% of the betting pool as the house percentage, and thus one has to do much better then the average bettor just to break even.

My simulation provides information on which outcomes are most likely. It does not by itself identify which are the best bets. A good bet depends both upon the likelihood of the event's occurring and the payoff when it occurs. Payoffs are decided by the rest of the betting public. To find the best bets to make, we will have to work a lot harder.

Generating Random Numbers

Finding a reliable source of random numbers is essential to making any Monte Carlo simulation work. A good random-number generator produces sequences of bits that are indistinguishable from random coin flips. This is much easier said than done. Generating random numbers is one of the most subtle and interesting problems in computer science because seemingly reasonable solutions can have disastrous consequences.

Bad random number generators can easily cause Monte Carlo simulations to give meaningless results. For example, suppose we tried a random-number generator that simply alternated heads and tails each time it was asked for another coin flip. This generator would produce a sequence of coin flips having some of the properties of a truly random sequence. For example, the expected number of heads after n random coin flips is $n/2$, and that is exactly how many will be produced by our simple generator.

But compare the following sequence of 50 real random flips (I used real pennies) with this "phony random" sequence:

real random	HTHHH	TTHHH	TTTHT	THHHT	HTTHH
	HTHHT	THHTH	THHTT	HTHHT	TTTHT
phony random	HTHTH	THTHT	HTHTH	THTHT	HTHTH
	THTHT	HTHTH	THTHT	HTHTH	THTHT

There are significant differences between the two sequences. First, the real random sequence has an unbalanced number of heads and tails (27 heads versus 23 tails). This is not surprising. In fact, 50 coin flips should end up as exactly 25 heads and 25 tails only 11.2% of the time. Likewise, in the real random sequence there is a run of four consecutive tails. A sufficiently long sequence of flips should have substantial runs of consecutive heads or tails *if* it is truly random. Such counterintuitive behavior helps explain why people are lousy at designing truly random-looking sequences. Many embezzlers, ballot stuffers, and quack scientists have been caught because their data or audit trails were too "random" to hold up to careful scrutiny.

Let's think through the consequences of using the phony-random generator with our simulation instead of a truly random generator. No matter how many games we simulated, only two different trifecta outcomes would ever be produced! Suppose that whenever the first coin was heads, we assigned player 1 to be the winner of the first point (against player 2). Whenever player 1 wins the first point, this means that the next "random" coin flip will always yield a tail, and thus the winner of the second point will always be predestined. In either case, the outcome of the first coin flip always decides the winner of the match, and thus the results of our simulation are completely meaningless!

How, then, do we generate truly random numbers on a computer? The short answer is that we can't. Computers are deterministic machines that always do exactly what that they are programmed to do. In general, this is a good thing, for it explains why we trust computers to balance our checkbook correctly. But this characteristic eliminates the possibility of looking to computers as a source of true randomness.

The best we can hope for are *pseudorandom* numbers, a stream of numbers that *appear* as if they had been generated randomly. This is a dicey situation. John von Neumann, the brilliant mathematician who is credited with designing the first modern computer, said it best: "Anyone who considers arithmetical methods of producing random digits is, of course, in a state of sin."

The pseudorandom-number generation algorithm of choice generates random numbers based on the same principle that roulette wheels use. In a roulette wheel, we start by rolling a ball around and around and around the outer edge of the wheel. After several seconds of motion, the ball loses enough energy that it drops into the bottom part of the wheel and then

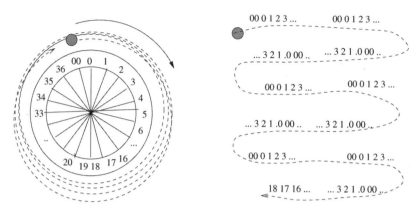

How roulette wheels generate random numbers.

comes to rest in one of the 38 equal-sized, labeled compartments at the bottom of the wheel.

Why do casinos and their patrons trust that roulette wheels generate random numbers? Why can't the fellow in charge of rolling the ball learn to throw it so it always lands in the double-zero slot? The reason is that the ball always travels a very long path around the edge of the wheel before falling, but the final slot depends upon the *exact* length of the entire path. Even a very slight difference in initial ball speed means the ball will land in a completely different slot.

So how can we exploit this idea to generate pseudorandom numbers? A big number (corresponding to the circumference of the wheel) times a big number (the number of trips made around the wheel before the ball comes to rest) yields a very big number (the total distance that the ball travels). Adding this distance to the starting point (the release point of the ball) determines exactly where the ball will end up. Taking the remainder of this total with respect to the wheel circumference determines the final position of the ball by subtracting all the loops made around the wheel by the ball.

This is the idea behind the *linear congruential generator*. It is fast and simple and (if set with the right constants a, c, m, and R_0) gives reasonable pseudorandom numbers. The nth random number R_n is a function of the $(n-1)$st random number:

$$R_n = (aR_{n-1} + c) \bmod m$$

To complete this analogy, the previous random number R_{n-1} corresponds to the starting point of the ball, and a and c dictate how hard the ball will be thrown. Finally, m stands for the circumference of the wheel. The mod function is just a fancy term for the remainder.

Lurking within my simulation is a linear congruential generator with carefully chosen constants that have been shown to produce reasonable-looking pseudorandom numbers.[2] The high correlation between the distribution of observed trifectas and our simulation results gives us faith in both our model and our random-number generator.

Passing Paper

I was a graduate student at the University of Illinois at the time I wrote this simulation. I was living in Daniels Hall, a graduate student dorm whose layout consisted of pairs of extremely small single rooms that shared a one-seat bathroom between them. To say these rooms were small was no understatement; there was no place in my room where I could stand without being able to touch at least three walls. I had a little couch that rolled out to be a bed, after which I could not stand regardless of how many walls I was willing to touch. The one saving grace in the tiny room was that my morning newspaper was delivered under my door, and I could pick it up and read it without ever leaving my bed.

But it is the shared bathroom that is the relevant part of this story. With two doors leading to a one-seat john, sooner or later you get to meet the other party. That year, my bathroom-mate was a guy named Jay French, a graduate student in the business school.

Jay went on to work for McDonnell Douglas Aerospace Corporation in St. Louis, and I've lost track of him over the years (give me a call, Jay, if you're out there), but he is the one who gave me the nerve to publish my jai alai results. As a future M.B.A., he had a professional interest in get-rich-quick schemes, and thus he was intrigued when I told him about my simulation.

"You know, I have just the place for you to publish a paper on that stuff. The Institute of Management Sciences publishes a semipopular journal, *Interfaces*. I'm a member, so they send it to me every other month. They have lots of articles analyzing optimal strategies related to sports."

---

[2] An effective way to ruin any linear congruential generator is to instantiate it with the wrong constants. Setting $a = 0$, $c = 0$ and $R_0 = 0$ simulates flipping a one-sided coin because every "random" number produced will be 0. See Knuth's book for a thorough discussion of the subtle problem of selecting the right constants to make things work.

He showed me a few back issues he had in his room. Daniels Hall rooms were so small you could only *store* a few back issues of anything. But indeed, there were articles whose depth and topics were comparable to what I had done.

"Is this a respected journal?," I asked suspiciously.

"Respected? No. But it is much less boring than the other journals they publish."

I took the bait and wrote up a paper with the results of my simulation. To give it a veneer of academic respectability, I claimed the paper was a study of the "fairness" of the Spectacular Seven scoring system. The Spectacular Seven scoring system is unfair because equally skilled players have an unequal chance of winning. I tried varying the position where double points first start (after the seventh point played in Spectacular Seven) so as to discover the point that leads to the greatest equality. After simulating 50,000 games for each possible doubling point, it became clear that doubling near the beginning of a cycle is the *worst* time if you want to ensure fairness because the already favored first or second players are likely to be the first to emerge or reemerge from the queue. Yet this is exactly what happens with the Spectacular Seven. It would be much better to double when the middle player is expected to leave the queue to play a point.

You might be curious about how academic journals work. Publication decisions are made on the basis of "peer review." When the editor of *Interfaces* received my submitted article in the mail, he or she skimmed through it and then came up with a list of two or three experts in the area to review it carefully. Identifying an appropriate set of referees for my article was probably somewhat difficult because there are few other academics with a clearly identifiable interest in jai alai. Instead, the editor probably sent it to experts in simulation or mathematical issues in sport.

Refereeing is one of the chores of being an active researcher. Whenever you submit a paper to a journal, you get your name stuck in that editor's database of possible future referees. It takes time to read a technical paper carefully and write a report stating its merits and identifying its flaws. Thus, many people try to dodge the work. But peer review is the best way to ensure that journals publish only research articles that are correct and of high quality.

These referee reports go back to the editor, who uses them to decide the question of acceptance or rejection. Copies of the reports are sent to the author of the paper, but with the names of the referee removed. Anonymity ensures that referees are free to speak their mind without worrying that vengeance will be taken at a later date. Referee reports contain ideas for improving the article, and thus even those papers recommended for acceptance are usually revised before publication.

My article, "A Fairer Scoring System for Jai-alai," appeared in *Interfaces* in November 1988. For my efforts, I received a modest amount of glory but no money. The authors of research papers receive no payment for their articles. To the contrary, researchers are often asked to contribute "page charges" to help keep the journal going. A specialized academic journal might have a circulation of only 1000 or so, which is not enough to realize any significant revenue from advertising. To cover the cost of production, libraries get charged a fortune for subscriptions to academic journals, which can run from hundreds to thousands of dollars a year. Nevertheless, most academic journals claim to lose money. I'm not sure I completely understand the economics of journals, but the point is that money is tight.

This tight money issue lead to an amusing incident with this particular paper. My *Interfaces* article contained several graphs of statistical data related to fairness, which I had drawn and printed using typical late 1980s computer equipment. The editor decided that the production quality of my graphs was too low for publication and that I had to hire a draftsman, at my expense, to redraw these graphs before the article would be accepted. My original graphs looked plenty good enough to me, and besides I wasn't happy about paying the draftsman. So I played the starving student routine. In my final letter responding to the journal I wrote as follows:

> Acting upon your suggestion, I found out that the university does indeed employ a graphics artist. Since I had no grant to charge it to, they billed me at a special student rate. The total cost, $26.25, meant that I only had to skip lunch for a week to pay for them. Thank you for your help and I look forward to seeing my paper in *Interfaces*.

A few weeks later I received an envelope in the mail from the managing editor of *Interfaces*. A stack of neatly cut out coupons to McDonald's, Dunkin Donuts, and seemingly every other fast food chain in existence was included. The note said

> Maybe the enclosed will help you with your lunch problem. We don't want you to go hungry.

A Fairer Scoring System for Jai-alai

STEVEN S. SKIENA

Department of Computer Science
State University of New York
Stony Brook, New York 11794

Several states permit paramutual wagering on jai-alai, a sport whose scoring system is based on a queue and can therefore be subject to analysis. Monte Carlo analysis of the "spectacular seven" scoring system shows that the post or starting position of the player strongly influences the results of the game. Alternative scoring systems can minimize the effect of post position.

ai-alai is a sport of Basque origin where opposing players or teams alternate hurling a ball against the wall and catching it, until one of them misses and loses the point. The throwing and catching is done with an enlarged basket or *cesta*, the ball or *pelota* is of goatskin and hard rubber, and the wall is of granite or concrete; all of which combine to lead to fast and exciting action. It is a popular spectator sport in Europe and the Americas. In the United States, jai-alai is most associated with the states of Florida, Connecticut, Nevada and Rhode Island, since they permit paramutual wagering on the sport.

Hollander and Schultz [1978] provide further information about jai-alai and its history.

As a paramutual sport, jai-alai has evolved to permit more than two players in a match. Typically, eight players or teams play in a match. The players are arranged in a FIFO queue, with two players playing each point. The loser of the point is added to the queue, with the winner staying on to play the team at the top of the queue. Play continues until one team totals some number of points, typically seven. Various tie-breaking strategies are used to determine the place and show positions.

GAMES/GROUP DECISIONS — GAMBLING
QUEUES — SIMULATION

INTERFACES **18**: 6 November-December 1988 (pp. 35-41)

My first publication on Jai-alai.

Perfect Evaluation

Computers are very fast and always getting faster. Instead of simulating 1,000,000 jai alai games, why not simulate 10,000,000 or more for greater accuracy? Even better, why not simulate *all* possible games?

In fact, there are only a finite number of possible ways that jai alai matches can unfold. Inherent in the Spectacular Seven scoring system is a tree of possibilities, the first few levels of which are shown here. The *root* of the tree represents the first point of any match, player 1 versus player 2. Each node in the tree represents a possible game situation. The left branch of each node means the lower-numbered player wins the point, whereas the right branch of each node means that the higher-numbered player wins the point. The *leaves* of this tree correspond to the end of possible games, marking when the winning player has just accumulated his seventh point.

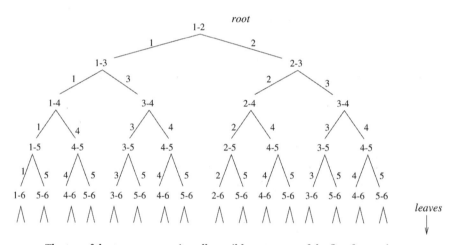

The top of the tree representing all possible outcomes of the first four points.

In such a tree, each path from the root to a leaf represents the sequence of events in a particular jai alai game. For example, the leftmost path down the tree denotes the outcome in which player 1 wins the first seven points to claim the match. After appropriately weighting the probability of each path (short paths are more likely to occur than long ones) and adding these paths up, we can compute the exact probability for each of the possible outcomes.

In fact, I once got e-mail from a fellow at Digital Equipment Corporation (DEC) who had built such an exact search program. His program built

65

the complete tree and analyzed all the possible outcomes in only a few seconds! Compaq, the leading personal computer manufacturer, recently bought out DEC in a multibillion dollar deal – presumably to get hold of this proprietary jai alai technology....

Why is the program so fast to play all possible jai alai matches? Because there are not so many possibilities. Moser built a program similar to that of the DEC guy and found that this game tree had only 422,384 leaves, or different possible sequences of events, even when factoring in the complicated tiebreaker rules. The number 422,384 is small in a world of computers that can process billions of instructions per second. A typical run of our Monte Carlo simulation played one million random games. This meant that we were playing many possible sequences more than once and presumably missing a few others. The net result is more work for the simulation.

So if brute-force evaluation is faster and more accurate than Monte Carlo simulation, why didn't we use it? The primary reason was laziness. Getting the brute force program to work efficiently and correctly would have required more time and intellectual effort that the naive simulation. We would have to reimplement all of those messy tiebreaking rules, which didn't seem like fun. Further, we would have to be careful to do our probability computations correctly, which requires more intricacy than the simple accumulations of the Monte Carlo simulation.

The reason we could get away with this laziness is that the Monte Carlo simulation is accurate enough for our purposes. It measures the probability

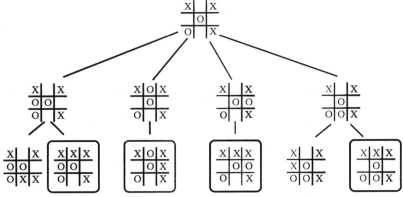

A portion of the tic-tac-toe game tree, establishing that *x* has a win from the position at the root of the tree.

of each betting outcome to within a fraction of a percent of its actual value. For example, our original simulation results agreed with Moser's complete evaluation to within 0.05% on each win-place-show entry. Any betting system that required finer tolerance than this would not be in a position to make much money in the real world, and there is no reason to lull ourselves into a false sense of security by overoptimizing one aspect of our system. I've always intended to build a brute-force evaluator, but our time always seemed better spent putting in more effort into the statistical analysis and modeling.

The idea of constructing a tree of all possible sequences of moves is the foundation of programs that play games of strategy such as chess. To evaluate which of the current moves is the best choice, the program builds a tree consisting of all possible sequences of play to a depth of several moves. It then makes a guess of the value of each leaf position and percolates this information back up to the top of the tree to identify the best move.

If such a program could build the complete tree of possibilities for a given game, as Moser did with jai alai, that program would always play as perfectly as possible. The game tree for tic-tac-toe is small enough to be easily constructed; indeed, a portion of this tree proving x has a win from a given position fits on a page of this book. On the other hand, the game tree for chess is clearly too large ever to fit in any imaginable computer. Even though the computer Deep Blue recently beat the human champion Gary Kasparov in a match, it is by no means unbeatable. The game of Go has a game tree that is vastly bigger than that of chess – enough so that the best computer programs are no match for a competent human.

When playing games, it is always important to pick on somebody your own size.

CHAPTER FOUR

THE IMPACT OF THE INTERNET

Many years passed. I received my doctorate in Computer Science from the University of Illinois with a thesis in computational geometry and found myself a faculty position in Computer Science at the State University of New York, Stony Brook.

Jai alai would have to wait awhile. As an Assistant Professor, your efforts revolve around getting tenure. Publish or perish isn't too far from the truth, but *what* you publish makes a big difference. I wouldn't have gotten tenure even if I had published 100 articles on jai alai because this work wouldn't (and shouldn't) carry much respect with the powers that be in academic computer science.

But 6 years later I found myself a tenured *Associate* Professor of Computer Science. Tenure gives you the freedom to work on whatever you want. You have to teach your classes, and you have to do your committee work, but otherwise what you do with your time is pretty much up to you. If I wanted to devote a little effort to an interesting mathematical modeling problem, well, nobody was going to stop me.

By now my parents had retired to Florida, and each winter my brother Len and I would pay them a visit. Each visit included an obligatory trip to watch jai alai, and so on January 17, 1995, we spent the evening at the Dania fronton. On arrival, our first action was, as always, to buy a

Pepe's Green Card. Our second step was to convince ourselves of its infallibility.

"Pepe's going to make us some money tonight."

"You bet. We've got nothing but winners here."

"Sure, Pepe's making money tonight. From bagel-heads like you who paid him good money for nothing." Dad remained a skeptic.

"Pepe's best bet is a 5–8–3 trifecta in Game 6. Remember when he gave us that winning trifecta when we were kids."

"Forget it. Pepe wins only once in a lifetime . . . ."

Game 6 started. After watching the early points play out, I looked at our ticket and thought ahead.

"Hey, if 8 beats 7, then 1, and then 2 he will be in first place. Player 4 can then beat 8 to stop the run. Player 3 wins the next point to move into second. If 5 then wins his next three points, we are in business."

Player 8 beat 7. Then 8 beat 1. Then 8 beat 2 to give him a total of five points.

"Player 8 needs to lose this point, or else they have won the match."

Player 4 beat 8.

"Player 3 has to win to stay ahead of 4."

Player 3 beat 4.

"Now all we need is for 5 to run it."

"Yeah, three more points and Pepe's got it."

Player 5 beat 3. My brother and I started giggling.

Player 5 beat 6. We were laughing hysterically. We didn't even have to watch the next point to know how it would turn out.

Player 5 beat 7.

This time the trifecta paid $148 and change. Again we took the folks out to dinner.

Each year, during our family fronton visit, I told my parents I could win at jai alai if only I spent the time to develop the method. They always said, "Big shot, so go do it." Finally I couldn't come up with a good reason not to. I came back from Florida with a suntan and a determination to move forward with predicting jai alai matches by computer.

The Coming of the Web

To proceed with the project, I needed to provide my computer with an extensive database of jai alai statistics and results. I needed three kinds of information:

- *Game schedules* – To perform an appropriate Monte Carlo simulation, I needed to know which players were playing, in which post positions, in which games, on which date. This meant obtaining the game schedules for a given fronton.
- *Player records* – To customize a Monte Carlo simulation for the particulars of a given match, I had to know the relative merits of the players in each post position. This meant obtaining enough game results and player statistics to rank the pelotaris with some level of confidence.
- *Payoff information* – To judge if a given bet was desirable meant I needed to know how much money each betting outcome would pay off if it won. This meant accumulating the prices paid to bettors over enough matches to predict the payoff without making the bet.

There seemed to be only two sources from which to get these statistics:

- *Directly from the frontons* – Running a pari-mutuel betting operation is very much an information-intensive business. Clearly, frontons use computers to compute payoffs and results; thus, I knew that all the information I wanted must have been on some computer at some time. However, except for general season statistics, frontons had no interest in keeping detailed records on each and every game. The public relations directors of every fronton I spoke to tried to be helpful, but they never had more than photocopies of records for the past few nights or old programs with last season's general statistics.
- *Directly from newspapers* – Several local newspapers in Florida and Connecticut print the results of jai alai matches each day. This means somebody at the newspaper must type them in in the first place. I figured that if I could get ahold of whoever did the actual typing, I could convince him or her to save the files for us to process.

But I was wrong. Nobody I spoke to ever kept more than a week's worth of data around. Local newspapers are in the business of producing newspapers and understandably could not be bothered with yesterday's news. Of course, I *could* have gone through old printed copies of the paper and retyped everything into the computer, but doing so for 1 or 2 year's worth of statistics would have been too great a task to bear.

Neither of these options was tenable. The jai alai project was dead in the water until the Internet and Worldwide Web (WWW) suddenly became popular.

As the WWW caught on, more and more companies asked themselves what information they could provide to their potential customers. Their first Web page probably only had the firm's address and phone number and maybe a copy of the public relations brochure. Eventually, however, someone had the imagination to say, "Hey, I can do more," and got to work building something interesting.

For jai-alai frontons, it was a no-brainer that they should provide schedules and results of play. Newspapers found the jai alai scores interesting enough to publish each day. The more information frontons could provide to the betting public, the more money the betting public would provide to the frontons. Milford's WWW site immediately started getting thousands of hits per month and kept growing.

Frontons on the net changed everything for this project. When several frontons started providing daily schedules and results in early 1997, we started downloading it. Retrieving a Web page by clicking a button on a browser such as Netscape or Internet Explorer is a simple task. It is not much more complicated to write a program to retrieve a given page without the mouse click. Using such a program, we convinced our computer to wake up early each morning and fetch the schedule of future matches from a given fronton's WWW site, as well as retrieve the winners of yesterday's matches.

For more than 3 years now we have collected schedules and results each night from the Websites of several frontons, including Milford, Dania, and Miami. Dania and Milford proved the most diligent about posting this information; therefore, all of our subsequent work was performed using data from these frontons. Our huge database of jai alai results promised to unlock the secrets of player skills – if only we could interpret them correctly.

Parsing

A Holy Grail of computer science is building computer systems that *understand* natural languages such as English. Wouldn't it be great if you could type something in like "schedule dinner with the Stark's for next Saturday night," and the machine could figure out what you meant and act accordingly?

Natural language understanding is an extremely hard problem for computers – so hard that for most applications it is easier to design an artificial language and teach people to use it instead of teaching the computer

English. This is why there are so many computer programming languages out there such as Java, C, Pascal, and Basic.

The first step in understanding any text is to break it into structural elements, which is a process known as *parsing*. Parsing an English sentence is equivalent to constructing a sentence diagram for it the way you did in elementary school. Your English teacher wrote a grammar on the board, probably something like the one below, and asked you to apply the rules to decode the structure of a sentence like "the cat drank the milk." The power of language grammars is that many different sentences with different meanings have the exact same underlying structure, such as "the mechanic fixed the car" or "the bookie fixed the match."

Parsing is only a first step in the process of understanding a natural language. *Understanding* means extracting meaning from a text, not just its structure. You can parse "the glaxtron bandersnatched the thingamabob" using essentially the same grammar, but you don't understand it. Understanding implies that you know what all the individual words mean in context, which is a difficult task because the same word can mean different things in different sentences. Recall the distinct uses of "fixed" in the previous example. Understanding implies that you know what the context of the discussion is. The meaning of the phrase "spit it out" differs greatly depending on whether you are in a courtroom or a dining room.

Such complexities partially explain why it is so hard to build computers that understand what we mean instead of what we say. People can make these distinctions, but they don't understand clearly enough *how* they do it to explain it to a computer. The field of artificial intelligence has attacked this problem for 50 years now with relatively little success. The Turing test, the generally accepted milestone by which to judge whether computers are

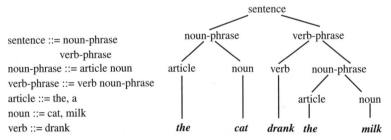

A grammar for parsing simple English sentences (on left) and the resulting parse tree when applied to "the cat drank the milk."

intelligent, asks whether a person in conversation with a machine is fooled into thinking that he or she is talking to another human. No computer has even come close to passing the Turing test. I do not anticipate a serious challenge to be made in my lifetime, even though the $100,000 Loebner Prize awaits the first program to pass.[1]

Although understanding natural language is a hopeless task, *parsing* some well-defined artificial language is part of almost every sophisticated computer program. This difference between parsing and understanding language is part of the vernacular of computer science. When a programmer comes out of a meeting saying "I don't understand what he is saying," the statement means that the programmer is confused. When a programmer comes out of meeting saying "I can't parse what he is saying," it means that the programmer is *very* confused.

One of my primary missions as a professor is to teach computer science students how to program. Programming is best learned by doing, and the best students are always looking for interesting projects to hone their skills and learn new things. Properly harnessed, this youthful eagerness to build things is a terrific way for professors to get students to work for them without pay. The trick is presenting students with a project so interesting they are happy to work for free.

Building a parser for WWW files to support a gambling system was a sexy enough project to catch any undergraduate worth his or her salt. I immediately thought of the best student in my previous semester's algorithms course, Dario Vlah. He was a soft-spoken 6-foot 8-inch Croatian with a small goatee and a tremendous eagerness to hack.

The language Dario had to parse was that which the frontons used to report the schedules and results on the WWW. Fortunately, these files were prepared by the fronton's own computers and thus had a fairly regular structure to them. For example, the start of a typical raw Milford schedule file looked like this:

```
Milford Jai-alai
Afternoon Performance - Sunday July 19, 1998
```

[1] Perhaps the most famous conversational program was *Eliza*, a 1960s attempt to simulate a Rogerian psychologist. *Eliza* briefly fooled surprisingly many people using very simple tricks that had nothing to do with intelligence. She met her match, however, when paired with another program designed to mimic a psychotic paranoid. *Eliza* failed to cure him but did succeed in sending a bill.

Game 1 Doubles/7 pts	Game 2 Singles/7 pts	Game 3 Doubles/7 pts
1 Ara-Fitz	1 Aja	1 Altuna-Edward
2 Tino-Edward	2 Douglas	2 Eggy-Fitz
3 Aja-Richard	3 Ara	3 Tino-Aritz
4 Aitor-Arrieta	4 Arrieta	4 Douglas-Capozzo
5 Jon-Alberto	5 Edward	5 Ara-Arrieta
6 Eggy-Alvarez	6 Richard	6 Liam-Guisasola
7 Iker-Guisasola	7 Tino	7 Aja-Alvarez
8 Douglas-Aritz	8 Aitor	8 Jon-Richard
SUBS Liam-Capozzo	SUB Eggy	SUBS Aitor-Alberto

Parsing such a schedule file means breaking each line into its basic elements. There is more subtlety to this task than immediately meets the eye. For example, how do we know that Aja–Richard represents a pair of teammates instead of the product of a modern, hyphenated marriage? The answer is that the heading above the column explains that this is a doubles match; consequently, we should be on the lookout for two players separated by a dash. How do we know that Eggy–Fitz is the second team in Game 3 as opposed to Game 1 or 4? We know that this particular file format lists players for up to three games on each line and that the position of the names on the line implies which game is meant. The first task in parsing such a schedule file is associating which text goes with which game – a problem complicated by different numbers of games being played on different days.

Each fronton posts its schedule and result information in different formats. To build a system capable of understanding each fronton's data, we had to build a separate parser for each one and write the data into a common, easy-to-understand format our analysis programs could use. Our translated version of this schedule file looked like this:

```
:FRONTON: Milford
:DAY: Sunday
:DATE: 07/19/1998
:GAME-COUNT: 15
:ABSOLUTE-DATE: 35994

:GAME: 1
:S/D: Doubles
:POINTS: 7
:POS-1: Ara-Fitz
```

```
:POS-1-ID: 42 73
:POS-2: Tino-Edward
:POS-2-ID: 11 85
:POS-3: Aja-Richard
:POS-3-ID: 13 86
:POS-4: Aitor-Arrieta
:POS-4-ID: 12 51
:POS-5: Jon-Alberto
:POS-5-ID: 44 63
:POS-6: Eggy-Alvarez
:POS-6-ID: 22 77
:POS-7: Iker-Guisasola
:POS-7-ID: 46 80
:POS-8: Douglas-Aritz
:POS-8-ID: 14 65
:POS-SUB: Liam-Capozzo
:POS-SUB-ID: 38 70
```

Our parser integrated certain additional information into this file. For example, it converted the calendar date (July 19, 1998) to an absolute date (35,994), which is precisely the number of days since January 1, 1900. Working with absolute dates can be much easier for computers than working with calendar dates.[2] For example, the absolute date 2 weeks from this one is computed simply as $35,994 + 14 = 36,008$, whereas figuring it out on a calendar requires knowing exactly how many days there are in July. The complexity of dealing with calendar dates was one of the primary reasons for the infamous though ultimately innocuous millennium bug.

The parser also added the uniform number of each player. We maintained a roster of all the players for each fronton, including their uniform number. The parser would check that each player it found on the schedule was on our roster and warned us if he wasn't. After all, an unknown player named Doubles or Afternoon probably meant that the parser got confused in its interpretation of the file, meaning we had a bug to fix rather than a player to add.

---

[2] Absolute dates can also be easier for people to work with. For example, to figure out what day of the week your birthday will fall on next year, simply add 1 to the day of the week it fell on this year, unless a leap day occurs between them (in which case you must add 2). The reason this works is that the 365 days of a given year equals 52 7-day weeks plus one additional day to add to the current absolute date.

75

In addition to schedules of who was to play, we needed to interpret the results of previous matches. Raw results files from Milford looked like this:

```
Milford Jai-alai Results
Afternoon Performance - Sunday July 19, 1998

Game 1 Doubles/7 pts                    Game 2 Singles/7 pts
8 Douglas-Aritz    29.70 16.50 6.90     1 Aja          21.30 8.70 5.40
4 Aitor-Arrieta          9.90 6.90      2 Douglas            8.40 4.20
1 Ara-Fitz                     5.70     8 Aitor                   12.00
Quiniela 4-8                  $51.60    Quiniela 1-2            $45.60
Exacta 8-4                    $69.00    Exacta 1-2            $102.90
Trifecta 8-4-1              $364.50     Trifecta 1-2-8       $640.80
```

The task of parsing results files is similar to that of parsing schedules. One important part of the result-parser's job is to warn us of possible errors in the files such as occasionally leaving out a decimal point in one of the numbers. Thinking that an 8–4–1 trifecta once paid off $36,450 instead of $364.50 could trick the program into forever hoping to repeat an event that never actually occurred.

After parsing, we ended up with a results file like the following:

```
:FRONTON: Milford
:DAY: Sunday
:DATE: 07/19/1998
:GAME-COUNT: 15
:HANDLE: 172952
:ABSOLUTE-DATE: 35994

:GAME: 1
:S/D: Doubles
:POINTS: 7
:WIN: 8
:PLACE: 4
:SHOW: 1
:WINNER: Douglas-Aritz
:WINNER-ID: 14 65
:WIN-PRICES: 29.70 16.50 6.90
:PLACER: Aitor-Arrieta
:PLACER-ID: 12 51
:PLACE-PRICES: 9.90 6.90
```

```
:SHOWER: Ara-Fitz
:SHOWER-ID: 42 73
:SHOW-PRICES: 5.70
:QUINIELA: 4-8
:QUINIELA-PRICE: 51.60
:EXACTA: 8-4
:EXACTA-PRICE: 69.00
:TRIFECTA: 8-4-1
:TRIFECTA-PRICE: 364.50
```

Languages of the Internet: Perl and HTML

It is an interesting phenomenon that most computer scientists go through a 5-year period early in their career when they think that computers and programming are really, really neat. They will kill enormous amounts of time customizing their personal computers to get everything to work just right and learn all the arcane details of the latest programming languages.

Students in this obsession phase are a joy to have around, largely because their professors have long since left it. These days, I am much more excited about finding interesting things to do with computers (like predicting jai alai matches) than I am in dealing with an upgrade from Windows 98 to Windows 2000. Fortunately, Dario did Windows, and a whole lot more.

Dario was particularly eager to learn the behind-the-scenes language that makes the Internet go, a programming language called Perl. Perl is not as much a reflection of hot new technology as it is a manifestation of old ideas freshly applicable to today's problems.

Although the explosive growth of the Internet has clearly been the most exciting recent development in computer technology, the dirty truth is that it really doesn't require much *computing* to make the Internet work. Throughout most of the information age, computers spent the bulk of their time crunching numbers (like predicting the weather) or in business data processing (doing things like payroll and accounting). Most applications ran on expensive, mainframe computers that kept busy around the clock and charged users for every minute of computer time.

Fast forward to today. Now millions of desks across the nation contain personal computers, each of which is vastly more powerful than the "big iron" of yesteryear. And what do we do with the billions of instructions per second that we have at our disposal? We run increasingly elaborate screen-saving programs whose shimmering images decorate our desks as they protect the phosphors on our monitors.

The truth is that the Internet is really about *communication*, not computation. Although the Worldwide Web has been dubbed the "Worldwide Wait" because of sluggish response times, the primary source of these delays is not insufficient processing power but the problem of too many people trying to use too few dedicated telephone lines – all at the same time.

An embarrassingly high percentage of the computing tasks associated with the Worldwide Web are basic bookkeeping and simple text reformatting. Perl is a language designed to make writing these conversion tasks as simple and painless as possible. Depending upon whom you believe, Perl is an acronym for either "practical extracting and reporting language" or "pathologically eclectic rubbish lister." The goal of its creator, Larry Wall, was to "make the easy jobs easy, without making the hard jobs impossible."

Perl programs are not particularly efficient, but they are particularly short. They are designed to be written quickly, plugged in place, and forgotten. No one would think of building a Monte Carlo simulation to simulate a million jai alai games in Perl because such high-performance number-crunching jobs must be carefully written to utilize the machine efficiently. Perl is for those quick-and-dirty, hit-and-run reformatting tasks that help programmers untangle the Web.

One of the common text-processing tasks in which Perl scripts are used is preparing WWW pages on demand from databases. Look up your favorite book (ideally, look up *my* book) on Amazon.com or some other on-line book dealer and you will see a customized page with the title and publisher, a picture of the cover, reader-supplied reviews, and even the current rank on the company's bestsellers' list. This WWW page was not written by a person but a computer program that extracts the relevant information from the database and adds formatting commands to make it look right on the reader's screen.

A second language of the Internet is HTML, an abbreviation for the "hypertext markup language." HTML is the language in which all WWW pages are written, that is, the text spit out by Amazon.com's Perl programs. It really isn't a computer programming language at all, for you can't write a program in HTML to *do* anything. This language provides a medium for an author (or computer) to specify what a WWW page should look like to the reader.

As we saw, Milford's schedule and results files were presented as unexciting-to-read but simple-to-parse text files. Dania Jai-Alai was more ambitious and used HTML formatting to present its results and schedule files. The following portion of a Dania schedule file illustrates HTML:

```
<HTML>
<HEAD>
<TITLE>Entries Shell</TITLE>
</HEAD>
<BODY BGCOLOR= "#FFFFff"TEXT = "#000000"LINK = "#FF0000"
    VLINK= "#0f4504">
<font color= "#ff0000">
<center><img src= "botlogo.gif"></center>
ENTRIES DANIA JAI ALAI AFTERNOON 07/19/98 14
GAMES</font>

<table cellpadding="15"align="top">
<tr align=left valign="top">
<td>

<!--column 1 entries -->

<table valign="top">
<tr valign=top align=left>
<td><font color="#ff0000">GAME 1 - Spec 7 -Tri,DD<br></font>
<font>1 Mouhica-Oyhara<br>
2 Blanco-Verge<br>
3 Scotty-Zuri<br>
4 Arecha-Inigo<br>
5 Rocha III-Ondo<br>
6 Aymar-Eneko<br>
7 Laucirica II-Bilbao<br>
8 Andonegui-Homero<br>
SUBS: Burgo-Ulises</font></td>
</tr>
```

The formatting commands of HTML appear within the angle brackets such as < TITLE>. This portion starts by presenting the title of this page and then specifies the color of both the background and the text (the actual colors are described by "names" like #ff0000). It then specifies that a picture named "botlogo" should be inserted, neatly centered in the middle of the line. The schedule of each game is formatted as a table in which each row presents the post number and the two members of each doubles team.

This HTML formatting may seem ungainly, but you weren't intended to read it – your WWW browser was. It would be tedious for a person to write all those formatting commands each day, but that was done by a Perl program, not a person. As is the case with Amazon.com, these WWW pages are produced by formatting the information in a database using a straightforward computer program. Because a computer program writes the actual HTML files, we can rely on the format to be the same day to day without any typing or formatting errors.

My student Dario did not have access to the fronton's private database containing the unformatted schedule and result information. However, he did have access to these HTML pages. By writing his own Perl program, he could carefully strip away all that formatting the fronton's program had diligently inserted. He could take the remaining data and format it just as we did with the Milford data, enabling us to add it each day to our library of jai alai scores. Once we had amassed enough data to work with, our fun could really begin.

Any discussion of the languages of the Internet would be incomplete without mentioning Java. At the risk of slightly oversimplifying things, Java is a programming language for writing programs that will run on *somebody else's* machine, typically using an Internet browser.

For example, suppose I want to put a facility on the WWW enabling you to calculate the amount of money you will pay each month if you take out a mortgage. I could create a WWW page that would prompt you to type in the interest rate, loan amount, and term of the loan, then calculate the number on *my* machine, and send this number to you on your machine. Alternatively, I could write a little program in Java my machine could give your machine, which, when run on *your machine*, would prompt you for the relevant numbers and do the calculation there. This second arrangement is better for me, in that it reduces the amount of interaction on my machine, and also better for you because I don't get to know how much money you are thinking of embezzling from the bank.

We don't use Java anywhere in our system because there is no program we want to run on somebody else's machine, and because no fronton's

WWW site provides a program that we want to run (as opposed to *data*, which we want to read). Still, Java is a good thing. In fact, it is such a good thing that Microsoft devoted considerable energy and resources trying to kill it.

Why Real Programmers Hate Microsoft

As the 900-pound gorilla of the software industry, Microsoft finds itself the subject of a great deal of attention. Always welcome is the interest of investors, whose enthusiasm has caused its stock to split each year like clockwork. Completely unwelcome has been the interest of the Justice Department, whose antitrust unit seeks to split the company instead of the stock.

It is fair to say that most *real* computer programmers hate Microsoft, but I've had a hard time explaining why to my nontechie friends. Most computer programmers have a warm spot in their heart for high-tech companies like Sun Microsystems, Netscape, Cisco, Apple Computer, and even Intel, but not for Microsoft. The usual motives for hatred (jealousy, fear, resentment) don't really suffice to explain this phenomenon:

- *Jealousy* – Why should I be jealous of their success? Hell, I'm proud to say I own some stock in Microsoft – enough to make me some money but not so much that I still can't root against them in the marketplace.
- *Fear* – What do I have to fear? I'm a tenured professor of computer science, and thus I have no reason to fear Microsoft will eat *my* lunch. This is one business Microsoft has shown no evidence of getting into. Indeed, Bill Gates has even donated money to Harvard and the University of Washington for new buildings to better house their excellent computer science departments. By the way, we could use a new building at Stony Brook, too, Bill.
- *Resentment* – Sure, Microsoft can be a pushy, arrogant company to do business with. It is well-known that no other company ever got rich dealing with Microsoft. But I don't *have* to deal with them. Some of my favorite former students have gone on to work for them. I wish them nothing but the best and indeed hope that they remember their alma mater when it comes time to be looking for tax shelters.

No, the usual reasons don't explain why real programmers hate Microsoft. The real problem is the unhealthy degree of control Microsoft exerts in shaping the way the rest of the computer world does business.

Its marketshare of the personal computer world is so high that it prevents the rest of the industry from doing new and interesting things.

These are strong words, but let me make things clear. Our entire jai alai project could never have happened if Microsoft controlled the Internet the way it does the personal computer world.

Why? The technical foundations of the Internet are a series of software standards enabling different hardware and software systems to talk to each other. As long as each component adheres to the standards, everyone can understand each other.

Back in the days when the public thought the Internet was an environmentally unsound practice of the fishing industry, the Internet was designed and run by a small group of techies who had no proprietary interest in the standards it employed. To establish a standard, you had to convince the other techies that your standard was better than theirs through open discussions. Eventually the community would reach a consensus, and the standard was adopted.

The language in which WWW pages are written, HTML, is perhaps the most familiar of these Internet technical standards. The goals of HTML were to make it easy to read and write WWW pages. Formatting commands are embedded within the raw text to be displayed, describing where to start paragraphs and how bold to make the titles.

Because HTML was designed as an open standard, it has no secrets to hide. Because every WWW page is written in an easy-to-understand language, any mortal can look at someone else's WWW page to see how he or she got it to look that way. This is nice. Want to know how to make a title blink on and off? Go to the WWW page of someone whose title is blinking and then view the source code to see how this was done. This open source policy makes it easy to learn from others, which is clearly a good thing for the entire community.

Our jai alai project got off the ground precisely because HTML is an open source language. Sure, the frontons that posted schedules and results each day only *intended* for these files to be viewed on the screen by potential bettors. However, because we were able to get the original HTML source files and parse them easily, we could understand the structure of the data they encoded. Because everything was open, clear, and consistent, we could write a parser to extract the information we wanted from each file and thus gather the statistics we needed. Although the potential of such open source documents was certainly not forseen by the frontons, it proved to be in their interest because we have placed a substantial number of bets with them via our program. The open standard enriches all by encouraging new ideas and applications.

Now let us return to Microsoft. It is the purveyor of the most dominant operating system in the world, running on 97% of all personal computers. Because Microsoft controls the software on the bulk of the machines out there, it is in a position to enforce whatever standards it wishes. Suppose Microsoft were to come out with a new standard "Microsoft-HTML," which *its* software used instead of real HTML. If you wanted your WWW page visible on 97% of the computers in the world, you would have to make it work with the Microsoft product. If you wanted to view all these WWW pages, you had *better* buy the Microsoft product because it is the only company supporting this new standard.

This creates two serious problems:

- *Quality and consensus are no longer part of the standards process –* There is no inherent reason the Microsoft standard has to be technically better to triumph in the marketplace. English is not an inherently better language than Serbo–Croatian, but because it is the standard more people write books in English than Serbo–Croatian. Because Microsoft has a monopoly, it can do whatever it pleases, and produce the de facto standard. With the appropriate changes to Microsoft Word, we could all be forced to write in hieroglyphics.

  Whenever another company comes up with a new or better idea for a standard, Microsoft always chooses to "embrace and extend" the standard, as it has done with Sun Microsystem's programming language Java. But this is the embrace of death, because these extensions serve primarily to make Microsoft's version incompatible with the rest of the world.

- *Microsoft has incentive to make its standards as obscure as possible –* A Microsoft standard analogous to HTML is the file format for Microsoft Word. Both provide ways to format text to make it look the way you want it to. But is the Microsoft standard open?

  Microsoft assumes that its users don't care what technical standards are used behind the hood – they just want to get their job done. Indeed, Microsoft products are great if you want to do exactly what Microsoft wants you to do. But can you take someone else's Word file and use it to figure out *how* to make your Word document look like that?

No, because the Word file format does not produce human-readable source. If you try to view a raw Word file on your screen, it will produce countless beeps and strings of gobledygook because of the machine-only control characters. You would learn nothing by reading it even if you could.

This problem is compounded because, instead of seeking clarity, Microsoft has an actual *incentive* to use as obscure and proprietary standards as possible. The Word file standard is defined by exactly what Microsoft's program reads. Why should Microsoft want to make it easier for other companies to use this format? Better you should be stuck using Microsoft-only software! Sure, technological and business opportunities will be lost because our standards are so restrictive, but they are lost primarily to the *other guy*.

So, what can be done about Microsoft? Either it is going to have to learn some manners, or else the real programmers of the world will eventually have to surrender. The former doesn't seem likely to happen unless the Justice Department succeeds in breaking up the company. The latter is highly undesirable because, frankly, it is the real programmers of the world who contribute the innovations for Microsoft to "embrace and extend." And it seems so unnecessary. Other corporations, like Sun Microsystems, have carved out very nice businesses while technically doing the right thing.

That, and not jealousy, is the reason real programmers hate Microsoft.

CHAPTER FIVE

IS THIS BUM ANY GOOD?

Every morning at 2 A.M., as professors sleep and graduate students arrive to pull all-nighters, my computer diligently makes the rounds of the Websites of all major frontons, downloading the latest schedules and results and then running these files through Dario's parsing programs. After a few months of retrieval we had built a large-enough collection of jai alai data to justify some serious analysis. Our goal was to use all this data to measure the relative abilities of jai alai players and incorporate this information into our Monte Carlo simulation to make customized predictions for each match.

To get this job done, I had to bring another student on to the project, Meena Nagarajan. Meena was a different type of student than Dario. As a married woman with a young child, she realized that there are other things to life besides computers. She was returning to school to get her master's degree with the express goal of getting a lucrative job with a financial services company associated with Wall Street, as indeed she ultimately did. She realized that building a program-trading system for jai alai was a great way to learn how to build one for trading stocks, and she therefore signed on to work on the project.

Her undergraduate degree back in India was in applied mathematics; thus, she brought to the table an understanding of the meaning and limitations of statistics.

Probability versus Statistics

Probability and statistics are related areas of mathematics that concern themselves with analyzing the relative frequency of events. Still, there are fundamental differences in the way they see the world:

- *Probability* deals with predicting the likelihood of future events, whereas *statistics* involves the analysis of the frequency of past events.
- *Probability* is primarily a theoretical branch of mathematics that studies the consequences of mathematical definitions. *Statistics* is primarily an applied branch of mathematics that tries to make sense of observations in the real world.

Both subjects are important, relevant, and useful. But they are different, and understanding the distinction is crucial in properly interpreting the relevance of mathematical evidence. Many a gambler has gone to a cold and lonely grave for failing to make the proper distinction between probability and statistics.

This distinction will perhaps become clearer if we trace the thought process of a mathematician encountering a craps game for the first time:

- If this mathematician were a probabilist, he or she would see the dice and think, "Six-sided dice? Presumably each face of the dice is equally likely to land face up. Now *assuming* that each face comes up with probability 1/6, I can figure out what my chances are of crapping out."
- If, instead, a statistician wandered by, he or she would see the dice and think, "Those dice may look OK, but how do I *know* that they are not loaded? I'll watch a while, and keep track of how often each number comes up. Then I can decide if my observations are consistent with the assumption of equal-probability faces. Once I'm confident enough that the dice are fair, I'll call a probabilist to tell me how to play."

In summary, probability theory enables us to find the consequences of a given ideal world, whereas statistical theory permits us to to measure the extent to which our world is ideal.

Modern probability theory emerged from the dice tables of France in 1654. Chevalier de Méré, a French nobleman, wondered whether the player or the house had the advantage in a variation of the following betting game.[1] In the basic version, the player rolls four dice and wins provided none of them are a six. The house collects on the even money bet if at least one six appears.

De Méré brought this problem to attention of the French mathematicians Blaise Pascal and Pierre de Fermat, most famous as the source of Fermat's last theorem. Together, these men worked out the basics of probability theory and established along the way that the house wins the basic version with probability $p = 1 - (5/6)^4 \approx 0.517$, where the probability $p = 0.5$ denotes a fair game in which the house wins exactly half the time.

The jai alai world of our Monte Carlo simulation assumes that we decide the outcome of a point between two teams by flipping a suitably biased coin. If this world were reality, our simulation would compute the correct probability of each possible betting outcome. But all players are not created equal, of course. By doing a statistical study of the outcome of all the matches involving a particular player, we can determine an appropriate amount to bias the coin.

But such computations only make sense if our simulated jai alai world is a model consistent with the real world. John von Neumann once said that "the valuation of a poker hand can be sheer mathematics." We have to reduce our evaluation of a pelotari to sheer mathematics.

Jai Alai Players and Baseball Players

How much of an influence does player skill have on the outcome of a jai alai match? Obviously this depends upon how great the skill difference between the players is. I am quite confident that the worst professional player, with his leg in a cast, would crush me 1001 times if we played a series of 1000 games against each other. The real question is whether the relatively minor differences in player skills on the professional level translate in a significant difference in the likelihood that the better player wins.

It is a simple matter to program our computer to tabulate the number of wins that each player had over the past year, but is the most successful player really most skillful? What is the right time span over which to analyze such statistics to measure the best current player? It needs to be a long enough time for the totals to be statistically significant i.e., for such

---

[1] He really shouldn't have wondered. The house *always* has the advantage.

random events as off-days and lucky bounces to cancel themselves out. And yet it cannot be too long a time interval, for certain player's skills will improve with training and experience whereas those of others erode with injury and aging.

There is clearly anecdotal evidence that certain jai alai players are better than other players. Joey, perhaps the greatest American jai alai player ever, led the Dania fronton in wins an amazing eight consecutive seasons from 1985 to 1989. (There are two seasons per year.) A look at the top 10 players at any fronton will reveal many names in common with the list from the previous year.

Table 5.1 shows significant variation in the success rate of players at Milford in 1998. Lander (a big star) won 16.3% of his games that year, which is a rate close to double that of Alberto (9.8%). Aragues was in the money (win, place, or show) 42.1% of the time, whereas the supporters of Tino were rewarded on only 32.9% of show bets.

Most Americans have a finely developed statistical sense about baseball. Let's use that sense to gain better intuition about the impact of player skills in jai alai. Baseball batting averages are well known to be meaningful statistics; indeed, a .300 hitter is the classical definition of a star player. Achieving a .300 average means that you managed to get 3 hits every 10 times at bat. Players' batting averages fluctuate over the season because they have good and bad games. So how successful is a player's current batting average at predicting how he will do in the future?

I will use batting averages from 1996 and 1997 to get a handle on this situation by building a scatterplot of the data (see Figure 5.1). Each data point represents the statistics of one particular player. Each of the major league baseball players who played regularly in both 1996 and 1997 (defined as at least 400 at bats each season) is represented by an (x, y) point, where x is the 1996 average and y is the 1997 average.

Let's think about what this means. If baseball players were completely consistent year to year, the two values would be identical, meaning that each point would lie perfectly on the diagonal line $y = x$. If batting averages were completely random and one year's performance completely independent of the next year's performance, these points would jump around like the darts we threw at Picasso's painting.

What my scatterplots show is that batting averages are fairly consistent from year to year. Eyeballing both the left (American League) and right

TABLE 5.1. Player Statistics from the 1998 Milford Jai-Alai Season

No.	Player	Games	1st	2nd	3rd	Win%	Money%
10	Altuna	647	80	76	79	.124	.363
11	Tino	1108	128	120	117	.116	.329
12	Aitor	1103	135	169	158	.122	.419
13	Aja	1071	120	138	137	.112	.369
14	Douglas	1065	133	122	120	.125	.352
18	Sorozabal	814	101	97	95	.124	.360
19	Xabat	934	115	110	111	.123	.360
21	Olate	1118	149	128	128	.133	.362
22	Eggy	876	107	140	111	.122	.409
23	Zarandona	976	115	120	116	.118	.360
24	Urquidi	1021	113	124	115	.111	.345
25	Tevin	1039	151	130	114	.145	.380
26	Goixarri	1154	164	156	157	.142	.413
31	Jandro	876	94	128	135	.107	.408
32	Beitia	1106	160	154	121	.145	.393
35	Alfonso	998	114	114	122	.114	.351
36	Aragues	749	109	102	104	.146	.421
38	Liam	1097	135	120	129	.123	.350
40	Lander	833	136	96	111	.163	.412
41	Iruta	1151	138	129	141	.120	.354
42	Ara	1070	119	168	145	.111	.404
44	Jon	1052	137	122	143	.130	.382
45	Borja	1151	134	137	131	.116	.349
46	Iker	1094	146	129	144	.133	.383
51	Arrieta	1101	145	119	137	.132	.364
54	Retolaza	449	48	55	60	.107	.363
55	Lasa	936	114	105	106	.122	.347
60	Brett	764	103	108	94	.135	.399
63	Alberto	966	95	122	135	.098	.364
65	Aritz	1100	147	146	145	.134	.398
66	Sergio	937	127	104	125	.136	.380
67	Ibar	856	109	127	99	.127	.391
68	Zabala	968	109	98	124	.113	.342
70	Capozzo	805	103	98	91	.128	.363
72	Azpiri	1091	128	128	125	.117	.349
73	Fitz	1080	127	150	139	.118	.385
74	Acin	1159	115	142	127	.099	.331
75	Matera	382	38	43	57	.099	.361
77	Alvarez	1039	140	130	143	.135	.397
80	Guisasola	1146	154	139	152	.134	.388
81	Wayne	1021	142	148	99	.139	.381
84	Arruri	1172	170	148	150	.145	.399
85	Edward	981	109	124	141	.111	.381
86	Richard	1067	130	155	150	.122	.408
88	Raul	1164	127	144	167	.109	.376
89	Baronio	1051	145	138	125	.138	.388
91	Jorge	1125	149	130	130	.132	.364
92	Badiola	980	123	106	127	.126	.363

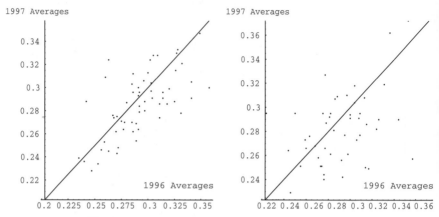

Consistency of batting averages between 1996 and 1997 for American and National League regulars.

(National League) plots shows that the points drift upward and to the left, indicating that players who did well in 1996 also tended to do well in 1997. Of course there are exceptions, flashes in the pan like Bernard Gilkey (who collapsed from .317 to .249), aging stars like Ellis Burks (who faded from .344 to .290), and developing youngsters like Delino DeShields (who grew from .224 to .295). But the exceptions seem equally likely to be above the line $y = x$ as below it.

How well a line fits the data is measured by a statistic called the *correlation coefficient*. When two sequences are completely related, their correlation coefficient is 1. When two sequences are completely unrelated, such as the price of tea in China against the ratings for the David Letterman show, the correlation coefficient is zero. The correlation coefficients are 0.588 for the American League data and 0.518 for the National League data. Correlation coefficients are not probabilities, and these are high values. Thus, they measure what we expect, that this season's batting averages are a good predictor for next year's.[2]

Now let us see how consistent jai alai player win percentages are across time. My next scatterplot gives the win percentages (the ratio of wins to

---

[2] For those not intimidated by formulas, the correlation coefficient of two sequences X and Y is given by

$$\text{corr}(X, Y) = \frac{\Sigma_i(x_i - \bar{X})(y_i - \bar{Y})}{\sqrt{\Sigma_i(x_i - \bar{X})^2}\sqrt{\Sigma_i(y_i - \bar{Y})^2}},$$

where $\bar{X}$ and $\bar{Y}$ are the means of sequences X and Y, respectively.

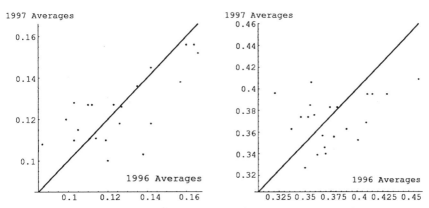

Consistency of Milford Jai-Alai players' win and in-the-money averages between 1996 and 1997.

games played) and in-the-money percentages (the ratio of wins, places, and shows to games played) for all regular players at Milford Jai-Alai in the 1996 and 1997 seasons.[3] By regular player, I mean somebody who played at least 400 games each season.

As you can see, the points in the plots also tend to increase as we move to the right, thus denoting a positive correlation. The correlation coefficients of 0.492 and 0.468, respectively, are slightly lower than the correlation of batting averages, meaning that this statistic is just slightly less useful in predicting future performance.

What is an example of sporting performance somewhat less consistent than that of jai alai players? How about major league pitching? The earned run average (ERA), the ratio of runs allowed to innings pitched, is considered to be the most reliable statistical measure of pitching skill. I created scatterplots for the 36 American League and 35 National League pitchers who threw at least 100 innings in both 1996 and 1997.

The correlation coefficient for American League pitchers was only 0.386, whereas the NL pitchers were somewhat more consistent at 0.503. These numbers reflect conventional baseball wisdom. Although "baseball is 90% pitching" and "you can never have too much pitching," teams are

---

[3] Note that as we aggregate more positions, our "in the money" statistic becomes progressively less informative. Indeed, the probability that a player finishes in the top eight of a given game correlates perfectly from year to year – because every player always finishes in the top eight of every game! This is a good example of why we must be careful in analyzing statistics, for even high correlation coefficients must be taken with a grain of salt.

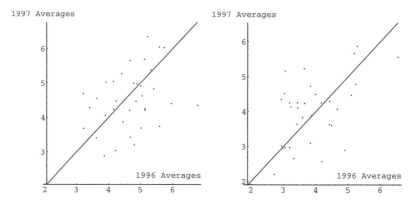

Consistency of earned run averages between 1996 and 1997 for American and National League pitchers.

historically much more reluctant to offer long-term contracts to pitchers than hitters. Their level of consistency just isn't the same. The difference between leagues may reflect the impact of the designated hitter rule. National League pitchers are often removed for pinch hitters, more sharply limiting how long they work in a typical ballgame. There is less incentive to remove an American League pitcher, and the accumulated work may wear him down over several seasons.

These numbers tell us something important about jai alai players. Star jai-alai players dominate their sport to about the same degree as star baseball players. Any reasonable system for predicting baseball games accounts for the difference in quality between the two team's players. Therefore, our system has to factor in the abilities of the players, not just post positions.

Estimating Player Skill from Statistics

How can we construct a useful measure of player skill from published statistics? We can't just use a player's win or in-the-money percentage, or even some combination of the two, as this measure. We need some number we can stick in our Monte Carlo simulation to tell us what the probability is that a given player (or team) P_1 beats another player (or team) P_2. The number of *game* wins is, by itself, fairly meaningless in terms of *point* wins. This is like using total wealth to estimate yearly salary. Sure, there is some correlation, but retired people and professional heirs have large wealth with no earned income, whereas compulsive gamblers can have large salaries but no wealth. We needed a way to estimate the point-win percentages accurately to enable our system to accumulate wealth.

Ideally, frontons would publish statistics on each player's point-win percentage, and thus we could use them directly. In fact, such statistics are kept but not published. The assignments of players to post positions are made by the fronton's player-manager, who traditionally handicaps the best players by putting them in the less desirable post positions. Player-managers keep track of point-win statistics to help in scheduling competitive matches, but unfortunately they keep these statistics to themselves.

So what information do we have at our disposal? Via the Internet, we have the schedules and results for all the games each player has played for the past year. For each player in every game, we know that player's initial post position and whether he finished first, second, or third. Unfortunately, the published results don't give the rest of the order, that is, the scores of players who don't win money.

It would be impractical for us to watch and tabulate the points scored by real jai alai players. But we can watch simulated players and see what happens to them. We played 1,000,000 simulated jai alai games and kept track of what every player scored from each starting position. We broke these down into a table of the points scored by simulated players (each of whom has equal likelihood of scoring) according to what post position they started in and where they finished. What can we observe?

■ Winners score more points on average than second- or third-place finishers, as one would expect. But the percentage of points scored by winners varies significantly, depending on their initial post position.

	Percentage of Points Won by Post Position and Outcome over 1,000,000 Random Games							
	Winner		Placer		Shower		Other	
Position	% won	total	% won	total	% won	total	% won	total
1	78.77%	966,964	63.52%	935,382	51.76%	774,133	27.26%	1,751,142
2	78.58%	950,603	63.29%	918,901	51.65%	766,861	26.73%	1,759,289
3	79.58%	797,630	66.16%	844,317	54.63%	729,834	27.91%	1,858,455
4	81.59%	700,431	67.75%	668,502	57.64%	665,485	29.45%	1,923,185
5	82.94%	574,348	70.32%	559,439	60.72%	610,894	30.83%	1,935,471
6	85.84%	545,218	70.18%	391,145	63.09%	509,161	31.80%	1,852,344
7	87.21%	471,896	72.05%	411,541	63.89%	414,517	31.76%	1,764,061
8	89.44%	528,948	70.41%	309,496	62.75%	346,252	29.96%	1,513,216
all	82.08%	5,536,038	66.88%	5,038,723	57.16%	4,817,137	29.48%	14,357,163

A player starting from the eighth post position has to win almost 90% of his points, on average, to win the game. Life is considerably easier for players starting in the first two positions, who can win only 79% of their points and expect to win the match.

■ The first two players can expect to be in the money even by winning only 51.7% of their points. This means they can lose almost as often as they win, whereas post positions 6 or 7 must win almost 2/3 of their points to show.

■ Winners from post positions 1 and 2 each play about twice as many total points as winners from post position 7. This is because there are almost twice as many winners from position 1/2 as there are from position 7. In addition, the points played by a typical position 1/2 winner are larger because they can accumulate a few more points at single scoring before each volley counts for two.

Interesting. But what can we do with it? For each player in every published game, we know which of the slots in the table he fell in. Thus, we could average the appropriate point-win percentages to get the number we need. Suppose Monolingual had played three games, winning in position 8, placing in position 7, and losing in position 6. His point-win average would be $(89.44 + 72.05 + 31.8)/3 = 64.43\%$. Suppose Bilingual had the same win-loss record but always started from position 2. His point-win average would be $(78.58 + 63.29 + 26.73) = 56.2\%$, which is not nearly as much to brag about. We should be careful, however. Averaging averages yields a meaningless number whenever the denominators are different. Your average speed on a cross-country car trip is not the average of your speeds in each state because you may travel far more miles in Texas than in Delaware. Thus, we should weigh each component average appropriately before averaging, using distance-traveled-per-state in the car example and expected-number-of-points-played-per-outcome for our jai alai problem.

This tells us how often each player should win points over the course of the simulation but doesn't completely resolve all issues. How can we compare a new pelotari who has only played three games with a workhorse who has played 400? Some form of compensation is needed. How can we account for performance in singles matches versus doubles matches? A stiff may accumulate a decent win total only because of being paired with terrific partners; alone such players are like lambs to the slaughter. This must also be compensated for.

Yet another consideration is the trade-off between serving versus receiving. In many racket sports, the server has a considerable advantage over the receiver. Certain tennis players, such as Goran Ivanisevic, have rocket serves but are relatively clueless if someone manages to hit the ball back to them. This effect in jai alai is not so pronounced. In fact, it appears that the receiving player has a small advantage over the server. This is suggested by the minor differences between the actual results of post positions 1 and 2 in the table on page 53. Unless you prefer a blue uniform to a red one, the only real difference between starting in 1 or 2 is that player 1 initially serves to player 2. Because post position 2 is slightly more successful in real life than player 1, presumably this server bias plays a small role in the outcome.

The Beauty of Curves

Although the French philosopher Descartes is best known for his statement "I think; therefore, I am," his enduring accomplishment is Cartesian geometry, the geometry of graphs drawn on an x–y plane. If you believe that souls live when instantiated in the memory of a living person, you can say of Descartes that "I graph, so he is."

Much of mathematics since Descartes can be described as the quest for simple descriptions of interesting curves. The simplest types of curves are straight lines, which can be described on a graph using *linear functions*, that is, formulas of the form $y = a \cdot x + b$ for given constants a and b. Linear functions are simple to work with and very useful in describing many aspects of the world. The linear function $y = (9/5)x + 32$ describes how to convert a temperature x in degrees Celsius to the temperature y in degrees Fahrenheit. For example, the boiling point of water is $(9/5) \times 100 + 32 = 212$ degrees Fahrenheit, whereas the freezing point is $((9/5) \times 0 + 32 = 32$ Fahrenheit. Similar linear functions are used to convert from inches to meters, pounds to kilograms, and euros to yen.

Although linear functions are good things, not all functions are accurately described by straight lines.[4] In particular, straight lines do a lousy job of approximating undulating curves such as the value of the Dow–Jones industrial average as a function of time. One way to try to predict the stock market would be to find a curve whose shape is as close

---

[4] A cynical mathematician's joke states that the best way to prove that a function is linear is to sample it at only two points.

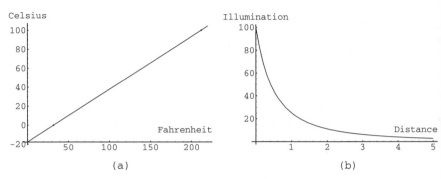

Examples of (a) linear (temperature conversion) and (b) nonlinear (illumination decay) functions.

as possible to reflecting past history and then to see what this function does in the future. We could try to fit the Dow–Jones average by a line, but because a line either goes up or down, such a predictor would always be either a bull or a bear.

To capture the more interesting shapes generated by the real world, we need a richer vocabulary of functions. Important classes of *nonlinear* functions include the following:

- *Polynomials* – Polynomials are the sum of functions of the form $y = x^c$, where c is some numerical constant. Thus, $y = x^2$ is a polynomial, as is $y = 4x^{3.5}$. The number of distinct handshakes among x people is given by the polynomial $y = (x^2 - x)/2$. As a "proof" by example, the $(4^2 - 4)/2 = 6$ handshakes possible among the four people (a, b, c, d) are ab, ac, ad, bc, bd, and cd. Polynomials are generalizations of linear functions with increasing freedom to create bumps and curves as the *degree c* and number of terms get larger.

  The number of possible handshakes *increases* with the square of the number of hands. Conversely, the amount of light one gets from a lamp *decreases* with the square of the distance, and thus moving from 10 to 20 feet away from the light leaves you with only 1/4 the degree of illumination instead of the 1/2 you would get if this function were linear.

- *Trigonometric functions* – Polynomial functions don't oscillate up and down forever; indeed, the number of bumps they can have is limited by their degree. However, many phenomena cycle up and down continuously, such as the rise and fall of ocean waves and the

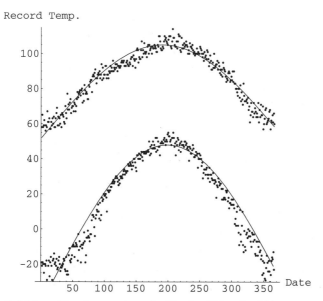

Record daily high and low temperatures for Omaha, Nebraska, fit to an appropriate sine function.

annual increase and decrease in temperature as summer comes and goes.

These kinds of curves can be appropriately modeled using the *sine* and *cosine* functions you suffered through in trigonometry. But this is why you suffered through them, even beyond their applications in computing the lengths of the sides of a triangle. We can fit the Omaha, Nebraska, record high and low temperatures (in Fahrenheit) for every day of the year to appropriate sine functions. The close fit between the curves and the points shows the accuracy of the model, whereas the high and low points on the two curves goes a long way in explaining why I'd be very reluctant to live in Omaha.

Different trigonometric functions are distinguished by their *period* (how rapidly do they alternate up and down?), *amplitude* (how high and low do they get?), and *phase* (where on each cycle does it start going up?). In fact, all interesting periodic curves can be constructed as the sum of trigonometric functions using a technique called *Fourier analysis*, and combining trigonometric functions with polynomials and other shapes opens up a new world of strange and wonderful curves.

- *Exponentials* – Some things go up faster than any straight line or even polynomial. Think of the growth of the Internet, at least in the early days. For a while, the number of Websites was doubling every few months according to a function like $y = 2^x$, where x is the number of seasons since the invention of the Web.

  Such multiplicative growth (or decline) defines an *exponential* function. Compound interest is the classic example of a function that grows exponentially. The value D' of D dollars accruing interest at a rate of r for y years is given by the formula

$$D' = D(1 + r)^y$$

Compound interest really adds up. Perhaps you recall the story of Peter Minuet, who bought the island of Manhattan from the Indians for $24 in 1626. Sharp New Yorker that he was, he even convinced the sellers to invest the money at an annual interest rate of only 6% ($r = 0.06$). Charting the progress of this investment over the course of the next 300 years shows that, as of this writing, the tribe has to make do with only $70 billion or so. This chart illustrates the most important characteristic of exponential functions, namely consistent explosive growth. Note that the shape of growth in each century is identical even as the totals always rapidly increase.

The explosive growth of exponentials brings up an important point. They can't be sustained. Within a few thousand years, the Indian investors above will have a dollar for every atom in the universe. Just try paying them off in small or even large bills! One wag used the sharp increase (10, 100, 1000, . . .) in the number of Elvis impersonators in the late 1970s to predict that by the late 1980s all U.S. males would sound and dress like the King. As with Elvis sightings, exponential functions are to be had wherever you look. But catch them quickly, before they leave the building.

- *Fractals* – Mathematicians continue their search for simple descriptions of new and interesting shapes. The computer has revealed a new aesthetic of what mathematical simplicity is. If a function is easy to program, then it is easy to describe. The new areas of fractals and cellular automata represent the latest ways to describe simple surfaces with simple mathematics. The modern answer to the question, How did the leopard get its spots?, is not with a just-so story but a simple cellular

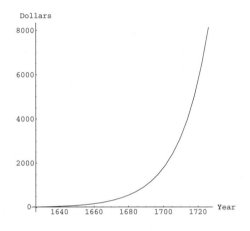

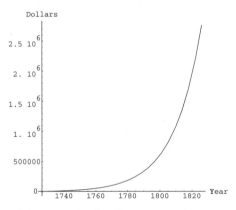

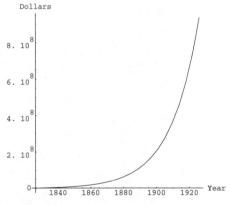

Three hundred years of compound interest (at 6% per year) applied to the proceeds from the sale of Manhattan.

automaton whose resulting patterns look astonishingly like leopard skin.

Fractals are curves that have certain self-reference properties. Zoom in on any portion of a fractal curve, and what you see will look suspiciously like the same curve at a larger scale. An interesting example of a fractal is Koch's *snowflake* curve. Start from a triangle and raise a triangular bump in each edge. Now repeat again with each edge of the new curve. And keep repeating. The results of this procedure look astonishingly like a snowflake even at arbitrary levels of magnification.

Such snowflake curves would be impossible to represent using the other mathematical functions have described. The uncanny resemblances between fractal curves and certain natural phenomena have led many to speculate on the birth of a new physics and the fractal geometry of nature. But certainly they provide an interesting tool with which to construct exciting new shapes.

Polynomials, exponentials, trigonometric functions, fractals – all these mathematically simple-to-describe curves are good for representing different families of shapes. Seventeenth-century mathematics was a gold rush of identifying and naming new families of curves and investigating their properties; they were given colorful names after their discoverers such as the ovals of Cassini, the witch of Agnesi, and the brachistocrone of Bernoulli.

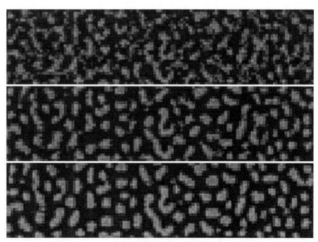

Leopard-skin patterns generated by Young's cellular automata model.

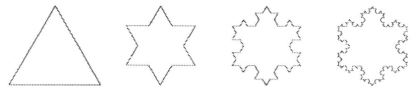

The first three iterations of the Koch snowflake curve.

The mathematical curves and surfaces they developed include many shapes of great beauty. Most university mathematics departments maintain collections of three-dimensional models of particularly interesting or important functions. Man Ray, the surrealist photographer, was intrigued by these mathematical shapes and wrote that "the formulas accompanying them meant nothing to me, but the forms were as varied and authentic as any in nature." Today, these models are being augmented with fantastic computer graphics imagery appearing both in textbooks and on T-shirts.

I conclude this digression to explain why I made it in the first place. In the next section, I will present our quest for a curve which, had I discovered it in the seventeenth century, might have been called the cesta of Skiena.

How Often Does X Beat Y?

In my humble opinion, the single most exciting sporting event in America is the first day of the NCAA Basketball Tournament. This tournament seeks to identify the best college basketball team in the nation starting from a field of 64 teams. The *last* day of the tournament, which pits the two surviving teams against each other to determine the champion, never holds much interest for me. However, in the first round we are treated to the spectacle of the highest seeded team (say the University of Kentucky, with a 31–2 record) playing the lowest seeded team (say Stony Brook, with an 11–19 record, which may have slithered into the field only through divine intervention). Why is this exciting? Kentucky knows Kentucky should win, and Stony Brook knows Kentucky should win, but somehow these expectations put the pressure on the better team. Every year the riff-raff scare the living hell out of the best teams in the land and sometimes beat them.

What does this have to do with jai alai? Suppose through our statistical analysis, we have decided that Lander wins, say 58.31% of the points he plays against the field, whereas Alberto wins only 45.11% of the points he plays. Now our Monte Carlo simulation tells us that Lander will play

101

the next point against Alberto. What is the probability that Lander wins the point?

This is a curious problem worth thinking about. Given that player A wins $\Pr(A)$ of his points played against everybody, and player B wins $\Pr(B)$ of his points played against everybody, what is the probability $\text{Prob}(A, B)$ that A beats B?

The answer must depend upon the nature of the contest. Suppose we want to predict the outcome of a battle of brute strength in which the stronger fellow always crushes the weaker one. Then the answer is simple. The probability that A beats B, $\text{Prob}(A, B)$, equals 1 if $\Pr(A)$ is bigger than $\Pr(B)$, and 0 if $\Pr(A)$ is less than $\Pr(B)$. But what about a more subtle sport in which upsets can occur, such as college basketball? This straightforward solution would clearly be inadequate.

In mathematical modeling, there are typically several different ways to approach a given problem. Good taste dictates that we consider the properties we want our solution to have and then find a function that does the job. Relevant properties for our points modeling problem include the following:

- *Integrity* – It is important that $\text{Prob}(A, B)$ be a real probability value, which means it must always lie between 0 and 1. The value of 0 means that A never defeats B, whereas a value of 1 makes A unbeatable. You would be surprised how often simple, reasonable-looking functions fail to yield real probabilities. For example, consider $\text{Prob}(A, B) = \Pr(A) - \Pr(B)$. This yields negative values whenever $P(A)$ is less than $P(B)$, which would be impossible for a probability value. Things can't happen less often than never!

- *Symmetry* – It makes sense that the probability that A wins should equal the probability that B loses. In other words, $\text{Prob}(A, B) = 1 - \text{Prob}(B, A)$.

- *Monotonicity* – A function f is *monotonically increasing* if $x \geq y$ implies that $f(x) \geq f(y)$ for all x and y. Our function should have certain monotonicity properties, namely that $\text{Prob}(A', B) \geq \text{Prob}(A, B)$ if $\Pr(A') \geq \Pr(A)$. Out of monotonicity and symmetry, we get for free...

- *Equality* – If $\Pr(A) = 0.45$ and $\Pr(B) = 0.45$, then it makes sense that A and B should have an equal chance of winning whenever they play each other. Thus, whenever $\Pr(A) = \Pr(B)$, $\text{Prob}(A, B) = 1/2$.

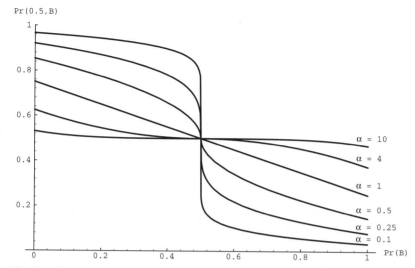

The family of point-win curves against an average player ($p = 0.5$), for $\alpha = \{0.1, 0.25, 0.5, 1, 4, 10\}$.

- *Generality* – We have seen that different types of contests will yield different types of functions. It is useful for our solution to consist of a function with a "fudge factor" that enables us to change the shape of the curve easily so that it is applicable in many different situations.
- *Simplicity* – Point scoring looks like it should be a simple problem, and thus we would expect a simple formula to result. Of course, many simple problems do not have simple solutions; life is a perpetual battle between Occam's razor and Murphy's law.[5]

What was our ultimate solution? The following function satisfies all of these requirements:

$$\text{Prob}(A, B) = \frac{1 + [\text{Pr}(A) - \text{Pr}(B)]^{\alpha}}{2} \quad \text{if} \quad \text{Pr}(A) \geq \text{Pr}(B)$$

$$\text{Prob}(A, B) = \frac{1 - [\text{Pr}(B) - \text{Pr}(A)]^{\alpha}}{2} \quad \text{if} \quad \text{Pr}(A) \leq \text{Pr}(B)$$

The constant $\alpha \geq 0$ is our fudge factor. Subtracting a small probability from a larger probability gives a number between 0 and 1, which

---

[5] *Occam's razor* is the philosophical principle that the simplest explanation of any phenomenon is best. *Murphy's law* is the philosophical principle that whatever can go wrong will go wrong.

is still a probability. Raising a probability to any power $\alpha \geq 0$ also leaves a probability. A large α means a small contribution from this term, whereas a small α implies the skill difference has a large impact on the outcome.

I illustrate this effect with a set of curves representing the probability that A will beat an average player B (i.e., $\Pr(B) = 1/2$) as a function of six different values of α. Each of these curves satisfies all of the properties listed above. Observe how the value of α provides us with a knob to tweak to generate a variety of different shapes from flat as a pancake to steep as a cliff. Though trial-and-error experiments, we determined that $\alpha \approx 0.4$ seemed to do the best job of predicting the winners of jai alai games, and that is what we generally will use from here on out.

The Hot-Hand Phenomenon

Is it reasonable to model human jai alai players merely as automata that output points according to a given probability distribution? We assume that each player always scores points uniformly at random according to his standard skill level with no correction for whether the simulated player scored the last point. Thus, our model ignores the possibility that players enter a mental zone in which they are unbeatable for the night or that they can be doomed to have a rotten day because of hangovers or pulled groins.

Certainly serious injuries will impair the performance of any athlete, but I think it is reasonable to assume that any pelotari is physically up to any match he plays in. If a player is not, why play and risk further injury when there are designated backups for each jai alai game? Missing one of 1200 games per season is not a serious problem. But our assumption that the results are completely independent of each other may seem more questionable. Isn't a player more likely to play badly after being the goat in the previous game? Conversely, any pelotari who just won three games in a row seems like a better than average bet to go for his fourth.

However, our model is supported by some fascinating studies of the "hot-hand" phenomenon of basketball. A time-tested strategy in basketball is to go with the hot hand, the fellow on the team who just can't seem to miss that night. Whenever a basketball player starts shooting the lights out, the basket looks like the opening of a dumpster to him – so big he can't miss. He's got confidence; he's shaking and baking and on a roll. The rest of the team just keeps feeding the ball to the hot hand – at least until the hot hand cools.

So if the hot hand works for basketball, why do we ignore it in our jai alai simulation? The reason is, surprisingly, that it doesn't really work in basketball! In a famous article, Gilovich, Vallone, and Tversky provided statistical evidence that cast doubt on the existence of hot streaks in sports. They examined the likelihood that a given NBA basketball player would make the $(k+1)$st shot in a row given that this player had made the last k. Careful statistical analysis of the sequences of shots showed that they did not differ in length from sequences that would be expected by chance alone.

But how can a phenomenon every basketball player has personally experienced just not exist? As we previously discussed, most people have a lousy understanding of how random sequences behave. If you make 50% of your shots on average, then by chance you are going to have long runs of baskets in exactly the same way a sequence of random coin flips will have long runs of tails. It is only human to feel on a roll when this happens, but it is a natural consequence of general shooting accuracy.

These counterintuitive results have sparked considerable debate, and follow-up studies provide some support for the concept of streaks in golf putting and professional pool. But in the absence of compelling evidence the other way, I am much happier using the simpler mathematical model of independence between games instead of trying to account for a phenomenon that may not even exist.

Correlation versus Causation

In a previous section, we used correlation coefficients to justify our assumption that we can use past results to predict future player performance. One of the tricky aspects of analyzing statistical data is distinguishing between correlation and causation. Two factors are *correlated* whenever a change in one of the sequences suggests that there will be a change in the other. Weight and height are well-correlated sequences in people. Tall people are likely to be heavier than shorter people. Education and income are also typically correlated. For the most part, people with greater education earn more money than those with less.

Properly interpreting correlations can be difficult. My favorite example is that the amount one exercises correlates positively with the probability of dying from cancer. Does this mean that exercise causes cancer? Of course not! It means that everybody dies of something. The physically fit are at increased risk of dying from a disease of old age (such as cancer) because they are at a decreased risk of an early death.

A sequence x has a *causal* relation to y if a change in the value of x is likely to impact the value of y. An example of a well-known causal relationship is that between interest rates and the price of stocks. Whenever interest rates rise, investors pull their money out of stocks to take advantage of this development, and stock prices drop. When interest rates decrease, investors take their money out of the bank and buy something that yields more of a return – typically stocks. Thus, not only are the sequences inversely correlated, but there is a reason for it – an honest causal relationship.

Two sequences can have high correlation without having a causal relationship between them. Consider the well-known connection between the winner of the Super Bowl and the fate of the stock market. The Super Bowl, held each January, pits the winner of the American Football Conference (AFC) against that of the National Football Conference (NFC). The stock market seems to be positively correlated with the fate of the NFC. When the NFC wins, the market goes up for the year, and when it loses the market goes down for the year. Since the Super Bowl began in 1967, this relationship has held an impressive 28 of 32 year, or 87.5% of the time.

If there was a causal relationship between the Super Bowl and the stock market, then we would be well justified in investing our money based on the outcome of the game. However, I for one am confident that this phenomenon is just a vagary of chance, a consequence of the fact that spurious correlations are certain to emerge whenever enough pairs of sequences are analyzed.

However, deciding whether a causal relationship between two factors *really* exists can be a very tricky business – indeed it can literally be a religious war. Consider the question of whether the Almighty acts on the prayers of the faithful. Countless people swear that the Lord heard their prayers and saved them. However, no statistical study worthy of the name has ever been able to convince nonbelievers. Is there a causal relation between faith and cure? What is the efficacy of prayer?

A notorious recent case is that of the "Bible code," mysterious messages apparently embedded in the Hebrew scriptures. A best-selling book by M. Droshin reported on patterns in the Torah (the first five books of the Bible) that predicted the assassination of Yitzhak Rabin and also encode other historical facts that would have been impossible for the authors of the books to know at the time. Unless of course, the authors of the Bible were divinely inspired . . .

This religious implication makes it impossible to convince any true believer that no causal relationship exists between divine authorship and the validity of the codes. Skeptics of the codes have instead focused on disproving the observed correlation instead of arguing against the causal relationship. By carefully analyzing the statistics associated with these observed patterns, they have convincingly shown the occurrences of them to be consistent with expectations in random texts. Indeed, they have found several amusing examples of "codes" in such holy scriptures as *Moby Dick* and *War and Peace.*

What's the Result?

The final products of our statistical modeling and curve plotting are player-pair point-win tables. I give examples of two point-win probability matrices generated for a given lineup of eight players. The players 1 through 8 in this example happen to be arranged in order of increasing skill, and their point-win probabilities against the entire field range from 0.4 to 0.6. These

Player-Pair Point-Win Matrices for $\alpha = 1.0$ and $\alpha = 0.4$

			$\alpha = 1.0$					
win %	0.40	0.425	0.45	0.475	0.5	0.525	0.55	0.60
.40	—	.488	.475	.462	.45	.438	.425	.4
.425	.512	—	.488	.475	.462	.45	.438	.412
.45	.525	.512	—	.488	.475	.462	.45	.425
.475	.538	.525	.512	—	.488	.475	.462	.438
.50	.55	.538	.525	.512	—	.488	.475	.45
.525	.562	.55	.538	.525	.512	—	.488	.462
.55	.575	.562	.55	.538	.525	.512	—	.475
.60	.6	.588	.575	.562	.55	.538	.525	—

			$\alpha = 0.4$					
win %	0.40	0.425	0.45	0.475	0.5	0.525	0.55	0.60
.40	—	.386	.349	.323	.301	.282	.266	.237
.425	.614	—	.386	.349	.323	.301	.282	.251
.45	.651	.614	—	.386	.349	.323	.301	.266
.475	.677	.651	.614	—	.386	.349	.323	.282
.50	.699	.677	.651	.614	—	.386	.349	.301
.525	.718	.699	.677	.651	.614	—	.386	.323
.55	.734	.718	.699	.677	.651	.614	—	.349
.60	.763	.749	.734	.718	.699	.677	.651	—

are fairly typical numbers. Each matrix presents the probabilities for each possible matchup between pairs of players.

The two matrices differ because they were generated with different values of the fudge factor α. The matrix on top used $\alpha = 1.0$, a very gentle skewing that actually reduces the degree of difference between these particular players. The bottom matrix used $\alpha = 0.4$, which our experiments suggest makes the simulation most accurately reflect reality.

Using the appropriate such matrix within a Monte Carlo simulation should yield reasonably accurate predictions of the outcome of jai alai matches. But that alone is still not enough information to venture an intelligent wager on the match. We must be able to estimate accurately what our payoff will be if we win. This requires that we delve much deeper into the economics of jai alai.

CHAPTER SIX

MODELING THE PAYOFFS

Economists are very concerned with the concept of *market efficiency*. Markets are efficient whenever prices reflect underlying values. Market efficiency implies that everyone has the same information about what is available and processes it correctly.

The question of whether the jai alai bettors' market is efficient goes straight to the heart of whether there is any hope to make money betting on it. All of the information that we use to predict the outcome of jai alai matches is available to the general public. Because we are betting against the public, we can only win if we can interpret this data more successfully than the rest of the market. We can win money if and only if the market is inefficient.

Analyzing market efficiency requires us to build a model of how the general public bets. Once we have an accurate betting model, we can compare it with the results of our Monte Carlo simulation to look for inefficiencies. Any bet that the public rates higher than our simulation is one to stay away from, whereas any bet that the simulation rates higher than the public represents a market inefficiency potentially worth exploiting.

The issue of market efficiency rears its head most dramatically in the stock market. Billions of dollars are traded daily in the major markets by tens of thousands of people watching minute-by-minute stock ticker reports. Quantitative market analysts (the so-called quants) believe that there are indeed inefficiencies in the stock market that show up as statistical patterns. Companies like D. E. Shaw and Renaissance Technology hire large teams of people with training like mine to perform analyses to find such patterns to invest in and exploit.

But are these patterns really present, and are they large enough to exploit? Many knowledgeable people believe that the behavior of the stock market is essentially random walk that is totally unpredictable. If so, it means these market inefficiencies don't really exist. And if they do exist, they will not exist for long. The quants have taken their beatings along the way.

Why should the situation be any different in jai alai than the stock market? My sense is that the average dollar in jai alai is spent in a less informed way than one invested in the stock market. I have never seen anyone hanging off the railing at the New York Stock Exchange yelling "You stink, ATT!" or "Miss it, TXN!" If the average bettor trusts oracles like *Pepe's Green Card* or knows as little about jai alai as I did before beginning this study – well, there are bound to be plenty of market inefficiencies. All we had to do was find them.

Pari-Mutuel Wagering

Accurately modeling payoffs requires us to face the question of exactly how the fronton makes its money. Running a professional jai alai fronton is an expensive proposition and involves several hundred people. Each fronton has a stable of at least 30 professional players who insist on being paid, as do the cashiers, cleaning people, management, and stockholders. Admission to a fronton costs only a few bucks; consequently, even 1500 paying spectators per match do not provide much of a revenue stream.

Much more than by selling tickets, refreshments, and copies of *Pepe's Green Card*, frontons make their money by taking a cut of the betting action. Jai alai frontons in the United States operate under the *pari-mutuel* system. Developed by a Frenchman, Pierre Ollier, in the middle of the nineteenth century, the pari-mutuel ("wagers among ourselves") system dispenses with odds makers who use their judgment to decide how much a given wager should pay. Ollier owned a perfume shop in Paris and developed his system in reaction to losing too much of his own money to bookies. Instead, all of the money wagered on the given type of bet is put into a single pool to be divided equally among the winning bets. However, *before* it is divided up, a house cut of roughly 20% is extracted from this pool and taken by the fronton (and its partner, the state government.)

Let's see an example of the system in action. Suppose the following amounts of money were bet on each of the eight possible winning outcomes:

Position	1	2	3	4	5	6	7	8
Amount Bet	$10	$20	$25	$40	$25	$20	$0	$10

The total amount of money in the pool is $150. After the house deducts its 20% cut, the pool is left with $120 in it. Suppose that number 1 wins the match. The payoff will be $120/$10 = $12 per dollar invested on the winner, and thus a bet of $3 would pay off $36.00. If number 4 had won the match, the payoff per dollar would be only $3, and thus a $3 bet would pay off $9.00. The odds reported in the newspaper or on the tote board refer to the amount paid off on the house's minimum allowable bet – typically $2 or $3.

Now suppose number 7 had won the match. Because no one bet any money on this possibility, typically the price of all win tickets would be refunded, although the exact policy depends upon local rules. This is a rare but not unheard of event; it occasionally happens in very early or late matches that have fewer customers.

Dividing up the place and show pools is a somewhat more complicated process. After the house extracts its cut, it sets aside an amount equal to the amount bet on all winning entries from the pool, and thus each winning bettor is assured of getting back at least his or her initial stake. The remaining money is split into equal-sized pools, one for each of the two (for place) or three (for show) different paying numbers. Each of these pools is divided among the dollars bet on the given number and returned along with the initial stake. Thus, the two different place payoffs in any match are usually different. In the example on page 76, 8 to place paid off at $16.50 whereas 4 to place paid only $9.90. Significantly more money was bet on 4 to place; consequently, its half of the pool had to be shared among more bettors.

In addition to the 15–20% deducted from the pool as house advantage, the fronton also profits from the *breakage*, the odd cents left over when dividing the pool. For reasons of either convenience, tradition, or greed, all payoffs at the track or fronton are given as multiples of 10 cents. You see payoffs of $14.40, but not $14.47. So what happens to that extra $0.07 per winning ticket whenever the pool works out that way? The answer is that it is deducted as breakage and is split between the state and the fronton according to prevailing local laws. These pennies certainly add up. The breakage works out to, on average, a nickel per winning ticket, thus adding another percentage point or two to the house advantage. This nickel works out as a lower percentage of exotic bets such as trifecta, because it is a negligible fraction of the payoff, but represents a more serious cut of the win, place, and show payoffs.

The computers used today crunch out these payoff computations in a fraction of a second. Thus, payoff results are typically posted within a minute of the completion of each match, which is somewhat faster than in years past. But in those precomputer days, the money counting and pool computations had to be done by hand. That they were performed quickly and accurately enough to satisfy impatient and suspicious gamblers was a feat worthy of our respect.

There are several interesting implications of the pari-mutuel system. First, the exact payoffs for any bet are not known to anybody in advance. To estimate the payoff you will receive, you really have to know how other people are betting. For this reason, every fronton or racetrack has an electronic scoreboard or monitor that flashes the current odds for each possible wager. Many "professional" gamblers make a careful study of the odds board and place their bet at the last possible minute, investing in players who seem undervalued by the rest of the betting population. Observe the difference from casino games, for you always know that a correct bet on black in roulette pays off at two-to-one regardless of how many other people have also invested on black.

Because of the pari-mutuel system, every bettor can theoretically pick the winner in jai alai, and the fronton *still* makes money.[1] This is not true of casinos and to my way of thinking makes frontons much friendlier places than casinos. Frontons want you to bet, whereas casinos want you to lose.

---

[1] This isn't completely true because many states guarantee bettors a minimum return (say 10%) on every winning bet, which would have to come from the house if everybody picked the same winner. This would be an unheard of situation in jai alai. Such minus pools do arise occasionally in horse racing – typically when a wonder horse goes up against thoroughly inadequate competition.

This may seem a meaningless distinction because casino odds are sufficiently stacked against you that the more you bet, the more you are almost certain to lose. However, it shows up clearly in how the house deals with systems bettors. Every casino employs a large security staff with sophisticated surveillance equipment who watch any successful bettor's every move. If the security force finds you using any forbidden equipment (like a computer in your shoe) or any successful mathematical technique (like card counting in blackjack), you will be tossed out on your rear hard enough to know *never* to come back.

Now conversely, suppose I showed up at the fronton with my laptop computer and a system guaranteed to make money betting on jai alai. Management would welcome me with open arms. The house keeps 20% of everything I wager, and I must spend money to make money. If I were successful, I would just be taking money from other bettors, but this is none of the fronton's concern.

Ollier's pari-mutuel system caught on quickly in France but was initially unpopular in the United States because bettors then (as now) wanted to be able to bet on long shots that paid off (if successful) at high odds. Under the pari-mutuel system, whenever many people bet on a long shot, it ceases to be one. Other bettors feared that the house would manipulate the calculations to skim off more than their allotted share.

Once the tide started shifting against them, bookmakers tried to compete by paying off at the same odds as those of the racetrack, with the added advantage that your bets would not depress the payoffs as they did when you bet at the track. Sharpies took advantage of the situation by investing relatively small amounts of money at the track on everything *except* the horse they wanted and then large amounts at the bookie on their favorite. Their preliminary wagers skewed the small pool so that their real horse paid off at greatly inflated odds, which the bookie then had to match. One by one, these bookies were put out of business, and now the pari-mutuel system reigns throughout horse racing and jai alai.

Estimating the Payoffs

Being able to pick winners in jai alai is not enough to make money. We need to be able to pick them better than other people.

Remember that glorious 4–2–1 trifecta triumph my brothers and I had via *Pepe's Green Card*. Sure, Pepe picked a winner, and we had a profitable evening. But the trifecta payoff of $124.60 for a $2 bet represents a terrible return on investment when we factor in risk. Essentially we got back $60 for every $1 we bet for successfully picking a 336-to-1 shot.

Why was the payoff so low? Every *yutz* who bought a *Pepe's Green Card* that night probably bet on the same 4–2–1 trifecta, which tremendously dampened the odds. The final payoff probably would have been three or four times higher without the influence of Pepe's disciples. Although it is impossible to predict who Pepe will pick, we can study past payoffs to get a handle on how the public bets.

We can model the behavior by properly interpreting the statistical evidence of previous payoffs. My belief is that there are three major factors that the betting public uses to decide where to place its bets:

■ *Estimates of player skills* – Every jai alai bettor is given the nightly program of matches as he or she walks into the fronton. In addition to the playing schedule, the program typically includes statistical measures of the performance of each entrant. Usually this consists of the win, place, and show record for each player this season sometimes supplemented by the entrant's record in the particular game number. For example, a reader of the program might learn that the team of Zarandona and Guisasola have a record of 7–4–9 as a doubles team in 47 games and that Guisasola has a personal record of 19–12–20 in the 139 Game 3's he played this season.

Personally, I cannot imagine why any bettor would find a pelotari's Game 3 record useful for predictive purposes any more than a baseball player's Tuesday average. But I don't have to. If I know that people are using this information to bet, it potentially provides some kind of edge for me if I am making more rational forecasts.

■ *Records of post positions* – The nightly program also includes tables showing how often each win, place, show, quiniela, exacta, and trifecta have occurred thus far this season. These tables alert the bettor to much of what we learned from our initial Monte Carlo simulation, namely that certain combinations occur much more often than others.

■ *Whims and fancy* – Here I might credit factors like *Pepe's Green Card* and all bets based on birthdays and lucky hotel room numbers. There doesn't seem to be very much one can do to model this sort of thing. Presumably these essentially random factors serve to cancel each other out. For every grandmother who bets on 4–8 quinielas because she likᵉ green and purple uniforms, there will be a granddaughter who thinks Olate has a cute butt.

The most straightforward approach to model how the public accounts for post position is simply to average the payoffs from all the times that the combination has occurred. By this point in the project, we had a logged the results of 7730 jai alai matches. This was a large enough database to provide some meaningful results. The average payoff of the 455 successful 1–2 quinielas was only $17.46 per dollar, whereas the average payoff of the 279 4–8 quinielas was $26.41 per dollar. These are enough results to convince me that a 4–8 quiniela bet should pay off substantially better than a 1–2 quiniela if, in fact, the combination wins.

Our payoff models are given in Tables 6.1–6.4. These payoffs are normalized to represent the amount returned per dollar invested so that we can properly combine the results from Dania and Milford. Because the two frontons have different minimum bet amounts, directly averaging payoffs from them would produce meaningless results.

What do these tables show?

- Table 6.1 presents the average payoffs for win, place, and show betting. As a citizen, I am gratified to see that the average payoff per dollar varies inversely with the number of times each result occurred. This means that the public is smart enough to understand that certain positions come in more often than others and bet accordingly. As a gambler, I find this somewhat less heartwarming because I become a better bettor the more wrongheaded the public is.

  The most interesting anomaly in these data is that the public prefers betting on 1 rather than 2. Two-to-win pays off 30 cents more per dollar than 1-to-win, even though 2 came in more often for win, place, and show.

- Table 6.2 presents the average payoff for quiniela bets. The payoffs per dollar range from $16.53 to $47.62, a much narrower band than the number of occurrences (86 to 455), which suggests that the public undervalues the most commonly occurring trifectas. This phenomenon also exists in horse racing and other types of sports betting in which it has long been recognized that the public tends to underbet the favorite.

- Table 6.3 presents the average payoff for exacta bets. There are twice as many betting opportunities with exactas as with quinielas, and evidence that the public does not evaluate exactas as well as the simpler

TABLE 6.1. Average Win, Place, and Show Payoffs from Dania and Milford

Bet Type	Bet	Dania Matinee Count	Dania Matinee Payoff	Dania Evening Count	Dania Evening Payoff	Milford Matinee Count	Milford Matinee Payoff	Milford Evening Count	Milford Evening Payoff	Totals Average Count	Totals Average Payoff/$
Win	1	194	$11.91	311	$12.10	266	$19.04	341	$19.34	1112	$6.23
Win	2	193	$12.70	321	$11.94	266	$20.00	371	$21.11	1151	$6.54
Win	3	177	$13.38	287	$12.58	207	$19.86	296	$22.05	967	$6.76
Win	4	165	$13.25	267	$14.39	228	$22.00	300	$22.25	960	$7.20
Win	5	150	$14.34	251	$15.02	228	$21.79	282	$20.29	911	$7.16
Win	6	159	$16.67	220	$16.73	223	$23.00	284	$24.41	886	$8.11
Win	7	126	$18.47	203	$17.54	230	$22.86	254	$22.67	813	$8.14
Win	8	153	$16.60	249	$15.66	248	$23.57	280	$24.42	930	$8.01
Place	1	417	$6.34	692	$6.00	592	$8.87	781	$9.26	2482	$3.04
Place	2	427	$5.93	730	$5.63	622	$8.70	779	$9.02	2558	$2.92
Place	3	404	$7.30	610	$7.02	536	$9.81	674	$10.14	2224	$3.44
Place	4	360	$7.60	546	$7.60	469	$10.59	606	$11.65	1981	$3.76
Place	5	302	$9.45	484	$8.29	456	$11.26	552	$11.24	1794	$4.02
Place	6	240	$9.03	391	$8.76	369	$12.76	482	$13.06	1482	$4.36
Place	7	227	$9.51	369	$9.84	371	$12.37	454	$12.53	1421	$4.45
Place	8	256	$10.51	396	$9.44	371	$12.91	468	$13.34	1491	$4.62
Show	1	641	$4.14	1022	$4.09	888	$5.72	1112	$6.11	3663	$2.01
Show	2	627	$4.11	1054	$4.09	882	$5.87	1118	$6.29	3681	$2.04
Show	3	593	$4.88	929	$4.96	826	$6.22	1038	$6.68	3386	$2.30
Show	4	527	$5.12	798	$4.96	725	$7.12	946	$7.15	2996	$2.44
Show	5	482	$5.72	755	$5.52	709	$7.50	885	$7.70	2831	$2.65
Show	6	388	$6.46	634	$5.76	560	$8.53	720	$8.34	2302	$2.90
Show	7	326	$6.19	559	$5.92	536	$8.69	637	$8.22	2058	$2.90
Show	8	388	$6.70	576	$6.08	498	$8.77	637	$9.14	2076	$3.07

bets. The spread on payoff-per-dollar (from $35.79 to $135.19) is only slight broader than that of quinielas, but the band of occurrences is much wider (17 to 269). Indeed, the average payoff for the rarest exacta (6–8) is substantially less than that of one that occurred more than three times as often (5–6).

■ Tables 6.4–6.7 present our model of trifecta payoffs. These payoffs were subjected to a grouping and averaging procedure (to be discussed later) that explains why trifectas 7–1–2 and 7–1–3 have the same projected Milford matinee payoff even though the former never occurred in the data.

In *The Gambling Times Guide to Jai-Alai*, Keevers reports that the trifectas 5–2–4 and 5–3–2 came up most frequently when he considered the question in 1982. Indeed, 5–2–4 and its twin 5–1–4 come up most frequently (74 and 71 times, respectively) over all of the trifectas.

TABLE 6.2. Average Quiniela Payoffs from Dania and Milford

| | Dania | | | Milford | | | Totals | |
| | Matinee | | Evening | | Matinee | | Evening | | Average | |
Bet	Count	Payoff	Count	Payoff	Count	Payoff	Count	Payoff	Count	Payoff/$
1–2	79	$29.17	138	$26.32	105	$70.82	133	$56.33	455	$17.46
1–3	67	$29.00	109	$26.82	82	$59.98	135	$60.49	393	$17.29
1–4	68	$33.09	105	$30.83	94	$61.62	135	$67.58	402	$19.19
1–5	60	$35.40	95	$34.22	111	$69.37	109	$57.66	375	$19.60
1–6	50	$40.77	100	$44.31	81	$77.55	111	$68.66	342	$23.01
1–7	37	$45.03	75	$44.57	60	$75.84	82	$69.34	254	$23.29
1–8	55	$48.75	70	$46.71	59	$82.60	78	$85.83	262	$26.07
2–3	65	$32.16	136	$29.07	91	$53.77	121	$53.94	413	$16.53
2–4	80	$32.51	118	$29.18	99	$59.46	116	$51.16	413	$16.86
2–5	64	$30.76	107	$32.55	101	$66.61	127	$54.59	399	$18.24
2–6	43	$39.36	70	$36.23	72	$92.75	117	$68.18	302	$23.18
2–7	50	$42.38	83	$41.73	79	$66.26	97	$68.23	309	$21.82
2–8	46	$46.40	78	$48.75	75	$85.59	68	$79.97	267	$25.92
3–4	61	$43.28	71	$44.85	66	$77.19	72	$73.95	270	$23.65
3–5	55	$41.35	95	$38.52	70	$65.03	93	$75.19	313	$21.77
3–6	56	$45.48	65	$46.40	72	$81.48	86	$71.28	279	$24.30
3–7	49	$45.93	64	$47.53	81	$72.57	83	$87.19	277	$25.34
3–8	51	$48.80	69	$45.52	75	$70.85	86	$87.32	281	$25.23
4–5	31	$62.65	55	$65.96	37	$99.76	67	$98.47	190	$32.71
4–6	43	$49.70	61	$50.57	53	$94.25	54	$91.53	211	$28.07
4–7	34	$45.94	55	$51.29	60	$70.49	68	$73.70	217	$24.29
4–8	41	$43.06	80	$49.56	62	$92.77	96	$80.83	279	$26.41
5–6	20	$84.39	40	$81.77	35	$126.30	38	$145.97	133	$43.62
5–7	31	$53.18	44	$68.15	48	$83.34	59	$79.21	182	$28.65
5–8	39	$51.14	48	$56.98	55	$98.05	64	$84.83	206	$28.99
6–7	14	$107.20	24	$93.71	28	$133.10	32	$145.25	98	$47.62
6–8	12	$91.92	28	$87.22	29	$106.61	47	$105.56	116	$38.42
7–8	12	$92.48	22	$100.88	18	$135.60	34	$123.77	86	$45.13

Further, 5–3–2 was no slouch, coming in 58 times and behind only 1–2–6 (58), 2–3–1 (60), 2–5–1 (65), 4–1–3 (68), 4–2–3 (67), 5–1–3 (64), 5–3–1 (60), 6–1–4 (63), and 6–2–5 (58). The payoffs for these high-flying triples were suitably depressed, although the expected payoff for 5–2–4 was inexplicably higher by almost $30 per dollar invested than 5–1–4.

Let's compare these results with our original Monte Carlo simulation, which assumed equal player skills. According to our simulation, the most frequently occurring trifectas should have been 1–4–2 and

117

TABLE 6.3. Average Exacta Payoffs from Dania and Milford

| | Dania | | | | Milford | | | | Totals | |
| | Matinee | | Evening | | Matinee | | Evening | | Average | |
Bet	Count	Payoff	Count	Payoff	Count	Payoff	Count	Payoff	Count	Payoff/$
1–2	41	$84.34	74	$80.27	57	$106.54	65	$110.83	237	$38.50
1–3	28	$90.33	50	$90.13	38	$107.27	58	$113.46	174	$40.63
1–4	25	$118.13	36	$106.99	27	$123.11	45	$124.23	133	$47.92
1–5	30	$101.86	35	$106.40	46	$145.09	42	$137.19	153	$49.25
1–6	21	$143.14	47	$146.86	34	$152.59	46	$137.37	148	$59.39
1–7	21	$167.16	37	$129.87	39	$152.52	47	$139.03	144	$57.77
1–8	27	$170.14	32	$160.12	26	$189.55	38	$154.26	123	$68.75
2–1	38	$90.25	64	$85.86	48	$109.84	68	$98.57	218	$38.78
2–3	28	$112.46	62	$100.05	49	$112.75	57	$112.97	196	$44.20
2–4	34	$123.56	42	$98.34	37	$131.41	42	$132.70	155	$49.32
2–5	29	$118.45	45	$101.25	45	$114.87	51	$128.12	170	$46.45
2–6	16	$126.39	29	$118.03	26	$145.95	60	$145.06	131	$52.59
2–7	25	$137.04	40	$140.43	31	$155.22	54	$140.84	150	$57.74
2–8	23	$152.13	39	$151.56	30	$158.24	39	$130.78	131	$60.97
3–1	39	$80.93	59	$84.02	44	$96.42	77	$92.18	219	$35.79
3–2	37	$90.01	74	$87.90	42	$88.46	64	$87.49	217	$36.97
3–4	25	$156.56	33	$147.48	24	$163.40	25	$183.76	107	$67.56
3–5	19	$126.57	35	$146.77	16	$170.64	34	$174.54	104	$64.03
3–6	14	$169.37	20	$144.81	20	$157.75	24	$204.25	78	$68.20
3–7	18	$148.67	35	$169.64	32	$143.67	33	$134.19	118	$61.99
3–8	25	$139.20	31	$143.71	29	$164.41	39	$159.77	124	$61.56
4–1	43	$99.31	69	$84.08	67	$88.73	90	$95.57	269	$36.75
4–2	46	$92.82	76	$85.20	62	$98.17	74	$85.92	258	$36.90
4–3	36	$125.46	38	$124.82	42	$133.13	47	$117.94	163	$51.18
4–5	9	$208.50	21	$232.33	18	$270.50	29	$277.83	77	$99.82
4–6	5	$154.98	15	$214.36	14	$224.40	8	$329.96	42	$93.39
4–7	12	$175.50	22	$203.50	9	$270.00	18	$162.03	61	$83.17
4–8	14	$179.08	26	$213.55	16	$203.42	33	$183.75	89	$80.18
5–1	30	$103.40	60	$108.72	65	$104.45	67	$103.97	222	$42.33
5–2	35	$83.38	62	$98.31	56	$99.26	76	$103.03	229	$39.17
5–3	36	$109.27	60	$110.85	54	$106.41	59	$110.82	209	$44.91
5–4	22	$180.09	34	$186.55	18	$163.68	38	$168.22	112	$73.80
5–6	7	$291.30	20	$349.29	15	$262.64	11	$365.29	53	$135.19
5–7	10	$224.29	11	$311.60	8	$255.71	20	$217.25	49	$101.34
5–8	8	$247.57	4	$192.45	10	$175.53	11	$200.24	33	$81.65
6–1	29	$141.97	53	$124.63	47	$123.25	65	$126.34	194	$51.70
6–2	27	$113.68	41	$123.73	46	$125.33	57	$113.48	171	$47.66
6–3	42	$107.02	45	$116.04	52	$105.22	62	$116.39	201	$45.21
6–4	38	$130.18	46	$140.95	39	$127.51	46	$137.15	169	$56.07
6–5	13	$305.17	19	$251.82	20	$239.44	27	$260.11	79	$105.23
6–7	8	$343.65	11	$264.68	14	$242.46	15	$273.66	48	$111.05
6–8	1	$196.00	3	$385.60	3	$260.60	10	$286.05	17	$111.21

	Dania				Milford				Totals	
	Matinee		Evening		Matinee		Evening		Average	
Bet	Count	Payoff	Count	Payoff	Count	Payoff	Count	Payoff	Count	Payoff/$
7–1	16	$133.91	38	$151.28	21	$133.34	35	$130.05	110	$58.15
7–2	25	$139.84	43	$128.55	48	$128.18	43	$123.68	159	$52.43
7–3	31	$151.80	29	$153.63	49	$127.10	50	$130.95	159	$55.59
7–4	22	$136.57	33	$144.72	51	$125.23	50	$124.85	156	$51.92
7–5	21	$175.19	33	$180.18	39	$139.18	39	$158.05	132	$65.73
7–6	6	$239.10	13	$365.74	12	$279.07	14	$222.58	45	$116.66
7–8	5	$301.44	12	$397.10	11	$287.51	21	$288.27	49	$126.70
8–1	28	$158.11	38	$127.23	33	$181.10	40	$143.85	139	$61.45
8–2	23	$138.05	39	$142.93	45	$150.31	29	$148.50	136	$59.30
8–3	26	$123.64	38	$123.44	46	$118.70	47	$123.59	157	$49.10
8–4	27	$102.99	54	$118.94	46	$128.93	62	$112.42	189	$47.10
8–5	31	$118.11	44	$147.63	45	$118.41	53	$119.04	173	$51.78
8–6	11	$262.31	25	$192.59	26	$239.85	36	$195.28	98	$84.41
8–7	7	$321.34	10	$374.70	7	$286.59	12	$260.05	36	$130.75

TABLE 6.3, continued

2–4–1, both of which should have occurred about 15% more often than 5–1–4 and 5–2–4. But they happened only 43 and 50 times, respectively. This difference between theory and practice presumably reflects the influence of the matchmakers, who consistently avoid putting the best players in the two most advantageous positions.

These expected payoff tables ignore the public's perception of player skills and reflect only the initial post positions. We performed some computer experiments to seek correlations between the average payoffs and our measure of player skills but didn't find any. This can be interpreted in one of two ways. Either the betting public does not consider who is a better player in selecting their investments or does not think much of how we model player skills. Either way, these results justify using our simple tables to predict payoffs.

Gambling and the Stock Market

Coupling the results of our Monte Carlo simulations with our expected payoff models gave us everything we needed to put together a betting system. To evaluate our method, we used our Monte Carlo simulation to replay all games from the previous year, incorporating our win-point probabilities to model player skills. The result of each game's simulation

CALCULATED BETS

TABLE 6.4. Average Trifecta Payoffs from Dania and Milford (1 and 2 to Win)

	Dania				Milford				Totals	
	Matinee		Evening		Matinee		Evening		Average	
Bet	Count	Payoff	Count	Payoff	Count	Payoff	Count	Payoff	Count	Payoff/$
1–2–3	4	$446.56	7	$435.82	6	$931.15	7	$1031.31	24	$278.63
1–2–4	8	$346.41	7	$435.82	7	$791.87	9	$772.16	31	$228.23
1–2–5	7	$389.97	13	$357.57	12	$600.65	8	$777.70	40	$204.14
1–2–6	9	$378.12	16	$274.83	15	$555.89	18	$541.67	58	$171.20
1–2–7	6	$390.86	12	$441.48	11	$600.41	19	$510.47	48	$192.83
1–2–8	1	$651.51	4	$532.54	6	$931.15	4	$1602.27	15	$359.30
1–3–2	6	$390.86	10	$357.56	7	$791.87	18	$541.67	41	$196.54
1–3–4	0	$651.51	1	$617.46	2	$1848.91	1	$1746.80	4	$530.90
1–3–5	5	$409.37	5	$547.30	2	$1848.91	12	$653.24	24	$259.88
1–3–6	3	$512.36	8	$379.95	7	$791.87	7	$1031.31	25	$261.70
1–3–7	7	$389.97	13	$357.57	12	$600.65	11	$661.04	43	$198.03
1–3–8	4	$446.56	7	$435.82	8	$821.88	9	$772.16	28	$247.38
1–4–2	8	$346.41	13	$357.57	7	$791.87	15	$559.60	43	$194.31
1–4–3	4	$446.56	3	$619.84	1	$1848.91	7	$1031.31	15	$323.04
1–4–5	1	$651.51	1	$617.46	0	$1848.91	1	$1746.80	3	$405.58
1–4–6	1	$651.51	3	$619.84	2	$1848.91	7	$1031.31	13	$376.50
1–4–7	3	$512.36	7	$435.82	7	$791.87	6	$1179.35	23	$282.62
1–4–8	5	$409.37	4	$532.54	9	$871.78	9	$772.16	27	$260.01
1–5–2	11	$267.35	14	$345.53	13	$609.87	13	$613.99	51	$180.25
1–5–3	7	$389.97	8	$379.95	16	$588.81	12	$653.24	43	$200.88
1–5–4	2	$554.06	3	$619.84	6	$931.15	3	$1795.16	14	$367.23
1–5–6	0	$651.51	0	$619.84	2	$1848.91	2	$1746.80	4	$599.28
1–5–7	4	$446.56	3	$619.84	2	$1848.91	5	$1179.35	14	$358.65
1–5–8	4	$446.56	3	$619.84	6	$931.15	7	$1031.31	20	$304.58
1–6–2	2	$554.06	12	$441.48	10	$705.09	11	$661.04	35	$227.92
1–6–3	2	$554.06	15	$373.82	14	$573.33	12	$653.24	43	$201.07
1–6–4	7	$389.97	5	$547.30	5	$892.28	15	$559.60	32	$219.32
1–6–5	1	$651.51	1	$617.46	3	$1424.04	2	$1746.80	7	$460.44
1–6–7	0	$651.51	1	$617.46	1	$1848.91	1	$1746.80	3	$502.43
1–6–8	0	$651.51	0	$619.84	1	$1848.91	5	$1179.35	6	$430.31
1–7–2	1	$651.51	8	$379.95	6	$931.15	5	$1179.35	20	$283.67
1–7–3	2	$554.06	10	$357.56	13	$609.87	17	$560.21	42	$194.27
1–7–4	5	$409.37	9	$398.43	7	$791.87	11	$661.04	32	$221.50
1–7–5	7	$389.97	5	$547.30	7	$791.87	10	$661.04	29	$233.94
1–7–6	1	$651.51	0	$619.84	6	$931.15	3	$1795.16	10	$398.32
1–7–8	0	$651.51	0	$619.84	0	$1848.91	1	$1746.80	1	$582.27
1–8–2	1	$651.51	0	$619.84	0	$1848.91	0	$1795.16	1	$325.75
1–8–3	5	$409.37	7	$435.82	5	$892.28	8	$777.70	25	$244.39
1–8–4	6	$390.86	7	$435.82	8	$821.88	13	$613.99	34	$222.07
1–8–5	5	$409.37	6	$496.42	10	$705.09	10	$661.04	31	$227.95
1–8–6	4	$446.56	2	$617.46	3	$1424.04	2	$1746.80	11	$372.65
1–8–7	1	$651.51	0	$619.84	0	$1848.91	3	$1795.16	4	$530.23

TABLE 6.4, continued

	Dania			Milford				Totals	
	Matinee		Evening		Matinee		Evening		Average
Bet	Count	Payoff	Count	Payoff	Count	Payoff	Count	Payoff	Count	Payoff/$
2–1–3	1	$651.51	5	$547.30	5	$892.28	5	$1179.35	16	$321.67
2–1–4	6	$390.86	8	$379.95	13	$609.87	10	$661.04	37	$203.75
2–1–5	4	$446.56	8	$379.95	15	$555.89	18	$541.67	45	$187.61
2–1–6	8	$346.41	14	$345.53	9	$871.78	20	$451.83	51	$184.94
2–1–7	4	$446.56	13	$357.57	6	$931.15	10	$661.04	33	$220.70
2–1–8	4	$446.56	4	$532.54	0	$1848.91	5	$1179.35	13	$301.83
2–3–1	8	$346.41	18	$352.25	15	$555.89	19	$510.47	60	$176.14
2–3–4	0	$651.51	1	$617.46	4	$1256.37	0	$1795.16	5	$396.78
2–3–5	3	$512.36	7	$435.82	10	$705.09	8	$777.70	28	$239.93
2–3–6	0	$651.51	10	$357.56	4	$1256.37	10	$661.04	24	$236.10
2–3–7	5	$409.37	6	$496.42	9	$871.78	9	$772.16	29	$256.71
2–3–8	9	$378.12	9	$398.43	7	$791.87	11	$661.04	36	$215.72
2–4–1	17	$248.74	10	$357.56	12	$600.65	11	$661.04	50	$174.57
2–4–3	2	$554.06	3	$619.84	10	$705.09	7	$1031.31	22	$283.66
2–4–5	1	$651.51	0	$619.84	0	$1848.91	1	$1746.80	2	$454.01
2–4–6	2	$554.06	3	$619.84	4	$1256.37	1	$1746.80	10	$374.12
2–4–7	3	$512.36	6	$496.42	5	$892.28	8	$777.70	22	$264.49
2–4–8	4	$446.56	11	$382.22	6	$931.15	14	$641.83	35	$224.37
2–5–1	9	$378.12	17	$209.13	19	$437.19	20	$451.83	65	$142.47
2–5–3	10	$423.17	8	$379.95	12	$600.65	14	$641.83	44	$205.31
2–5–4	2	$554.06	1	$617.46	9	$871.78	3	$1795.16	15	$351.55
2–5–6	0	$651.51	0	$619.84	2	$1848.91	2	$1746.80	4	$599.28
2–5–7	2	$554.06	4	$532.54	3	$1424.04	2	$1746.80	11	$382.52
2–5–8	2	$554.06	5	$547.30	0	$1848.91	10	$661.04	17	$242.69
2–6–1	5	$409.37	8	$379.95	6	$931.15	16	$559.60	35	$211.15
2–6–3	4	$446.56	10	$357.56	10	$705.09	24	$452.54	48	$180.24
2–6–4	3	$512.36	4	$532.54	5	$892.28	9	$772.16	21	$268.44
2–6–5	1	$651.51	3	$619.84	2	$1848.91	4	$1602.27	10	$462.45
2–6–7	0	$651.51	0	$619.84	2	$1848.91	3	$1795.16	5	$605.55
2–6–8	0	$651.51	0	$619.84	0	$1848.91	4	$1602.27	4	$534.09
2–7–1	3	$512.36	7	$435.82	10	$705.09	11	$661.04	31	$228.00
2–7–3	4	$446.56	9	$398.43	7	$791.87	14	$641.83	34	$221.44
2–7–4	3	$512.36	8	$379.95	6	$931.15	17	$560.21	34	$215.45
2–7–5	5	$409.37	5	$547.30	8	$821.88	8	$777.70	26	$256.05
2–7–6	0	$651.51	1	$617.46	0	$1848.91	1	$1746.80	2	$445.50
2–7–8	0	$651.51	1	$617.46	0	$1848.91	2	$1746.80	3	$491.09
2–8–1	0	$651.51	2	$617.46	0	$1848.91	2	$1746.80	4	$445.50
2–8–3	2	$554.06	6	$496.42	4	$1256.37	12	$653.24	24	$263.81
2–8–4	6	$390.86	10	$357.56	7	$791.87	5	$1179.35	28	$241.92
2–8–5	2	$554.06	7	$435.82	12	$600.65	10	$661.04	31	$215.66
2–8–6	6	$390.86	6	$496.42	4	$1256.37	7	$1031.31	23	$293.19
2–8–7	0	$651.51	0	$619.84	2	$1848.91	2	$1746.80	4	$599.28

TABLE 6.5. Average Trifecta Payoffs from Dania and Milford (3 and 4 to Win)

	Dania				Milford				Totals	
	Matinee		Evening		Matinee		Evening		Average	
Bet	Count	Payoff	Count	Payoff	Count	Payoff	Count	Payoff	Count	Payoff/$
3–1–2	7	$389.97	11	$382.22	8	$821.88	11	$661.04	37	$218.45
3–1–4	5	$409.37	8	$379.95	8	$821.88	17	$560.21	38	$208.14
3–1–5	7	$389.97	9	$398.43	10	$705.09	15	$559.60	41	$202.59
3–1–6	7	$389.97	8	$379.95	6	$931.15	11	$661.04	32	$224.09
3–1–7	6	$390.86	10	$357.56	6	$931.15	9	$772.16	31	$230.29
3–1–8	3	$512.36	6	$496.42	6	$931.15	14	$641.83	29	$245.35
3–2–1	6	$390.86	11	$382.22	10	$705.09	8	$777.70	35	$219.97
3–2–4	9	$378.12	7	$435.82	7	$791.87	11	$661.04	34	$220.54
3–2–5	7	$389.97	18	$352.25	9	$871.78	15	$559.60	49	$203.03
3–2–6	4	$446.56	10	$357.56	5	$892.28	18	$541.67	37	$200.49
3–2–7	2	$554.06	10	$357.56	6	$931.15	6	$1179.35	24	$273.45
3–2–8	4	$446.56	9	$398.43	5	$892.28	6	$1179.35	24	$272.16
3–4–1	8	$346.41	7	$435.82	3	$1424.04	10	$661.04	28	$233.52
3–4–2	6	$390.86	8	$379.95	12	$600.65	8	$777.70	34	$210.85
3–4–6	1	$651.51	2	$617.46	1	$1848.91	1	$1746.80	5	$428.36
3–4–7	0	$651.51	2	$617.46	1	$1848.91	3	$1795.16	6	$504.82
3–4–8	3	$512.36	5	$547.30	7	$791.87	3	$1795.16	18	$321.09
3–5–1	7	$389.97	13	$357.57	7	$791.87	11	$661.04	38	$209.49
3–5–2	9	$378.12	9	$398.43	5	$892.28	17	$560.21	40	$203.90
3–5–4	0	$651.51	1	$617.46	0	$1848.91	0	$1795.16	1	$308.73
3–5–6	0	$651.51	0	$619.84	1	$1848.91	1	$1746.80	2	$599.28
3–5–7	0	$651.51	0	$619.84	2	$1848.91	2	$1746.80	4	$599.28
3–5–8	2	$554.06	4	$532.54	1	$1848.91	2	$1746.80	9	$377.77
3–6–1	7	$389.97	5	$547.30	5	$892.28	10	$661.04	27	$237.92
3–6–2	6	$390.86	8	$379.95	11	$600.41	10	$661.04	35	$202.78
3–6–4	0	$651.51	0	$619.84	0	$1848.91	3	$1795.16	3	$598.39
3–6–5	0	$651.51	0	$619.84	1	$1848.91	0	$1795.16	1	$616.30
3–6–7	0	$651.51	0	$619.84	2	$1848.91	1	$1746.80	3	$604.96
3–6–8	0	$651.51	0	$619.84	1	$1848.91	0	$1795.16	1	$616.30
3–7–1	6	$390.86	6	$496.42	10	$705.09	8	$777.70	30	$236.20
3–7–2	2	$554.06	12	$441.48	4	$1256.37	7	$1031.31	25	$291.38
3–7–4	7	$389.97	6	$496.42	11	$600.41	9	$772.16	33	$223.40
3–7–5	1	$651.51	4	$532.54	3	$1424.04	4	$1602.27	12	$412.60
3–7–6	1	$651.51	0	$619.84	4	$1256.37	3	$1795.16	8	$474.51
3–7–8	0	$651.51	1	$617.46	0	$1848.91	1	$1746.80	2	$445.50
3–8–1	6	$390.86	4	$532.54	11	$600.41	4	$1602.27	25	$263.02
3–8–2	7	$389.97	3	$619.84	5	$892.28	9	$772.16	24	$254.09
3–8–4	4	$446.56	8	$379.95	5	$892.28	8	$777.70	25	$238.96
3–8–5	1	$651.51	7	$435.82	3	$1424.04	10	$661.04	21	$260.89
3–8–6	2	$554.06	1	$617.46	3	$1424.04	7	$1031.31	13	$361.02
3–8–7	0	$651.51	0	$619.84	1	$1848.91	1	$1746.80	2	$599.28

MODELING THE PAYOFFS

TABLE 6.5, continued

Bet	Dania Matinee Count	Payoff	Evening Count	Payoff	Milford Matinee Count	Payoff	Evening Count	Payoff	Totals Average Count	Payoff/$
4–1–2	7	$389.97	10	$357.56	13	$609.87	17	$560.21	47	$190.85
4–1–3	6	$390.86	22	$197.62	21	$270.37	19	$510.47	68	$124.59
4–1–5	10	$423.17	11	$382.22	6	$931.15	22	$520.23	49	$201.95
4–1–6	4	$446.56	4	$532.54	10	$705.09	10	$661.04	28	$232.57
4–1–7	4	$446.56	6	$496.42	5	$892.28	13	$613.99	28	$233.22
4–1–8	4	$446.56	7	$435.82	12	$600.65	9	$772.16	32	$223.05
4–2–1	6	$390.86	14	$345.53	11	$600.41	14	$641.83	45	$195.29
4–2–3	11	$208.75	19	$205.64	17	$351.94	20	$451.83	67	$121.02
4–2–5	10	$423.17	8	$379.95	10	$705.09	11	$661.04	39	$215.63
4–2–6	3	$512.36	12	$441.48	7	$791.87	10	$661.04	32	$233.39
4–2–7	3	$512.36	8	$379.95	6	$931.15	6	$1179.35	23	$283.01
4–2–8	7	$389.97	7	$435.82	11	$600.41	13	$613.99	38	$204.01
4–3–1	7	$389.97	15	$373.82	10	$705.09	12	$653.24	44	$207.54
4–3–2	10	$423.17	8	$379.95	12	$600.65	8	$777.70	38	$213.48
4–3–5	1	$651.51	3	$619.84	6	$931.15	3	$1795.16	13	$377.92
4–3–6	3	$512.36	1	$617.46	2	$1848.91	5	$1179.35	11	$388.68
4–3–7	3	$512.36	1	$617.46	9	$871.78	6	$1179.35	19	$318.49
4–3–8	4	$446.56	4	$532.54	3	$1424.04	13	$613.99	24	$251.79
4–5–1	2	$554.06	8	$379.95	8	$821.88	12	$653.24	30	$229.28
4–5–2	4	$446.56	2	$617.46	7	$791.87	10	$661.04	23	$241.81
4–5–3	0	$651.51	2	$617.46	3	$1424.04	7	$1031.31	12	$370.66
4–5–7	0	$651.51	1	$617.46	0	$1848.91	0	$1795.16	1	$308.73
4–5–8	0	$651.51	1	$617.46	0	$1848.91	0	$1795.16	1	$308.73
4–6–1	1	$651.51	1	$617.46	1	$1848.91	1	$1746.80	4	$458.26
4–6–2	1	$651.51	3	$619.84	4	$1256.37	2	$1746.80	10	$409.52
4–6–3	1	$651.51	2	$617.46	8	$821.88	4	$1602.27	15	$351.42
4–7–1	3	$512.36	6	$496.42	4	$1256.37	1	$1746.80	14	$322.52
4–7–2	3	$512.36	6	$496.42	2	$1848.91	5	$1179.35	16	$341.00
4–7–3	3	$512.36	2	$617.46	2	$1848.91	11	$661.04	18	$280.13
4–7–5	1	$651.51	1	$617.46	1	$1848.91	0	$1795.16	3	$416.93
4–8–1	2	$554.06	3	$619.84	2	$1848.91	7	$1031.31	14	$365.92
4–8–2	2	$554.06	2	$617.46	6	$931.15	7	$1031.31	17	$320.01
4–8–3	3	$512.36	6	$496.42	5	$892.28	15	$559.60	29	$225.62
4–8–5	0	$651.51	2	$617.46	3	$1424.04	4	$1602.27	9	$464.21
4–8–6	1	$651.51	0	$619.84	0	$1848.91	0	$1795.16	1	$325.75

CALCULATED BETS

TABLE 6.6. Average Trifecta Payoffs from Dania and Milford (5 and 6 to Win)

	Dania				Milford				Totals	
	Matinee		Evening		Matinee		Evening		Average	
Bet	Count	Payoff	Count	Payoff	Count	Payoff	Count	Payoff	Count	Payoff/$
5–1–2	4	$446.56	4	$532.54	13	$609.87	10	$661.04	31	$219.50
5–1–3	6	$390.86	18	$352.25	19	$437.19	21	$451.83	64	$160.54
5–1–4	4	$446.56	19	$220.06	22	$342.25	26	$287.00	71	$112.41
5–1–6	1	$651.51	5	$547.30	5	$892.28	5	$1179.35	16	$321.67
5–1–7	2	$554.06	2	$617.46	5	$892.28	2	$1746.80	11	$347.56
5–1–8	3	$512.36	5	$547.30	1	$1848.91	3	$1795.16	12	$379.02
5–2–1	4	$446.56	13	$357.57	6	$931.15	10	$661.04	33	$220.70
5–2–3	7	$389.97	9	$398.43	12	$600.65	20	$451.83	48	$178.60
5–2–4	12	$349.10	15	$373.82	19	$437.19	28	$308.52	74	$142.52
5–2–6	1	$651.51	6	$496.42	6	$931.15	9	$772.16	22	$272.44
5–2–7	4	$446.56	2	$617.46	7	$791.87	5	$1179.35	18	$295.77
5–2–8	4	$446.56	7	$435.82	6	$931.15	4	$1602.27	21	$305.58
5–3–1	12	$349.10	10	$357.56	19	$437.19	19	$510.47	60	$164.74
5–3–2	6	$390.86	18	$352.25	13	$609.87	21	$451.83	58	$174.97
5–3–4	3	$512.36	5	$547.30	9	$871.78	7	$1031.31	24	$298.27
5–3–6	2	$554.06	3	$619.84	4	$1256.37	2	$1746.80	11	$393.05
5–3–7	0	$651.51	2	$617.46	4	$1256.37	5	$1179.35	11	$387.11
5–3–8	3	$512.36	6	$496.42	5	$892.28	5	$1179.35	19	$300.55
5–4–1	8	$346.41	10	$357.56	9	$871.78	8	$777.70	35	$224.65
5–4–2	7	$389.97	10	$357.56	5	$892.28	13	$613.99	35	$208.58
5–4–3	2	$554.06	4	$532.54	3	$1424.04	7	$1031.31	16	$340.60
5–4–6	0	$651.51	0	$619.84	0	$1848.91	1	$1746.80	1	$582.27
5–4–7	0	$651.51	0	$619.84	1	$1848.91	3	$1795.16	4	$602.87
5–4–8	0	$651.51	2	$617.46	1	$1848.91	6	$1179.35	9	$399.37
5–6–1	1	$651.51	1	$617.46	7	$791.87	1	$1746.80	10	$306.44
5–6–2	1	$651.51	3	$619.84	2	$1848.91	4	$1602.27	10	$462.45
5–6–3	1	$651.51	1	$617.46	5	$892.28	3	$1795.16	10	$391.68
5–6–4	0	$651.51	2	$617.46	1	$1848.91	3	$1795.16	6	$504.82
5–7–1	0	$651.51	1	$617.46	5	$892.28	1	$1746.80	7	$339.73
5–7–2	1	$651.51	3	$619.84	1	$1848.91	4	$1602.27	9	$445.35
5–7–3	4	$446.56	0	$619.84	3	$1424.04	7	$1031.31	14	$337.40
5–7–4	0	$651.51	1	$617.46	0	$1848.91	7	$1031.31	8	$339.39
5–8–1	0	$651.51	0	$619.84	0	$1848.91	1	$1746.80	1	$582.27
5–8–2	0	$651.51	0	$619.84	1	$1848.91	0	$1795.16	1	$616.30
5–8–3	3	$512.36	3	$619.84	5	$892.28	2	$1746.80	13	$334.61
5–8–4	1	$651.51	0	$619.84	3	$1424.04	4	$1602.27	8	$485.77
5–8–6	0	$651.51	0	$619.84	1	$1848.91	3	$1795.16	4	$602.87

TABLE 6.6, continued

	Dania				Milford				Totals	
	Matinee		Evening		Matinee		Evening		Average	
Bet	Count	Payoff	Count	Payoff	Count	Payoff	Count	Payoff	Count	Payoff/$
6–1–2	2	$554.06	4	$532.54	6	$931.15	3	$1795.16	15	$351.77
6–1–3	5	$409.37	11	$382.22	5	$892.28	9	$772.16	30	$230.97
6–1–4	9	$378.12	14	$345.53	19	$437.19	21	$451.83	63	$159.55
6–1–5	5	$409.37	10	$357.56	14	$573.33	23	$388.92	52	$162.85
6–1–7	2	$554.06	2	$617.46	3	$1424.04	5	$1179.35	12	$380.10
6–1–8	0	$651.51	2	$617.46	0	$1848.91	4	$1602.27	6	$458.97
6–2–1	2	$554.06	4	$532.54	4	$1256.37	6	$1179.35	16	$353.31
6–2–3	4	$446.56	4	$532.54	2	$1848.91	5	$1179.35	15	$343.76
6–2–4	10	$423.17	8	$379.95	17	$402.04	13	$613.99	48	$178.63
6–2–5	6	$390.86	13	$357.57	14	$573.33	25	$388.58	58	$162.25
6–2–7	1	$651.51	2	$617.46	5	$892.28	5	$1179.35	13	$338.15
6–2–8	1	$651.51	0	$619.84	3	$1424.04	3	$1795.16	7	$506.42
6–3–1	17	$297.52	9	$398.43	11	$600.41	17	$560.21	54	$179.59
6–3–2	8	$346.41	10	$357.56	8	$821.88	17	$560.21	43	$198.60
6–3–4	1	$651.51	4	$532.54	5	$892.28	9	$772.16	19	$273.39
6–3–5	4	$446.56	8	$379.95	16	$408.86	10	$661.04	38	$178.87
6–3–7	1	$651.51	0	$619.84	8	$821.88	6	$1179.35	15	$325.08
6–3–8	1	$651.51	4	$532.54	4	$1256.37	2	$1746.80	11	$384.59
6–4–1	12	$349.10	10	$357.56	10	$705.09	16	$559.60	48	$192.03
6–4–2	6	$390.86	12	$441.48	11	$600.41	10	$661.04	39	$210.93
6–4–3	9	$378.12	7	$435.82	7	$791.87	8	$777.70	31	$230.60
6–4–5	2	$554.06	5	$547.30	2	$1848.91	4	$1602.27	13	$407.02
6–4–7	2	$554.06	2	$617.46	4	$1256.37	3	$1795.16	11	$421.99
6–4–8	1	$651.51	0	$619.84	4	$1256.37	5	$1179.35	10	$396.65
6–5–1	3	$512.36	2	$617.46	7	$791.87	4	$1602.27	16	$335.63
6–5–2	2	$554.06	2	$617.46	5	$892.28	7	$1031.31	16	$316.56
6–5–3	1	$651.51	6	$496.42	3	$1424.04	9	$772.16	19	$292.40
6–5–4	1	$651.51	0	$619.84	2	$1848.91	6	$1179.35	9	$435.23
6–5–8	0	$651.51	0	$619.84	2	$1848.91	1	$1746.80	3	$604.96
6–7–1	0	$651.51	1	$617.46	4	$1256.37	1	$1746.80	6	$427.69
6–7–2	0	$651.51	0	$619.84	1	$1848.91	4	$1602.27	5	$550.53
6–7–3	3	$512.36	2	$617.46	4	$1256.37	4	$1602.27	13	$399.81
6–7–4	0	$651.51	1	$617.46	4	$1256.37	5	$1179.35	10	$394.95
6–7–5	0	$651.51	0	$619.84	3	$1424.04	1	$1746.80	4	$501.58
6–8–1	0	$651.51	0	$619.84	0	$1848.91	2	$1746.80	2	$582.27
6–8–3	0	$651.51	0	$619.84	1	$1848.91	1	$1746.80	2	$599.28
6–8–4	1	$651.51	1	$617.46	0	$1848.91	5	$1179.35	7	$371.44
6–8–5	0	$651.51	0	$619.84	1	$1848.91	3	$1795.16	4	$602.87

TABLE 6.7. Average Trifecta Payoffs from Dania and Milford (7 and 8 to Win)

| | Dania | | | | Milford | | | | Totals | |
| | Matinee | | Evening | | Matinee | | Evening | | Average | |
Bet	Count	Payoff	Count	Payoff	Count	Payoff	Count	Payoff	Count	Payoff/$
7–1–2	1	$651.51	1	$617.46	0	$1848.91	5	$1179.35	7	$371.44
7–1–3	2	$554.06	1	$617.46	2	$1848.91	1	$1746.80	6	$446.28
7–1–4	0	$651.51	4	$532.54	2	$1848.91	7	$1031.31	13	$361.85
7–1–5	5	$409.37	13	$357.57	8	$821.88	14	$641.83	40	$213.36
7–1–6	4	$446.56	16	$391.46	7	$791.87	6	$1179.35	33	$249.43
7–1–8	0	$651.51	2	$617.46	2	$1848.91	2	$1746.80	6	$502.43
7–2–1	0	$651.51	4	$532.54	2	$1848.91	4	$1602.27	10	$443.40
7–2–3	1	$651.51	4	$532.54	7	$791.87	1	$1746.80	13	$293.91
7–2–4	4	$446.56	6	$496.42	11	$600.41	10	$661.04	31	$218.95
7–2–5	7	$389.97	11	$382.22	14	$573.33	18	$541.67	50	$187.85
7–2–6	5	$409.37	12	$441.48	13	$609.87	9	$772.16	39	$221.32
7–2–8	0	$651.51	1	$617.46	1	$1848.91	1	$1746.80	3	$502.43
7–3–1	2	$554.06	6	$496.42	11	$600.41	7	$1031.31	26	$255.82
7–3–2	5	$409.37	6	$496.42	8	$821.88	8	$777.70	27	$251.05
7–3–4	4	$446.56	0	$619.84	6	$931.15	4	$1602.27	14	$349.41
7–3–5	9	$378.12	6	$496.42	12	$600.65	14	$641.83	41	$209.48
7–3–6	4	$446.56	7	$435.82	9	$871.78	14	$641.83	34	$236.15
7–3–8	1	$651.51	0	$619.84	3	$1424.04	3	$1795.16	7	$506.42
7–4–1	5	$409.37	6	$496.42	15	$555.89	15	$559.60	41	$197.32
7–4–2	6	$390.86	7	$435.82	13	$609.87	12	$653.24	38	$209.31
7–4–3	2	$554.06	4	$532.54	8	$821.88	10	$661.04	24	$250.59
7–4–5	2	$554.06	2	$617.46	5	$892.28	5	$1179.35	14	$330.30
7–4–6	2	$554.06	4	$532.54	5	$892.28	6	$1179.35	17	$321.47
7–4–8	2	$554.06	1	$617.46	5	$892.28	2	$1746.80	10	$351.45
7–5–1	3	$512.36	3	$619.84	13	$609.87	11	$661.04	30	$225.50
7–5–2	3	$512.36	6	$496.42	8	$821.88	9	$772.16	26	$260.23
7–5–3	8	$346.41	10	$357.56	11	$600.41	7	$1031.31	36	$216.15
7–5–4	2	$554.06	3	$619.84	6	$931.15	9	$772.16	20	$283.13
7–5–6	0	$651.51	0	$619.84	1	$1848.91	0	$1795.16	1	$616.30
7–5–8	0	$651.51	0	$619.84	0	$1848.91	3	$1795.16	3	$598.39
7–6–1	0	$651.51	1	$617.46	2	$1848.91	2	$1746.80	5	$541.17
7–6–2	0	$651.51	3	$619.84	2	$1848.91	2	$1746.80	7	$475.27
7–6–3	2	$554.06	1	$617.46	3	$1424.04	3	$1795.16	9	$453.55
7–6–4	0	$651.51	3	$619.84	3	$1424.04	5	$1179.35	11	$392.67
7–6–5	0	$651.51	0	$619.84	1	$1848.91	3	$1795.16	4	$602.87
7–6–8	0	$651.51	0	$619.84	1	$1848.91	0	$1795.16	1	$616.30
7–8–1	0	$651.51	1	$617.46	0	$1848.91	1	$1746.80	2	$445.50
7–8–2	0	$651.51	0	$619.84	1	$1848.91	4	$1602.27	5	$550.53
7–8–3	0	$651.51	0	$619.84	3	$1424.04	3	$1795.16	6	$536.53
7–8–4	0	$651.51	0	$619.84	1	$1848.91	6	$1179.35	7	$425.00
7–8–5	0	$651.51	2	$617.46	3	$1424.04	5	$1179.35	10	$400.71
7–8–6	0	$651.51	0	$619.84	1	$1848.91	0	$1795.16	1	$616.30

TABLE 6.7, continued

	Dania				Milford				Totals	
	Matinee		Evening		Matinee		Evening		Average	
Bet	Count	Payoff	Count	Payoff	Count	Payoff	Count	Payoff	Count	Payoff/$
8–1–2	0	$651.51	1	$617.46	2	$1848.91	1	$1746.80	4	$530.90
8–1–3	0	$651.51	1	$617.46	0	$1848.91	1	$1746.80	2	$445.50
8–1–4	3	$512.36	3	$619.84	5	$892.28	3	$1795.16	14	$355.76
8–1–5	8	$346.41	8	$379.95	7	$791.87	8	$777.70	31	$220.23
8–1–6	8	$346.41	6	$496.42	12	$600.65	18	$541.67	44	$193.81
8–1–7	5	$409.37	11	$382.22	6	$931.15	9	$772.16	31	$235.63
8–2–1	2	$554.06	1	$617.46	0	$1848.91	1	$1746.80	4	$361.26
8–2–3	1	$651.51	1	$617.46	3	$1424.04	2	$1746.80	7	$460.44
8–2–4	2	$554.06	4	$532.54	1	$1848.91	3	$1795.16	10	$403.06
8–2–5	5	$409.37	5	$547.30	14	$573.33	13	$613.99	37	$208.86
8–2–6	6	$390.86	12	$441.48	14	$573.33	9	$772.16	41	$214.96
8–2–7	2	$554.06	6	$496.42	13	$609.87	1	$1746.80	22	$239.47
8–3–1	2	$554.06	1	$617.46	3	$1424.04	6	$1179.35	12	$387.13
8–3–2	3	$512.36	7	$435.82	5	$892.28	8	$777.70	23	$254.56
8–3–4	1	$651.51	1	$617.46	4	$1256.37	2	$1746.80	8	$434.27
8–3–5	5	$409.37	7	$435.82	7	$791.87	11	$661.04	30	$227.34
8–3–6	6	$390.86	11	$382.22	20	$495.33	10	$661.04	47	$186.82
8–3–7	6	$390.86	8	$379.95	7	$791.87	10	$661.04	31	$217.53
8–4–1	2	$554.06	7	$435.82	12	$600.65	10	$661.04	31	$215.66
8–4–2	7	$389.97	13	$357.57	8	$821.88	12	$653.24	40	$212.34
8–4–3	0	$651.51	10	$357.56	10	$705.09	8	$777.70	28	$221.86
8–4–5	4	$446.56	3	$619.84	5	$892.28	8	$777.70	20	$269.19
8–4–6	4	$446.56	8	$379.95	5	$892.28	12	$653.24	29	$224.59
8–4–7	4	$446.56	2	$617.46	6	$931.15	12	$653.24	24	$249.41
8–5–1	5	$409.37	6	$496.42	10	$705.09	9	$772.16	30	$239.32
8–5–2	4	$446.56	14	$345.53	7	$791.87	8	$777.70	33	$219.19
8–5–3	5	$409.37	8	$379.95	11	$600.41	17	$560.21	41	$193.15
8–5–4	5	$409.37	3	$619.84	6	$931.15	10	$661.04	24	$250.79
8–5–6	2	$554.06	1	$617.46	3	$1424.04	4	$1602.27	10	$442.32
8–5–7	0	$651.51	2	$617.46	8	$821.88	5	$1179.35	15	$318.31
8–6–1	2	$554.06	4	$532.54	3	$1424.04	3	$1795.16	12	$403.19
8–6–2	0	$651.51	2	$617.46	8	$821.88	10	$661.04	20	$250.63
8–6–3	1	$651.51	9	$398.43	6	$931.15	6	$1179.35	22	$288.17
8–6–4	3	$512.36	3	$619.84	6	$931.15	13	$613.99	25	$248.85
8–6–5	0	$651.51	1	$617.46	3	$1424.04	4	$1602.27	8	$483.64
8–7–1	0	$651.51	2	$617.46	0	$1848.91	2	$1746.80	4	$445.50
8–7–2	1	$651.51	0	$619.84	1	$1848.91	1	$1746.80	3	$508.11
8–7–3	2	$554.06	0	$619.84	0	$1848.91	3	$1795.16	5	$469.84
8–7–4	1	$651.51	1	$617.46	3	$1424.04	2	$1746.80	7	$460.44
8–7–5	0	$651.51	0	$619.84	3	$1424.04	3	$1795.16	6	$536.53
8–7–6	0	$651.51	0	$619.84	0	$1848.91	1	$1746.80	1	$582.27

was a probability distribution predicting the likelihood of each possible betting outcome. Using the payoff model, we could predict what the payoff should be for each outcome and make a simulated bet if its expected value was sufficient to justify the investment.

The expected value of a given dollar bet on x with probability p_x and model payoff m_x is given by the formula

$$E(x) = p_x \times m_x - \$1$$

This captures the notion that we get paid only if x happens, but we must buy the $1 ticket regardless. If $E(x)$ is greater than zero, then x is a bet offering positive returns. If $E(x)$ is negative, we should avoid that bet like the plague.

Our initial betting strategy was to place simulated wagers on all bets offering sufficient positive return. And our first attempt at simulated betting using these average payoffs was amazingly successful. We made a *simulated* $15,000 profit on a simulated investment of only $20,000. Meena was, understandably, quite happy with these results. But the key word is simulated. Our simulated success was due to an overly simplistic betting model.

To be a first-rate programmer, it is important to be very suspicious. You learn to trust no one and question everything. Any program can fail because of bugs, and a mathematical model is particularly problematic because, even if the program is "correct," the model can fail to capture some important aspect of reality. It is essential for any programmer to anticipate problems and not to trust numbers that happen to be spit out. As Intel's longtime chairman Andrew Grove says, "Only the paranoid survive." As my mother could have told me, if we were making too much money too easily, there had to be a catch.

What was the catch? Under the pari-mutuel system, the payoff for any match is a function of both how much money was wagered in total and how much of this pool was invested on the successful outcome. Whenever we add winning money to the pool, it will necessarily reduce the amount that will be paid off per dollar to the other winners. If we simply average the payoffs we have seen from the WWW site, we miss the fact that our bets themselves will change the payoffs. As we will see in the discussion that follows, this factor can be very significant.

Investing in the stock market bears considerable similarity to gambling and in particular works more like a pari-mutuel system than one governed by odds makers. Yet all serious investment money is put into stocks, not horses. Why hasn't anyone started a jai alai or racetrack mutual fund to bet on these sports? There are two fundamental reasons why pari-mutuel wagering cannot be considered to be a solid investment vehicle:

- *The cost per transaction* – We have seen that the house keeps about 20% of each bet as a cost for each transaction. This means that we must do 20% better than the average bettor *just to break even*. By comparison, the cost per transaction is just pennies per share in major stock markets, particularly for large transactions. Thus I can prosper with even a slight increase in the value of my stock.

  Low transaction fees are one of the important reasons for the success of computer trading systems for stocks, which react instantaneously to price changes in the market and look to benefit from minor fluctuations. A typical stock price might vary 5% per day or less, and thus large commissions would kill any short-term trading strategy.

- *The size of the pool* – Large investors like the stock market because it can absorb great amounts of capital with relatively little reaction. Suppose I wanted to buy 1000 shares of Microsoft. According to my newspaper almost 600,000 shares were traded yesterday. My 1000-share trade will only be a blip in this market, yet it would represent an investment on the order of one million dollars. By comparison, one lousy $3 jai alai bet to win will significantly reduce the payoff for everyone else who bet on the same number to win. Thus, even when I find an excellent betting opportunity in jai alai, I can't put enough money on it to take significant advantage of my insight.

  The so called "penny stocks" that trade on small stock exchanges are subject to this same phenomenon or even worse malfeasance and chicanery. Small companies are, by definition, small. Hence, the total value of all the stock is relatively low. The current price of any stock is exactly what the last person paid for it. Suppose I own a significant amount of a cheap stock that has relatively little trading in it each day. I can sell a small part of my holdings back and forth to my co-conspirator, raising the price each day. Eventually, honest bettors will see that the stock is moving and want to get some of the action. I will be happy to sell them all of my holdings at this artificially high price, hoping to get rid of it before the market crashes.

With these two facts in mind, why did I devote so much time and effort to develop a betting system for jai alai? Frankly, it can't be justified on any cold, analytical basis. I did it because it was a very cool thing to do. I once read a description of an infamous boxing promoter as a man who would prefer to steal one dollar than earn two dollars honestly. That motivation, in a much more benign sense, probably also applied to me. All of us, I think, get a perverse thrill that comes only from beating the system. Making money gambling is a form of beating the system because we know that the odds are stacked against us. This project represents my effort to beat back the forces of nature through understanding and intellectual effort.

If you remain unconvinced, think of it this way. Building this system was my attempt to steal one dollar. Writing this book was my attempt to earn two dollars honestly. Which of the two do you think was a more exciting venture to contemplate?

Measuring Our Impact on the Pool

How we can compensate for the fact that our own bets impact the payoffs we receive? The first order of business is to estimate the size of the betting pools that we are impacting.

The single best measure of the financial health of any track or fronton is not its attendance but its *handle*. The handle is the total dollar amount that has been wagered over the course of the day. Because the fronton takes 20% of the handle as its cut, this is the number that matters to them.

Milford Jai-Alai posts the handle with the other results of each day's matches. These numbers provide interesting insights into the financial state of the jai alai industry. I plotted the the amount of money bet at Milford each night over a 2-year period in six graphs partitioned according to the day of the week.

I always find it exciting to see a large amount of data presented in a small amount of paper in such a way that it can be understood. I refer all fellow mathematical graphics fans to Tufte's *Visualization of Quantitative Data*, a coffee-table quality book illustrating the beauty of properly represented data.

The handles presented in this figure are for all the evening sessions at Milford in 1997 and 1998. Matinee (afternoon) sessions, which are typically played on Sunday, Monday, and Wednesday, are not included. From this data, it is clear that Friday and Saturday are the big nights at Milford. The handles are almost twice as large on weekends as on Monday night. Early in 1998 they tried to solve the slow Monday night problem by moving the Monday evening session to Tuesday. But Tuesday handles proved no better and in fact seemed to depress the take from Thursday. Restoring the status quo did no lasting damage, for both the Monday and Thursday handles quickly recovered to their previous levels.

But the most ominous shadows are cast by the trends in the data, which show a slight but perceptible decrease in the handle as a function of time.

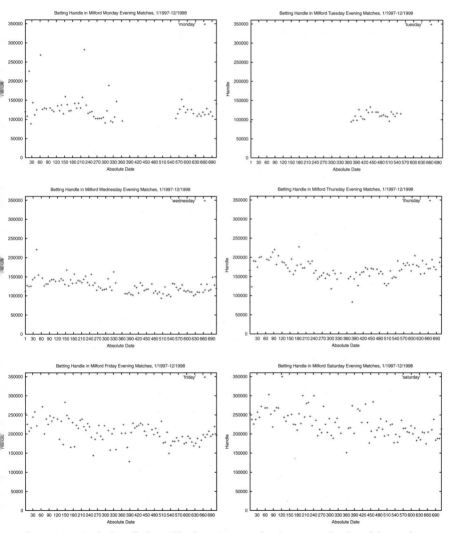

Fluctuations in the handle for Milford evening matches in 1997–98 by day of the week.

131

These numbers are best put in perspective by comparing them with the boom days of jai alai 20 years ago. In 1978, the *average* handle at Milford was $349,360, a figure reached exactly once over the past 2 years, on an average attendance of over 3000 people. Today's handle and attendance are about half of what they were 20 years ago.

This data can be used to model how much money would be bet at the fronton on a given night. But that isn't all we need. Each night's handle is a total of all the pools over all the matches. We had to break this total into its components to predict the size of each betting pool. We could estimate the amount of money bet on each match by dividing the handle by the total number of matches in the session. We could further divide the money per match into its component pools *if* we knew what fractions of the handle went into win, place, show, quiniela, exacta, and trifecta pools.

Once we knew how much money was invested in a given pool, it was easy to figure out our impact on it. From the pool size and our payoff-per-dollar estimation, we could work backwards to figure out how much of the pool money would have to have been invested on the winner for it to pay off at the estimated rate. By adding our (minimum allowable) bet to this winning pool amount, we can now divide the total pool among the winners, including, it is hoped, ourselves.

These formulas gave us the ability to estimate the impact of our bets on the entire pool, but we needed the right fractions to predict how much money was invested in each betting pool. This information wasn't available on the Internet. We had to go back to the source.

Field Trip to Connecticut

My then-fiancé, now-wife Renee had heard me babble about jai alai almost from the moment we had met, but she had never been to see a game. It seemed like a good idea to let her see what she was missing and show Dario and Meena what the sport was really about.

Therefore, on May 28, 1997, we went on a field trip to Connecticut. Bridgeport, which used to be the fronton closest to where I live, had recently gone out of business after a disastrous attempt to turn it into a dog racing track. Milford, the only remaining fronton in Connecticut, is a 2-hour drive from Stony Brook. Renee and I swung by to pick the two students up, and then we rounded New York City and drove into the Nutmeg State.

From our discussions in the car, it became clear that neither Dario nor Meena had any real understanding of the physical nature of jai alai. All they knew of the sport was what I had told them, and what I told them was a mathematical abstraction. To Dario and Meena, jai alai players were Basque-speaking automata who randomly scored points according to a given probability distribution. They found it somewhat disorienting to discover that the players were people. It was a reversal of the standard movie zombie story – the body snatchers came and suddenly there was flesh and blood on what yesterday had been much-loved machines.

We arrived at an attractively landscaped building designed by award-winning architect Herbert S. Newman. Although Milford has been called the "Tiffany of frontons," its concrete bulkiness betrayed the 1970s construction. Milford dates back to the time when betting on jai alai first became legal in Connecticut.

We cruised down the Galleria, beneath a series of colorful Basque-style banners. The thin early crowd seemed to consist mostly of retired people. Not too many working people can take the afternoon off to watch jai alai. The spectators projected the same aura of modest seediness that you find in any race track or casino. There was just enough light, glitter, and spectacle about the room to ward off the undercurrent of gloom that lurks wherever people are losing money. Renee wandered off to explore while the rest of us took care of business.

I had arranged for us to meet with Milford Jai-Alai's public relations director, Bob Heussler. He turned out to be a tall, friendly fellow who treated us as honored guests. Bob escorted us to the clubhouse, a small bar and restaurant with the best seats in the house, and offered us drinks on his tab. He even seemed a little disappointed when none of us ordered anything stronger than orange juice. I guess his usual clientele does not include students and their professor.

We spent an hour watching and talking jai alai. Times had gotten a lot harder for Milford the instant that the Pequots had opened up their nearby Foxwoods casino. First the Hartford and then the Bridgeport frontons got scalped by the Indians, leaving Milford as the only remaining outpost in the state. Milford inherited the dates and some of the customers of the previous frontons, which helped. Their finances were stable, but still, it wasn't like the old days.

"I don't understand these people," Bob said, shaking his head sadly. "We offer an exciting game with lots of action. But people just seem to want to throw their money into slot machines. We can't take their money from them as fast as the casino can, so they stay away."

I looked around the hall. It was an early game of a Wednesday matinee, perhaps the slowest period of the week. Only a couple hundred spectators lined the stands, although more would file in later. The thought that several times as many people were sullenly feeding quarters to the Pequots just an hour's drive away filled me with despair.

"We've been lobbying the state to let us offer slot machines and poker on the side. That would help bring back the public."

My students and I had come primarily to learn what we could about betting patterns at Milford. Les Trotto, the director of mutual operations, dropped by to give us copies of the handle summary sheets for the past few days.

This data was extremely interesting. The total handle (i.e., the total amount bet) for Sunday afternoon, May 25, was $222,670. With a good Memorial Day weekend crowd of 1542 on hand, this worked out to $144.40 bet per head. This figure is somewhat inflated because roughly a quarter of the handle comes from off-track betting (OTB). Indeed, enough people had looked up from their slot machines at Foxwoods to contribute $5,475 to the pool.

Still, these average handles sounded awfully high to me. The typical bettor was doing much more than placing one minimum $3 wager on each game.

The early games of the session had by far the smallest pools, presumably because most of the spectators had not yet shown up at the fronton. The handle picked up as the day progressed, eventually reaching almost twice that of the opening session. It peaked three or four games from the end as the crowd started going home. There was a blip in the last game, however. It featured a high payoff "superfecta" bet for which the object is to pick the first *four* players in the correct order.

"We like to have an exotic bet at the end of the session to keep the crowd in the house," Bob explained.

Indeed, the higher the payoff, the more popular the bet seemed to be. Roughly 60% of the total handle was wagered on trifectas. Quinielas accounted for 25% of the pool, and 10% was invested in exactas. The remaining 5% of the handle was split between win, place, and show as well as the exotic bets. Bob and Les confirmed that these patterns were typical.

"Trifectas are the most popular type of bet. People are attracted by the big payoffs and then lose all their bets. They get frustrated and don't come back. We wish more people would bet win–place–show so they have something to show for the day. Keep them coming back."

"Any ideas on what kind of systems people use to bet?," I asked, looking for an edge.

"Our customers do all kinds of things. Some people play their favorite number or color. Others watch the players. We have a few people who watch the odds boards and bet on numbers which have very little money in them."

"How do they do?"

"The odds guys? Pretty good, I guess. Some of them have been here for years."

I had heard that there were people at tracks who made a living picking up winning tickets that had been erroneously discarded by the people who bought them. "What happens to unclaimed winning tickets?" I asked him.

"Good question. Each year there are about $100,000 worth of winnings which are not claimed. You get exactly one year to cash in any winning ticket. Unclaimed winnings money is retained by the house, but it is not money we are looking for. We urge patrons to cash winning tickets immediately. The state used to keep that money until several years ago."

"Tell me," I asked. "Who is Pepe, of *Pepe's Green Card*, and how does he make his picks?"

Bob laughed. "I hate to tell you this, but there is no Pepe. The *Green Card* picks are usually made by the public address announcer. I've filled in for him on occasion when he went on vacation."

The truth sometimes hurts. It was a good thing we were working on a system to eliminate our dependence on Pepe.

After Bob and Les left, Renee joined us at our table. It was time to teach my fledglings how to bet. They had been watching the numbers closely for almost a year now. Now was the time to test what they had learned.

"How about 2 to show?," Dario suggested. My adventurers had picked the safest bet in the house. It was the second game, a singles match.

I bellied up to the cashier and invested $3 on Baronio to Show.

Baronio came in second, and so we won. We watched with interest as the result was posted. Number 2 to show paid off at $3.60. We had cleared 20% on this wise investment in less than 15 minutes, which was probably better than either Bill Gates or Warren Buffet have ever done with their money.

I sauntered up to the cashier to collect my winnings. I asked the cashier what the biggest ticket she ever cashed was. She told me this wasn't it. Indeed, pocketing only 60 cents' profit left a somewhat empty feeling behind. Now I understood better why more people didn't bet win–place–show. The thrill of victory loses some of its luster when all you collect is change. Quinielas and trifecta offer payoffs sufficient to justify the effort of rooting and the excitement of figuring out the permutations of what might happen. When you have a bet on only one player, only a small fraction of the points played will have an immediate consequence on your investment.

"If we stop betting now we finish ahead." Dario pointed out. But I bet on a few quinielas to show them how much more interesting the game could be. I lost them all, illustrating how a high roller gets steamrollered.

We left early to avoid getting caught in rush hour traffic from the city. But we spent the whole trip back discussing how to incorporate what we had learned from our expedition into the system.

The Problem of Overfitting Data

Suppose that you are given the job of distinguishing likely Democratic party voters from likely Republican voters on the basis of age and income.

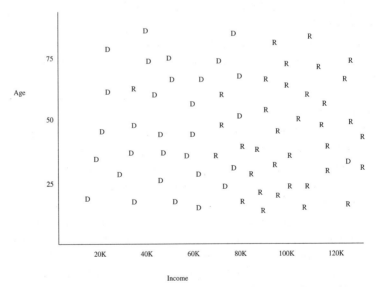

A scatter plot illustrating political party affiliation as a function of age and income.

To give you the basis to make such a decision, you have polled 100 people and obtained their age, income, and party affiliation and put the results in a scatterplot.

How can you generalize from this data to predict political affiliation based only on people's age and income? The simplest approach would be to carve up the age–space plane into two regions and assign each of these regions to one of the political parties. We present two possible divisions on page 138. On the top is the best possible Democrat–Republican discriminator that can be built from a single straight line. It cuts the space completely according to income; anyone who makes less than $80,000 a year is a classified a Democrat, whereas anyone who makes more than that is called a Republican.

Such a simple-minded division makes mistakes, of course. Indeed, three of the Democrats and four of the Republicans ended up on the wrong side of the line. On the bottom we provide a different divider that correctly classifies for all the compassionate rich and misguided poor in our test set, but it has to jump around a lot in order to do so.

Which of these two classifiers do you think does a better job distinguishing Democrats from Republicans? Even though it makes a few mistakes, I prefer the simpler model on the left. Its simplicity helps guard against *overfitting* the data, that is, building a model that so completely reflects the weirdnesses of the training data that it misses the larger picture. The classifier on the right distorts its shape to classify the outliers, correctly whereas the classifier on the left mislabels these oddballs on the assumption that they are, in fact, oddballs without predictive value.

Properly modeling the expected trifecta payoffs required care to guard against overfitting our data. Recall that we averaged the results of all previous payoffs to predict future returns. This method worked well for most bet types such as win, place, show, and quiniela. However, the results of simple averaging are not so easy to believe in the case of trifectas. There are 336 different trifecta combinations, and thus the average trifecta should have occurred roughly 23 times during our sampling interval. But this average is misleading because there is a high *variance* in the number of occurrences.

The mean or average is a statistical measure of the most likely value of a sequence, whereas variance, and its close cousin *standard deviation,*

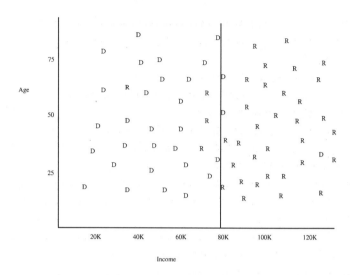

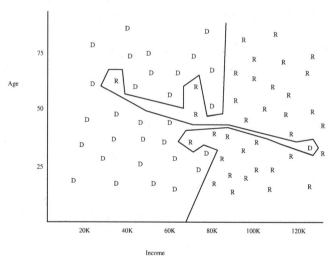

Two dividers that discriminate between Democrats and Republicans.

measure the consistency of values in a sequence. Let us consider the annual salaries (in thousands of dollars) of 10 people in each of 2 different professions. The first sample comes from unionized postal workers in Omaha, Nebraska:

$$33, 27, 39, 25, 26, 24, 36, 28, 32, 30$$

and the second sample comes from people in the telemarketing industry (a large fraction of whom happen to operate out of Omaha):

19, 30, 20, 24, 108, 17, 23, 19, 22, 18

Both of these sequences have the same average (30K). But the variance of the telemarketers is considerably higher because it is thrown off by the inclusion of one high-paid member of management. The standard deviation in salaries at a union shop is likely to be much lower than one in which management feels free to oppress the masses and appropriately oil the squeaky wheel.

The high variance of payoffs associated with rare trifectas becomes a problem in trying to estimate their expected return accurately. Suppose we were to pick a single random element of each of the two sets of salaries above. Which random salary would more accurately reflect the average of the group? There is less chance that a random element of the low-variance sequence will do a bad job representing his cronies than one from the more diverse sequence. Picking the manager as a typical representative of the telemarketing industry would be seriously misleading, but is just as likely as picking the single fellow who is right on the average.

Simply averaging the payoffs for rare, high-variance trifectas doesn't make much sense. Over the last 2 years the trifecta 8–7–6 came in only five times at Milford, paying at $3708.60, $4568.40, $4574.70, $1975.50, and $1293.00 for a $3 bet. What about even rarer trifectas that may have come in only once or never? What should they pay off at?

To do a better job of estimating the payoff of rare trifectas, we partitioned them into groups with similar occurrence frequencies and then averaged all the payoffs within each group. This meant all of the low-probability trifectas in a given group were assigned the same expected payoff. Damping the projected payoff from the highest-return singleton payoff was essential to keep our betting system from being burned like a moth attracted to a flame. If one trifecta had a projected payoff of $2000 per dollar invested based on only one or two actual occurrences, the system would be liable to keep chasing what was probably a fluke payoff instead of a real quirk in the public's betting strategy.

Mathematical Modeling Techniques

I digress here to explain more about the broad range of mathematical modeling techniques used in science and industry. None of these techniques is directly employed within our jai alai system, so follow the bouncing pelota

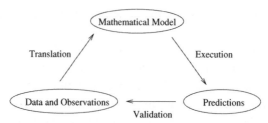

The cycle of mathematical modeling development and validation.

to the next chapter if you really want to get on with the story. But I urge you to stick with me for a better understanding of how models are built in the real world.

The process of creating and validating any mathematical model is characterized by three primary steps:

- *Translation* – Express observations of the real world in some form of mathematical language or implementation.
- *Execution* – Use this model on training or real-world data to make new predictions or conclusions about the world.
- *Validation* – Interpret and test the resulting predictions to assess the extent to which the model reflects reality.

As shown by our experiences, the validation process typically leads us to new observations that must be translated back into the model, thus generating a cycle of activity that may require several rounds to get right.

Our system employs two different types of mathematical model techniques, namely Monte Carlo simulation and statistical analysis. In this section, we will introduce several other important approaches to mathematical modeling. The resulting models can be classified according to a variety of basic properties and characteristics. My taxonomy of models is based on the following traits:

- *Discrete versus continuous models* – Certain models manipulate *discrete* entities, which are those that cannot be further divided into fractional parts. Our jai alai model was discrete, for each point scored was a distinct minimal event with exactly one winner. Traffic flow simulations deal with quanta of individual vehicles. But other models deal with inherently *continuous* quantities such as temperature, speed, time, force, and salary where there are no possible gaps between allowable values. Whatever speeds x and y are traveling at say, 65.231 and 65.232 mph, respectively, there is room for someone to get between them (say, at 65.2315 mph).

Calculus, algebra, geometry, and trigonometry all revolve around continuous functions, and so the full weight of classical mathematics can be brought to bear in modeling continuous functions.

■ *General versus ad hoc models* – Certain types of models use ad hoc techniques carefully customized for the given application. In the course of developing our jai alai simulation, not for one moment did we ever forget that we were simulating jai alai. It would be very difficult to adapt our model to another application – even another pari-mutuel sport such as horse racing.

Other mathematical modeling techniques are not so fussy. They are typically designed to work with general statistical data, hunting for patterns and correlations. They couldn't care less whether you feed them stock market data, baseball scores, electrocardiograms, or astrological charts. Of course the quality of the resulting model depends heavily upon the quality of the input data – garbage in, garbage out.

The surprise is that the performance of such *general* techniques is often very competitive with carefully crafted, problem-specific models. Which approach is better depends upon the quality of the statistical data you have to work with and how much the proper interpretation of this data depends upon idiosyncrasies of the application.

■ *Black box versus descriptive models* – *Descriptive* modeling techniques give us more than just an answer. They provide additional information to let us know how the model reached its decision and how much to believe it. Many statistical models come with measures of the strength of correlations and the significance of the results.

Black box methods apply some form of magic to data, yielding answers but not necessarily a reason to trust them. Applying any modeling method you don't fully understand yields a black box model. The name should conjure up the image of a device that takes data in and spits answers out but whose internal mechanisms are hidden from view by the container in which it is housed.

Black box methods can be very useful despite this inherent mystery – particularly if there is independent data on which to validate the resulting models. Indeed, we will see that the opaqueness of such popular modeling techniques as neural networks can be an important part of their charm.

■ *Simulation versus data-driven models* – Simulations attempt to recreate nature from first principles. Conversely, data-driven models attempt to interpret nature by analyzing statistical data.

The actuarial tables used by insurance companies are constructed by classical data-driven models. A simulation approach to predicting your life expectancy might be to model the set of all events that could happen to you each and every day, play them out, and see which one happens to kill you. By repeating the experiment millions of times in a Monte Carlo fashion, the model could estimate the probability distribution of when and how you will die.

But the range of activities you may engage in over the course of your life is clearly much too varied to be simulated accurately, particularly because the fate of the entire insurance industry depends upon the results. Instead, actuaries use a statistical approach to predicting your life expectancy, not by predicting what will happen to you but by observing what has happened to people like you. Do you smoke? Do you drive more than 15 miles to work each day? Well, the actuaries have extensive records on millions of people, and they know just what happened to people just like you. They predict your future not by preplaying it but by putting you in the right pigeonhole and reporting what happened to the rest of the flock.

■ *Randomized versus deterministic models* – Certain mathematical models are *deterministic*, meaning that the answers they give are completely defined by the input data. If we give exactly the same input twice, we expect to see the same results twice. My high-school football prediction program *Clyde* is a good example of a deterministic model.

Randomized models, such as our Monte Carlo simulation, incorporate some level of randomness into their execution. Thus, running the model twice on the same players and post positions will yield two slightly different distributions of who wins with what probability.

That there is usually only one *right* answer to any given problem yields an aesthetic appeal to deterministic models. But remember Ralph Waldo Emerson's credo that "a foolish consistency is the hobgoblin of little minds." Randomization give us the power to run a model many different times, enabling us to vote for solutions that come up most frequently or explore the space of possibilities. Such a distribution can be more useful than a bald assertion that X is the best solution possible.

I will now introduce a variety of modeling techniques whose advantages and disadvantages can best be understood in the light of these attributes.

CURVE-FITTING MODELS

We have seen that the mathematical modeler has a menagerie of curve shapes available to work with. A simple but powerful modeling paradigm is to find the curve that most closely agrees with the shape of your data at hand and use it to predict future trends or the values of points you haven't been able to measure.

Modeling the high and low temperatures in Omaha by sine curves (see page 97) is an excellent example of curve fitting in action. We can use this technique to predict which temperature records are most likely to be broken by noting which highs lie below and which lows lie above the fitted curves. This works because the curve tells us what the real values "should be." A reasonable way to predict how much warmer it will be a month from now would be to measure how much higher the fitted curves cross that date relative to the present.

The basic curve type to use for fitting a given data set can identified by either eyeballing its gross shape or using a general theory. In the first approach, the modeler studies the data set and selects a curve whose shape the data remind him of. In the second, the modeler posits a curve that *should* underlie the data according to the laws of physics or man.

Once the given curve type has been identified, the appropriate parameters must be set to best match the data. The number of parameters for any curve type is counted by its number of *degrees of freedom*. A straight line, $y = ax + b$, has two degrees of freedom, namely the slope a and intercept b. The best parameter values to fit a given curve to a given data set can be found using a black box mathematical technique called *linear regression*, which is programmed in many pocket calculators these days.

The more degrees of freedom a curve has, the more flexibility it has to be wrapped around a given data set. With this power comes the danger of overfitting, that is, constructing a curve that so completely accounts for the noise in your data it ignores the larger trends. Robust fits use small numbers of degrees of freedom to account for large numbers of data points. The sine curves so carefully fitting our Omaha temperature data use only four parameters (height, amplitude, frequency, and phase) to fit 365 points accurately.

NEAREST NEIGHBOR PREDICTORS

Nearest neighbor models use a simple but compelling idea. To predict something about you, find someone similar to you and *observe* that property in them.

Let's say a telemarketing company wants to know your salary but is too polite to ask.[2] The company no doubt has a large database of customers who have previously been hassled as well as some information about you. Thus, they can hunt through their database to find the person who seems most similar in the aspects they know about. If person x is similar to you in several aspects, say your age, amount of education, and geographic location, why shouldn't he or she be similar in other ways as well? Thus, if the telemarketers knew person x's salary, they probably have a reasonable idea of what you are making.

Nearest neighbor classifiers work by carving up the space of possible inputs into cells such that each cell consists of the portion of space closest to that of a single training point. The entire cell takes on the identity of the training point, thus enabling us to classify the entire space of possibilities. I give such a cell decomposition (also called a Voronoi diagram) for a training set of Democrat–Republican data. This type of system is used by Amazon.com and other Websites to predict what products I might like by matching me with people who have made similar purchases.

Despite their elegance and simplicity, nearest neighbor models have two serious drawbacks. First, finding the right measure of similarity is often an ill-posed problem. Is a 39-year-old New Yorker with a Ph.D. more similar to a 45-year-old high-school dropout from Chicago or a 79-year-old retired professor on Barbados? Somehow your distance function will have to score that appropriately. The simplest class of distance functions assigns each feature a numerical value and mimics the geometric distance function in the plane

$$d(a, b) = \sqrt{(X_a - X_b)^2 + (Y_a - Y_b)^2}$$

---

[2] Sure ... if only they were too polite to interrupt my dinner.

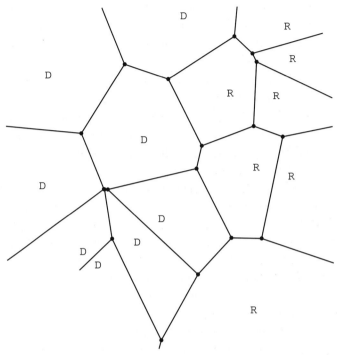

A nearest-neighbor predictor distinguishing between Democrats and Republicans.

with as many dimensions as input features and perhaps adjustments to make certain features more important than others.

A second issue with nearest neighbor models is a relative lack of robustness. The nearest neighbor to a given query may be, like some neighbors you encounter in real life, a weirdo who does not resemble anyone else around. Such outliers make lousy predictions. A more robust alternative might be to take a vote among all close neighbors to get a consensus.

SYSTEMS OF EQUATIONS

A wide class of mathematical models are constructed from systems of equations. You have probably developed your own equational model if you have ever used a spreadsheet program such as Microsoft Excel. Spreadsheets consists of rows and columns of cells, and each cell contains either input data or an equation operating on data or other equation cells.

Budgets are perhaps the model most frequently implemented on spreadsheets. Such models can be used to establish how high you can jack up your own salary while maintaining corporate profitability or to determine the impact of a tax cut on the fate of a project.

Indeed, spreadsheet programs make wonderful environments in which to experiment with your own mathematical models. Modern spreadsheets have the graphical capability to make plots, statistical routines for data analysis, and even fairly general data entry formats. I hope inspired readers will go on to tackle their own modeling projects, perhaps starting from my suggestions at the end of this book.

Econometrics is the science of building models of the economy. Say the director of the Federal Reserve Bank wants to know what will happen if he raises interest rates one point. Instead of trying it on the real economy to see if the stock market crashes, he can experiment with an econometric model. Such models are essentially giant spreadsheets with thousands of equations incorporating vast amounts of economic data and experience.

Similar models are maintained by large companies such as airlines to predict the sales impact of raising or lowering prices. By incorporating optimization techniques such as *linear programming* these models can yield pricing schemes that maximize profits. Indeed, the rapidly changing and seemingly irrational ticket prices that airlines set for different seats on a given plane are a tribute to the power and flexibility of such models.

DIFFERENTIAL EQUATION MODELS

Perhaps the most important mathematical model ever developed was Newton's laws of motion. The success of these laws in predicting the motion of planets had a radical effect on humanity's conception of how the universe works. Like any good mathematical model, Newton's laws oversimplified reality (they were superseded by Einstein's general theory of relativity) but yielded very accurate predictions on a wide variety of problems.

The proper models for many physical phenomena are based on *differential equations*. They are used in modeling fluid flows and heat dissipation, analyzing electronic and magnetic fields, and predicting changes in human or animal populations. These differential equations provide the underpinnings of weather forecasting, nuclear weapons design, and epidemiology – to name just a few killer applications.

The basic idea behind differential equations is the observation that quantities can be expressed in terms of changes. Suppose you know the value of a function $f(x)$ at time t_1 and can predict the change $\Delta(t_2 - t_1)$ between this value over the short time interval from time t_1 to time t_2. Then $f(t_2) = f(t_1) + \Delta(t_2 - t_1)$ by definition. If we wanted to compute the value of this function further in the future, we could sum up many of these small steps, that is,

$$f(t_k) = f(t_1) + \sum_{i=0}^{k-1} \Delta(t_{i+1} - t_i)$$

Calculus is the branch of mathematics that specializes in summing up changes over tiny time intervals known as differentials. Indeed, Newton had to invent calculus in order to develop his laws of motion.

The discerning reader may catch a whiff of a circular argument here. If you can indeed correctly predict small differences in the state of a system, then surely you can add them up to predict large changes. But how do you correctly predict the small changes? Here formulas from the appropriate branch of physics come into play. In weather prediction, for example, the temperature at a location might change according to the temperature of neighboring locations and the rate at which heat is conducted in the atmosphere. The ultimate accuracy of weather prediction models depends upon how accurately and completely the current conditions can be observed as well as the fidelity of these formulas at predicting small changes.

A proper appreciation of differential equation models requires substantial training in physics and mathematics. But such models govern our interaction with nature and account for the vast bulk of cycles used on the most powerful supercomputers around. They will *always* consume as much computer power as they can get, because they can be made more accurate by summing up over smaller and smaller time intervals.

NEURAL NETWORKS

Neural networks are an approach to mathematical modeling inspired by the architecture of the human brain. The intuition is that since brains are good at solving problems, machines built in the same way should be, too.

Brains are very good at learning and recognizing certain patterns. At the risk of gross oversimplification, learning in brains seems to work by adding connections between different pairs of brain cells called neurons

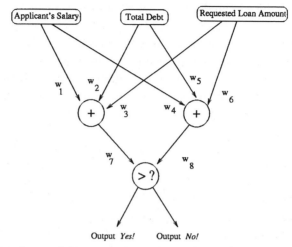

A simple neural network for mortgage authorization. The values of the constants w_1 through w_8 govern the strength of each connection and are determined by the test data used to train the network.

and changing the strengths of the connections. Modifying connection strength in response to training examples provides a natural way to "train" a neural network.

Neural nets prove a reasonable approach to classification and forecasting applications such as optical character recognition and stock-market time-series prediction when you have a large amount of data to experiment with and no particular ideas of what to do with it. You train the net on the data and watch what happens.

For example, suppose that a bank wants to build a computer model to recognize loan candidates who are likely to default and hence are not good risks to lend money to. No doubt the bank has a database of loans it has made in the past, from which a suitable set of successful and unsuccessful loan applications can be extracted. Each loan application is described by a natural set of features the loan officer and our model should use to make their decisions such as annual income, amount of previous debt, credit rating, dollar amount of collateral, and the amount of money requested. The neural network training algorithm takes your training data and produces a classification function that will say either thumbs up or thumbs down for any given loan application.

But there is a problem. Neural networks are black boxes with the strength of edges adjusted only by the training examples according to some magic learning algorithm. Because your classifier was developed by a black box, you never really know why it is making its decisions, and thus you can't know when it will fail. An interesting case was a system built for the military to distinguish between images of cars and tanks. It performed very well on test images but disastrously in the field. Eventually, someone realized that the car images had been filmed on a sunnier day than the tanks had been filmed on, and the program was classifying solely on the basis of clouds in the background of the image!

That it is difficult to figure out why neural networks make the decisions they do can actually be perceived as an advantage in certain applications. *Redlining* is the illegal practice of making loan decisions on the basis of addresses. Redlining is illegal because it has often been used as a cover to discriminate against members of the given minority group that happens to dominate the particular neighborhood. If a loan officer were to reject a loan on the basis of zip code, the bank could have a serious lawsuit on its hand. But if the loan officer rejects the loan because the mathematical model tells him to, all is covered. An unscrupulous banker can train a neural network to hate Hispanics by feeding it a selection of many bad loans from bad neighborhoods and know that his or her tracks are covered by the opaqueness of the black box.

ENGINEERING THE SYSTEM

There is a big difference between building a prototype system and a piece of production software. In his classic book *The Mythical Man-Month*, Fredrick Brooks estimates that it takes nine times the effort to create a complete, reliable system as opposed to an initial program that starts to do the job.

With Meena's graduation, I needed a fresh student to turn our prototype into a production system. I got to know Roger Mailler when he took CSE 214, undergraduate Data Structures, with me in the fall of 1997. Roger was the bored-looking student in the front row – too bright and knowledgeable to get very much from the course, but too disciplined to cut class or hide in the back. Roger finished first out of the 126 students in the course (by a substantial margin) and was untainted by a programming assignment cheating scandal that claimed many of his classmates.

Roger is an interesting fellow whose career path to Stony Brook followed a very non-standard course. His first attempt at college (at the Rochester Institute of Technology) was, to be charitable, unsuccessful. In one year at RIT he amassed a grade point average (GPA) of 0.96, where 4.0 is an A and 1.0 is a D. Any mammal with a pulse ought to be able to do better. Indeed, this is the lowest GPA I've ever seen sustained over a full academic year because students capable of such performance usually manage to get themselves expelled before the year is out.

Roger clearly had some growing up to do. He did this in the U.S. Air Force while stationed in Korea. There he started computer programming and found his calling. He worked on a system that automatically monitored e-mail to prevent the release of classified information. Working Air Force security is perhaps the best place to develop that productively suspicious nature needed to produce high-reliability software.

After his enlistment ran out, he returned to college, this time at Stony Brook. He went on to earn a 3.96 GPA here, which is about as high as you can get and a hell of a lot better than I ever did. Such academic turnarounds occur surprisingly often with older returning students who have finally figured out what they want from life. They are Exhibit A for the importance of allowing people second chances, which is one of the many noble missions for state universities like Stony Brook.

After incorporating the pool adjustments of the previous chapter, our program was losing simulated money. This is better than losing real money but still not a satisfactory state of affairs. It was now up to Roger to turn our system around, as successfully, it was hoped, as he had his GPA.

Elegance in Software Systems

I often get the sense that people trained in the humanities have an image of computer scientists as Neanderthals with knuckles dragging on the ground. They see our mismatched clothes and our taste for Jolt Cola instead of wine as the stigmata of the geek and manifestations of a downtrodden people.

However, the quest for beauty and elegance occupies a substantial place in the hearts and minds of software engineers. There can easily be two programs that solve exactly the same problem, one of which is beautiful and the other of which is ugly. And although beauty is only skin deep, ugliness goes clean to the bone as far as software is concerned.

What goes into making a beautiful program?

■ *Readability*–An understandable program is a pretty program. Explaining what makes programs readable is as easy (and hard) as it is to explain what makes English text readable. You have to break the program properly into files and subroutines, which are analogous to chapters and paragraphs in English. You have to add meaningful documentation and variable names much as you have to define any unusual vocabulary for the reader. You have to structure the program properly on the page just as you must use the proper fonts and formatting for your English document.

The importance of readable programs is emphasized by an Internet tradition, the annual International Obfuscated C Code Contest. The enormously powerful programming language C incorporates the potential to write indecipherable programs. The goal of the Obfuscated C contest is to write short programs that do useful or interesting things but in such a way that no skilled programmer would be able to identify these things are by reading the program. The Best of Show winning program by Carl Banks is a particularly outstanding combination of beauty and illegibility. To see other inspiring winners, visit the contest's official WWW page at http://www.ioccc.org/.

Comparing this code with that of our Monte Carlo simulation should convince you that clarity and legibility have their own beauty – especially if you are trying to make something work.

Creating readable programs is particularly essential in a world in which software gets passed from its author to those charged with maintaining it. Dario's programs got passed to Meena, who passed them to Roger. Much of the trouble associated with the millennium bug was due to the unreadable programs Generation IX left to Generation X.

■ *Generality* – A beautiful program is one that can easily be made to do more than it was intended to do. This is a testament to the soundness of its underlying design more than it is about the programmer's ambition or the ability to anticipate what needs will be made of the system in the future.

The distinction between programs and data is a fundamental one; programs are descriptions of how to do something, whereas data is a passive entity being acted on. In a well-written program, we can easily change the data without changing the program acting on it. A good word processor can be used to edit English as well as Chinese text, computer program source code as well as tables of numbers. The key is thinking generally enough about the task at hand to encompass a broader set of goals than may originally have been conceived.

An example of the quest for generality was Roger's rewrite of Meena's programs to tabulate statistics for each different type of bet – win,

```
#include                    <math.h>
#include                    <sys/time.h>
#include                    <X11/Xlib.h>
#include                    <X11/keysym.h>
                            double L ,o ,P
                            ,_=dt,T,Z,D=1,d,
                            s[999],E,h= 8,I,
                            J,K,w[999],M,m,O
                            ,n[999],j=33e-3,i=
                            1E3,r,t, u,v ,W,S=
                            74.5,l=221,X=7.26,
                            a,B,A=32.2,c, F,H;
                            int N,q, C, y,p,U;
                            Window z; char f[52]
                          ; GC k; main(){ Display*e=
    XOpenDisplay( 0); z=RootWindow(e, 0); for (XSetForeground (e,k=XCreateGC (e,z,0,0) ,BlackPixel(e,0))
    ; scanf("%1f%1f%1f",y +n,w+y, y+s)+1; y ++); XSelectInput(e,z= XCreateSimpleWindow(e,z,0,0,400,400,
    0,0,WhitePixel(e,0) ) ,KeyPressMask); for(XMapWindow(e,z); ; T=sin(O)){ struct timeval G={ 0,dt*1e6}
    ; K= cos(j); N=1e4; M+= H*_; Z=D*K; F+=_*P; r=E*K; W=cos( O); m=K*W; H=K*T; O+=D*_*F/ K+d/K*E*_; B=
    sin(j); a=B*T*D-E*W; XClearWindow(e,z); t=T*E+ D*B*W; j+=d*_*D-_*F*E; P=W*E*B-T*D; for (o+=(I=D*W+E
    *T*B,E*d/K *B+v+B/K*F*D)*_; p<y; ){ T=p[s]+i; E=c-p[w]; D=n[p]-L; K=D*m-B*T-H*E; if(p [n]+w[ p]+p[s
    ]== 0|K <fabs(W=T*r-I*E +D*P) |fabs(D=t *D+Z *T-a *E)> K)N=1e4; else{ q=W/K *4E2+2e2; C= 2E2+4e2/ K
    *D; N-1E4&& XDrawLine(e ,z,k,N ,U,q,C); N=q; U=C; } +p; } L+=_* (X*t +P*M+m*1); T=X*X+ 1*1+M *M;
    XDrawString(e,z,k ,20,380,f,17); D=v/1*15; i+=(B *1-M*r -X*Z)*_; for(; XPending(e); u *=CS!=N){
                            XEvent z; XNextEvent(e ,&z);
                            ++*((N=XLookupKeysym
                            (&z.xkey,0))-IT?
                            N-LT? UP-N?& E:&
                            J:& u: &h)); --*(
                            DN -N? N-DT ?N==
                            RT?&u: & W:&h:&J
                            ); } m=15*F/1;
                            c+=(I=M/ 1,1*H
                            +I*M+a*X)*_; H
                            =A*r+v*X-F*1+(
                            E=.1+X*4.9/1,t
                            =T*m/32-I*T/24
                            )/S; K=F*M+(
                            h* 1e4/1-(T+
                            E*5*T*E)/3e2
                            )/S-X*d-B*A;
                            a=2.63 /1*d;
                            X+=( d*1-T/S
                            *(.19*E +a
                            *.64+J/1e3
                            )-M* v +A*
                            Z)*_; 1 +=
                            K *_; W=d;
                            sprintf(f,
                            "%5d %3d"
                            "%7d",p =1
                            /1.7,(C=9E3+
    O*57.3)%0550,(int)i); d+=T*(.45-14/1*
    X-a*130-J* .14)*_/125e2+F*_*v; P=(T*(47
    *I-m* 52+E*94 *D-t*.38+u*.21*E) /1e2+W*
    179*v)/2312; select(p=0,0,0,0,&G); v-=(
    W*F-T*(.63*m-I*.086+m*E*19-D*25-.11*u
    )/107e2)*_; D=cos(o); E=sin(o); } }
```

Best of Show Winner in the 1998 Obfuscated C Contest – an actual working flight simulator program by Carl Banks.

CALCULATED BETS

```
/*                         Monte Carlo Simulation of Jai-Alai

        This program simulates the results of a large number of jai-alai
        games to see if the Spectacular Seven scoring system inherently
        favors certain starting positions.

        Steven Skiena -- January 18, 1987
                Simulation of win, place, and show probabilities as a
                function of post position.

        Dario Vlah -- March 12, 1997
                Enhance simulation to support players with non-uniform
                point win probabilities.
*/
#define TOTALPLAYERS         8         /* number of players per game */
#define TOTALWINPOINTS       7         /* number of points to win */
#define MAXLENGTH          100         /* maximum length of a game */

int queue[TOTALPLAYERS+1];             /* next player queue */
int queuesize;                         /* number of items in the queue */
int p1, p2;                            /* active players */
int points[TOTALPLAYERS+1];            /* scoring for a game */
int doublepoint;                       /* how many points until doubling? */
int scoreperpoint;                     /* single or double points? */
int ngames;                            /* number of games in simulation */
int i;                                 /* counter */

int results[TOTALPLAYERS+1][TOTALPLAYERS+1][TOTALPLAYERS+1];
        /* total outcomes */

int wins[TOTALPLAYERS+1], places[TOTALPLAYERS+1],
        shows[TOTALPLAYERS+1];         /* cumulative outcomes in simulation */

        /* Added by Dario Vlah */

double winprob[TOTALPLAYERS][TOTALPLAYERS];
        /* winprob[A][B] is the probability that A wins a point against B */

/*****************************************************************/
/*      This procedure identifies the winner and loser of each point,
        according to the player win probabilities
*/

void playpoint(int p1, int p2, int *winner, int *loser) {
        if (random_number() > winprob[p1-1][p2-1]) {        /*p2 wins point */
                *winner = p2;
                *loser = p1;
        } else {                                            /*p1 wins point */
                *winner = p1;
                *loser = p2;
        }
}

/*      Add the given player to the bottom of the queue. */

void addtoqueue(int loser) {
        queuesize = queuesize + 1;
        queue[queuesize] = loser;
}
```

An initial section of our Monte Carlo jai-alai simulator program.

place, show, exacta, quiniela, and trifecta. Once Meena got the first program working (say to calculate win statistics), she basically copied this program and changed the word "win" everywhere it appeared to "show". She then repeated this process five times to build six separate programs, each computing results for one type of statistic. This was a reasonable response at the time to an unreasonable professor who wanted results yesterday, but this approach was not conducive to building small, reliable programs.

Roger looked at all six of the slightly varying programs and replaced them by a single program that did the right thing for each by only changing one word in a data file, say from "win" to "show". This made the program much more general, because we could add functionality to all bet types by changing one program file instead of requiring us to make the change to all six of them. Roger's change shortened the program by several hundred lines, and you can't have bugs in lines you don't have.

■ *Robustness* – A pretty program is robust and reliable. It detects problems like faulty or unexpected data without crashing and burning. Instead, it smoothly compensates for the defective data and alerts the user as to the nature of the problem.

Anticipating the unexpected and developing a plan to respond to it are hallmarks of a top-notch programmer. I have said before that a good programmer must be paranoid, but that is not enough. You cannot get trapped in conspiracy theories, frozen by the impossibility of looking everywhere and seeing everything. You must be creative enough to eliminate the causes of your paranoia, or at least bottle them up so these demons are constrained to a small part of the system.

Smoking Out Bugs

How can we find bugs in programs when we don't know what the answer should be? This was the case in our system. We certainly did not know how successful we *should* have been at predicting the outcome of jai alai matches when we wrote the program. For every problem we encountered, there would be two distinct sources of possible error:

■ Our underlying mathematical model did not accurately describe the real world. This meant a fundamental problem in the design of our system.

■ The computer program did not implement the mathematical model as we had intended. This presumably meant a problem that could be solved by rewriting the appropriate portion of the program. But we had to find it first.

The most frustrating aspect of debugging our system was figuring out which of these possibilities were the real source of our problem. At this point, our simulated betting strategies reported that we were losing money at a rate of about 20% per bet. This suggested that we were doing no better than any grandmother betting on her favorite color would. It was not clear whether we had bugs that could be fixed or if in fact Grandma had a good thing going relative to us.

This form of uncertainty occurs in interpreting the results of any simulation or mathematical model. Every so often you read that physicists have performed supercomputer simulations of what happens when galaxies collide, the results of which inexorably imply that the Big Bang did (or did not) happen. It is prudent to be highly suspicious of such simulations unless the physicists can also bang two actual galaxies together to see what *really* happens.

Finding and fixing bugs in computer programs are very tricky things to do, even in applications in which you know exactly what the program is supposed to do and how it works. A company like Microsoft employs roughly one full-time tester for every computer programmer in order to boost the reliability of its products. Still, this programmer can create bugs at a faster rate than the tester can discover them.

A good programmer can anticipate bugs in a system by identifying what he or she did not know how to do in a clean, correct manner. I was once privileged to witness the spectacle of Stephen Wolfram demonstrating his *Mathematica* computer algebra system to William Kahan, who is perhaps the world's leading authority on performing accurate numerical computations. Now Wolfram is a *very* bright guy – winner of the MacArthur Foundation genius award and recipient of his Ph.D. at age 20 – and *Mathematica* is an excellent product. But Kahan is no slouch, either. Within a few minutes of stepping up to the console, Kahan had *Mathematica* merrily proving that $0.9999 = 1$ and that $-1 = 1$. From there, he proved that day was night, as Wolfram shrank in horror.

I've heard the following tale told of IBM's OS 360, the biggest software development project of its time. A large staff of programmers set to work repairing bugs as they were found by users, gradually improving the reliability of the product. Eventually, their progress slowed and ceased with roughly a thousand known bugs still infesting the system. No matter how hard they worked at it, fixing these bugs created other bugs, just as painting the walls leaves drips on the floor.

The Millennium Bug

As we were developing our system, the specter of the millennium bug (or the Year 2000 problem) slowly but surely eased its way into the consciousness of the general public. People became aware that computer systems around the world were at serious risk of failing on the morning of January 1, 2000, owing to what sounded like the most ridiculous and trivial of programmer errors. My personal favorite doomsday scenarios included the following:

- *December 31, 1999: Grand Ballroom, Waldorf–Astoria Hotel* – The cream of New York society, powerful gray-haired men in tuxedos with diamond-studded trophy wives, gather to drink and dance in the new century. 10–9–8–7–6–5–4–3–2–1! We have reached the twentyfirst century!

  Suddenly several men around the room start clutching their chests, unable to breath. Inside their bodies, pacemakers programmed with the millennium bug have begun to party like it's 1999...

- *December 31, 1999: United States Strategic Air Command Headquarters* – Renegade General Duke Hazard lights up a victory cigar deep within a top-secret bunker under the Colorado Rockies. The clock strikes 9 P.M. It is the moment he had spent 5 years planning for, waiting for. The rotation of the earth has already changed the century throughout Europe and Asia, and the United States now awaits its turn to ring in the century with a bang.

  But not anywhere near the bang General Hazard had in mind! He knows that the militaries of every other power on earth lie paralyzed by the millennium bug. With one all-out nuclear strike we could eliminate the threat of China, Russia, Iraq, Libya – once and for all. He caresses the button that will irrevocably send off the missiles and bombers when he pushes it. The true Manifest Destiny of the United States is being on the right side of the International Dateline at the right time, he muses.

But outside his bunker, a crack team led by Bruce Willis attacks the hardened concrete, racing against time to save the world from utter destruction...

Fortunately, neither of these scenarios was destined to happen; indeed in retrospect Y2K seems much ado about nothing. However, billions of dollars had to be spent fixing programs to ensure that business and society continued to function properly at the start of the century.

The millennium bug was usually described as the result of a programmer's ill-advised attempts to save the memory space it took to store the "19" at the front of every year. Thirty years ago, this may have been true. But in fact, the most insidious occurrences of the bug were not a result of space parsimony so much as a human inability to anticipate trouble in something that seemed like it was working correctly.

Lurking within our jai alai system was a good example of a millennium bug. Each night our program fetched the next day's schedules and yesterday's results, and this data had to be stored in files. We gave each file a name that encoded as much information as possible about what it was. For example, we named the Milford Afternoon results and schedule files for a particular date ma-08-22-98.res and ma-08-22-98.sch, respectively. In various contexts, our program assumed two-digit dates because they read better than the full four-digit dates. Sure, the extra two digits were wasted space, but who cares about the cost of such a tiny amount of memory. But the extra digits were a pain for the people who had to read the dates.

Two-digit dates don't necessarily present a problem, provided they are computed correctly from four-digit dates. The obvious algorithm is to take the given year and subtract 1900 from it. Obvious but wrong! Sure $1996 - 1900 = 96$, but $2000 - 1900 = 100$, which is no longer a two-digit number! Extra logic has to be added to chop it down to two digits.

After making such changes, Roger assured me that the system will continue to predict jai alai matches into next century, and indeed it came through New Year's Day 2000 like a champ. We should now be in the clear until 2096, when the earliest of the data we collected will start to have file names that will collide with our latest retrievals. At this point, I do not trust our system to work after 2096, but we can take care of this in due time. Of course, this is the kind of thinking that got us in trouble with the millennium bug in the first place, but I will be very happy if I get to deal with the problem at that time.

Program Trading in Jai Alai

Roger diligently beat on the jai alai system, fixing bugs, tightening the code, making sure he understood how every line of the program works.

With the system clean and stable, he now systematically conducted experiments on its performance. He took 3 months' worth of schedules and results and evaluated a raft of different betting strategies on them. Each betting strategy was described by three parameters: (1) the subset of games we were studying (evenings, matinees, or both for a given fronton), (2) the α value described earlier regulating how aggressively we favored the stronger player, and (3) the expected-return threshold that regulated how advantageous a bet had to be before we were willing to risk it. In principle, the higher we set our expected-return threshold, the greater the percentage of our profits should have been. However, a lower threshold might return greater total profits by enabling us to place more money-making bets even if the yield-per-bet was less. We needed to find the right point to skim off the most cream.

Roger kept our computers busy for a week trying every possible betting strategy. The results were clear and consistent. There was no cream to skim with any of them. All lost money at about the same rate as random chance.

How could this be? We racked our heads trying to figure out what was wrong with the model. I repeatedly sent Roger away in search of bugs, but he kept coming back giving the program a clean bill of health.

If our programs didn't have bugs, the problem had to be in our model. But where could it be? Our Monte Carlo simulation was straightforward enough to trust, but what about our assessment of player skills? It dawned on us that almost 90% of all jai alai matches are doubles matches, yet we were maintaining statistics about individual players, not teams. To predict how good a team was, we averaged the skills of the two athletes involved. But did this make sense? It was easy to imagine pairs of highly talented players who couldn't stand each other, and other pairs whose skills complemented each other so they were better as a team than as individuals. Certainly teams with more experience were likely to do better than a pair thrown together for the first time.

We decided to give the system one last chance and use team records to measure player skill. This presented some minor problems because the number of teams is potentially enormous. Note that a stable of 50 players could generate up to $50 \times 49/2 = 1225$ teams to keep track of, but in fact most possible pairings never occurred.

To give ourselves the best possible chance, we also incorporated trifecta box betting. By betting on the box 1–2–3, we had bets on all six possible orderings (permutations) of the three numbers. But the minimum bet on a trifecta box at Milford was $9 versus $3 per trifecta. Although we would get paid off as if we only made a $1.50 bet on the winning trifecta, this enabled us to reduce our impact on the pool in the event of successful bets, which is what seemed to be killing us. Of course, we had to place bets on nonoptimal trifectas to get the volume discount, but if the stars were properly in alignment this could be a much better deal.

After incorporating the team statistics and trifecta boxes, Roger again fired up the program to search for successful betting strategies. Again the computer ground away for a week. But this time, there was sunshine at the end. Indeed, there was a strategy offering positive expected returns. We had been doing such a lousy job evaluating teams that the entire system was lost in the fog. But now we had reason to believe.

Now that we had something worth working with, Roger set up the program to run in a daily production mode. Each morning, the program sent me e-mail with a list of possible bets and results for next day's matches. For example, on a particular Wednesday in November the system sent me this list of recommended bets:

```
FRONTON: milford
SESSION: ma
DATE: 11-04-1998
YOUR FAVOURABLE BETS ARE
*****************************************************
 9 BOX 2-4-6 9 6.36
12 BOX 2-3-4 9 6.70
12 EXACTA 4-2 3 9.10
12 PLACE 4 3 1.70
12 QUINIELA 2-4 3 7.62
12 WIN 4 3 1.35
14 WIN 1 3 1.81
```

The first number represents the game number of the desired bet, and the second field the type of bet recommended. Field three gives the recommended post position to invest in followed by the amount of money to bet. The last field gives an inflated estimate of the expected return of the given wager.

Assuming that the fronton posted the results in a timely manner, the next morning I would get e-mail telling me how the system had done. This particular Wednesday proved to be an especially successful betting session:

```
RESULTS OF YOUR BETS
****************************************************************

milford 11-04-1998 ma

game bet bet_spec amount result payoff_per_dollar final_amount
*******************************************************************
9     BOX       2-4-6   9   6-4-2   180.6   249.15
12    WIN       4       3   2       11.2    -3.00
12    PLACE     4       3   2-8     3.4     -3.00
12    BOX       2-3-4   9   2-8-3   297.8   -9.00
12    QUINIELA  2-4     3   2-8     19.7    -3.00
12    EXACTA    4-2     3   2-8     94.9    -3.00
14    WIN       1       3   8       8.4     -3.00

*******************************************************************
total_win          6                        -6.000
total_place        3                        -3.000
total_show         0                         0.000
total_quinel       3                        -3.000
total_exac         3                        -3.000
total_trifec       0                         0.000
total_box         18                       231.150

*******************************************************************
```

As a result of Roger's experiments, we were now ready to go into business.

The Jai Alai Maven

We now had in place a system that appeared to predict the results of the next day's jai alai matches accurately. Each day, our program woke up at 2:30 A.M. and then again at 4:30 A.M. to look at the schedule of games to be played that day at Milford and Dania. For each pair of opposing players or teams P_1 and P_2 in each scheduled game, the program used statistics for the past year to estimate the probability that P_1 would win the point played against P_2. Once it had all these probabilities, the program would simulate each game 250, 000 times and then produce a list of all the bets that it felt offered a sufficiently high return to warrant betting on.

The 2:30 A.M. version of the program differed from the 4:30 A.M. version only in the value of the fudge factor α. The early program used a conservative $\alpha = 1$, whereas the late program used the more aggressive $\alpha = 0.4$. By comparing the two results, we could see whether the early program caught the worm.

Each invocation of the program provided a fairly long list of bets it assessed as offering reasonable returns. Betting on all of them would have cost me over $1000 a day in bets, which was much too rich for my blood and too much data for me to be able to keep track of how well the system was doing. For this reason, I wrote a short program to merge the conservative and aggressive selections and identify a more exclusive subset of good bets under the following criteria:

- Make any win, place, or show bet the conservative program thought offered positive returns *or* the aggressive program thought offered at least $0.50 profit per dollar bet.
- Because the system offered up considerably more quiniela and exacta betting possibilities, make any quiniela or exacta bet the conservative program thought offered positive returns *and* the aggressive program thought offered at least $5.00 profit per dollar bet.
- Because trifecta box bets were more expensive than the other bets (they cost us $9 at Milford instead of $3), we needed an even stricter investment criteria. The system would make any trifecta box bet the conservative program thought offered positive returns *and* the aggressive program thought offered at least $6.00 profit per dollar bet.

I named this selection program *Maven*, which is a Yiddish word for "self-proclaimed expert." After final tuning, my jai alai Maven and I were ready for the test.

On the Wire

I live in New York, and the nearest jai alai action resides a 2-hour drive from me in Connecticut or a 2-hour flight from me in Florida. I'm not such a self-destructive gambler to incur such transit times just to make a bet – particularly for a system that seeks to bet only a modest amount each day. But to test the system, we had to find someone to take our money. I thought about striking a deal with local people in Connecticut and Florida to serve as my betting agents, but then I would have had to give them a cut of the action. Eventually, I found a simpler, more elegant solution.

Many states provide off-track betting (OTB) facilities that enable people who can't make it to the racetrack to put down bets legally. These OTB parlors are usually fairly seedy-looking places filled with low-life characters watching TV screens that show how their latest investments are paying off. In the 1970s, OTB services were touted as a way to help the horse-racing industry, which was suffering as state lotteries began siphoning off much of their action. When casino gambling began spreading through the land, OTB offices tried to compete by offering simulcasting, the ability to watch and bet on any race (or fronton) anywhere in the country, not just at local tracks.

Simulcasting helped, but not enough. The fiscal health of racetracks, frontons, and the OTB itself continued to deteriorate. Indeed, certain politicians in New York have recently been making hay complaining that only state government could manage to *lose* money running a bookie operation. Because the OTB parlors themselves are as popular as the plague in most of the neighborhoods they reside in, more creative thinking was required.

The Connecticut OTB, in cahoots with its partner Autotote Enterprises, rose to the occasion by starting *On the Wire* telephone betting services. Who needs an OTB parlor at all when you can call in your bets from home or office? *On the Wire* enables its customers to speak with live operators eager to take their bets or to dial bets in manually using an interactive voice-response system. Indeed, the *On the Wire* WWW page (http://www.ctotb.com) stresses the advantages of the latter technology for married or employed compulsive gamblers:

> Bet using the touch tone key pad on your phone and no one around you will be aware you are placing a wager through your phone account.

All the bets are made using a toll-free telephone number, which presumably has the additional advantage of never appearing on anyone's telephone bill.

I sent in an initial $250 deposit to Autotote Enterprises and a few days later was rewarded with a letter containing my account number and instructions on how to bet. Deposit and withdrawal tickets were provided as with any other financial institution. The seven deposit and only four withdrawal tickets made for an ominous asymmetry, but one probably well justified given the nature of Autotote's business. A cheaply mimeographed sheet listed all the betting events for the coming month, including horse racing at a variety of tracks as well as Dania and Milford jai alai.

A careful reading of its literature made clear the special nature of this financial institution. Checks drawn on business or corporate accounts are not accepted, which is a lesson presumably learned from hard experience. The Internal Revenue Service (IRS) insists on tax withholdings of 28% whenever winnings exceed $5000. All betting conversations are recorded on tape to prevent customers from later disowning their unsuccessful investments.

Dialing bets in via *On the Wire* was fairly easy. A call to their toll-free phone number was answered by a cheerful four-note jingle and a soothing recorded voice:

```
Welcome to On the Wire automated teller. Enter your
account number, followed by the pound key.
```

The proper stream of digits yielded the soothing voice again:

```
Enter your personal identification number, followed
by the pound key.
```

After entering this four-digit code, the system would pause a while to check me out. If all was in order, the voice would inform me of my holdings:

```
Your account balance is two hundred and fifty dollars.
For track conditions enter 99 pound.
```

A harsher, metallic voice now set down to business:

```
Track?
```

It wanted the code of the fronton session where we wanted to bet. Milford matinees and evenings were 78 and 79, respectively. Dania matinees and evenings were 92 and 93, followed of course by the pound key.

```
Race?
```

Which game did you wish to bet on? Presumably this was a number between 1 and 15.

```
Bet amount?
```

Here we could type in any amount we wanted, in dollars, subject to the minimum allowable bet. The "*" key was available to serve as a decimal point if needed, as on trifecta box bets.

```
Bet type?
```

Each possible type of bet had a numerical code associated with it. The code for a win was "11," while "32" would get you a trifecta box.

```
Runners?
```

Here the system would prompt you for the post position numbers (between 1 and 8) of the players you wished to bet on. For quiniela, exacta, and trifecta bets that involved more than one post position, the entries were separated with the "*" key.

```
You have requested Milford Jai-Alai, evening, game 5,
for one dollar fifty cents on trifecta box 3-5-6. Press
1 to confirm.
```

On confirming the bet, the system would inform you of the size of your now diminished balance and return to "Track?" Entering a "*" or just hanging up the phone would end this session. Personally, I preferred entering a "*" so I could listen as their machine thanked me for my business.

Otto the Autodialer

Dialing in bets may have been easy, but it was also mind-numbingly boring. This was the kind of boredom that ruined far more blackjack card counters than casino security ever did. Imagine you were an intelligent, restless sort of person who knew enough mathematics to develop or master some kind of intricate card-counting system. This system turns the odds in your favor instead of the house's, offering, say, a 1.5% per hand positive return. Now seat this intelligent, restless sort of person at a blackjack table, where his or her disciplined, intense play pays off at up to $50 per hour. For the first few hours, the card counter will think, "Cool! I am sitting here taking the casino's money."

But over the course of the next 100 hands or so, reality will gradually but inevitably set in. Your eyes will start to get glassy from the glare of the lights off the cards, your fingers will start to cramp from handling the cards, and your head will start pounding from the strain of keeping track of all those numbers. "What the hell am I doing here? I never wanted to be a bank clerk, even at $50 an hour!" You will storm out of the casino and buy a book on the stock market, or preferably this one, on jai alai.

The same thing happened to me in the course of phoning in my bets, and it didn't take a hundred hands. Five or six was more like it. Phoning in each bet took close to a minute of punching in a list of digits printed out by a machine and then waiting until another machine read back my bets and asked for my confirmation. It didn't take long before the glamor wore off. There was no way I would spend the 15–20 minutes per day of mindless dialing it would require to really test our system out.

It was time to put technology to work for the betterment of man. When computers want to talk on the telephone, they use a device called a *modem*. A modem, short for modulator–demodulator, is a device that translates arbitrary text and data into tones suitable to be sent down a phone line and converts another modem's tones back into its original text and data. Anyone who has ever tried talking to a fax machine or interrupted junior's AOL session by picking up the phone has some idea what these tones sound like. But other computers don't mind listening to them, and such communication is the real foundation of the Internet revolution.

My first modem was a 300-baud acoustic coupler model for which you hand dialed the phone number of the computer you wanted to reach, listened for the squeal, and then tried to jam the handset of the telephone into the two black rubber cuffs fast enough to establish a connection before the other machine cut you off. If you got lucky, you were rewarded with text streaming across your computer screen at the speed of a slow typist.

From these humble beginnings, modem technology has matured in a big way. Acoustic cuffs disappeared years ago in favor of jacks plugging directly into phone lines, thus increasing reliability and speed. Today's modems operate at 56 kilobaud on standard telephone lines, roughly 200 times faster than what I started with.

Eliminating the acoustic couplers meant that the modem had to be smart enough to dial the phone for itself. This required the modem to understand a command language with instructions to dial numbers, detect whether a phone answers or is busy, wait prescribed amounts of time before issuing new commands, and hang up.

Turning modems into programmable devices opened up new worlds of possibilities for those bold enough to grasp them. By programming your modem to speed-dial a radio station repeatedly, you could increase your chances of getting through to win some kind of prize. You could use your modem for political expression. I recall a bloke who programmed his modem to call up the Reverend Jerry Falwell's toll-free fund-raising number once every minute for several months. This saddled poor Jerry with quite a phone bill because toll-free calls are paid by the recipient, not the sender. "Reach out and touch someone," was the bloke's motto, at least until the courts shut him down. While he was still in high school, my old roommate Luke programmed his home computer to conduct an early-morning search for telephones answered by computers. Over the next few months, he systematically woke up every single person in his home town of Baton Rouge, Louisiana, exactly once.

Fortunately for Luke, those were the days before the caller ID option was offered by the telephone company. Today, such activities, called "scanning" or "war-dialing," are illegal in many places. In particular, the law in Luke's current hometown of Colorado Springs, Colorado, makes it illegal to place a call "without the intent to communicate."

What I had in mind wasn't so unsavory. I wanted to program the modem to dial our bets into *On the Wire* so I didn't have to phone them in myself. I needed free access to a modem attached to our departmental computer systems. This was a problem. In justifiable fear of creative students like Luke, our system's staff would not let anybody but themselves play with the modems. They did inform me that one of our faculty members has his own modem hooked to his own personal computer in his office.

Because this professor is Gene Stark, I knew that he would help me with this project. Why? Well, first Gene is a terrific hacker in the best sense of the word, and thus I knew that he would get a kick out of it. Second, Gene has had high-tech gambling experience of his own; he was the colleague I told you about who devised his own card-counting system in blackjack.

Gene was intrigued enough with the project that he wrote the autodi-aler program himself. Its job was to take a file of bets and phone them into Autotote. It was a pleasure watching Gene program, a master at work. His big hands would dance over the small keyboard, bang–bang–bang, and he issued commentary as he pecked away.

"Parse the input file, initialize the modem, emit the dialing commands." Bang–bang–bang . . .

"Need some structure. Modularize this sucker. One routine to make each kind of bet." Bang–bang–bang . . .

Gene was disciplined enough to do things right, not just get something working. "Always aim for more structure. Nah, that is too crufty. Try it this way." Bang–bang–bang…

"Good. Let's see if it talks to the modem." We could hear garbled sounds coming through the cheap speaker on his modem. Hiss, bleep, whine. "Doesn't work. Why not? The modem is hung trying to talk to the other machine. It doesn't get the carrier. Why not? Of course. It's not trying connect, just pumping out dial commands." Bang–bang–bang…

"Try it again."

Hiss, bleep! Welcome to On the Wire automated teller. Enter beep-beep-beep-beep your account number. I did not understand your account number. Please try again.

"Our pause timing is off here. Sleep another 5 seconds and try it again." Bang–bang–bang…

One of the most critical aspects of the autodialer was figuring out how long to wait before issuing various commands. We were trying to program the modem to use an interface designed to be used by people. People phoning in bets would listen to the system prompts and enter the data when the machine told them it was ready for it. If they goofed, the machine would tell them why and what to do from that point. But our modem was deaf and didn't understand English. It could not hear any prompts from the system, let alone understand them. All it could do was pump out touch-tones at prescribed intervals in time. By timing the On the Wire system with a stop watch, we could estimate how long it would take the system to react and pause accordingly between data items.

Hiss, bleep! Welcome to On the Wire automated teller. beep-beep-beep-beep, . . ., beep-beep-beep-beep, Your account balance is now two hundred and forty seven dollars...

"Ha-ha-ha," Gene laughed. "It just spent your money. I sure hope you know what you're doing with this jai alai thing."

We sat there for a while listening to the two machines talking to each other. The modem would issue commands, wait patiently until its partner stopped talking and then dial in its next request. I've had conversations like that, when someone is babbling so much that I just remove the phone from my ear and wait until he or she is finished talking. But here, it was a machine doing the talking as well. It was the dumb talking to the deaf.

Gene's only stipulation was that our computer had to be off his phone by the time he came into the office each morning. This meant that we had to start dialing in our bets by about 7:30 A.M. or so to be sure we finished on time. This was before *On the Wire* officially opened for business, and thus about half the time our bets didn't take. Still, it was well worth this amount of shrinkage to avoid the drudgery of phoning the bets in by hand.

Phoning the bets in that early may also have had an advantage, because it might scare off any bettor watching the odds board. Our bets could serve to depress the preliminary odds enough that these bottom-feeders would be induced to pick other options instead, thus reducing our competition. Considerations like this made it impossible to simulate exactly how the system would perform in real life. We had to place actual bets to see if we knew what we were doing.

I'd occasionally get to work early enough to catch the modem phoning in the bets. Whenever I did, I'd press my ear against Gene's office door to hear what was going on. I'd hear foggy touch-tones going `beep-beep-beep-beep` followed by a muffled, synthesized voice thanking an empty room for its business.

Cryptography and Security

Gene never let any program that he didn't understand run on his computer. "I don't trust it," he'd say.

We had to insulate Gene's machine from the entire jai alai system while getting him the bets. The solution was to e-mail the bets to a special address on his office machine and have his e-mail handling software respond appropriately to it.

How does your email ultimately get to you, and you alone? Suppose you send mail to skiena@jai-tech.com. The stuff to the right of the @ specifies a machine that knows about the fellow whose account name is to the left of the @. Internet routing computers keep tables of the addresses of important machines on the network and eventually ship the mail to the specified machine. This machine runs software that looks at each incoming message, identifies which account it is for, and then looks to see how mail for this account should be processed.

For most people, this processing means adding the mail to their unread mail file and perhaps raising a "you've got mail" flag. For our special jai alai account, this meant taking the given mail message, stripping off any header information, and then invoking Otto the Autodialer on the given set of bets.

Gene's system was now safely protected from my jai alai program, although this nifty e-mail interface exposed my money to a certain amount of extra risk. Suppose someone else sent an appropriately formatted e-mail message to this account. Otto would be just as happy to phone in these bets as it would be to phone in mine. Indeed, an evil person could drain all my money away making 6–8–7 trifecta bets if he or she were appropriately informed and devious.

This introduces us to an important and surprisingly intricate problem of contemporary computer science, namely, "convince me that you are who you say you are." I needed to find a way to prevent Otto from listening to anyone except me. How could I convince it I was who I said I was?

The most common approach to solving such identification problems involves the use of a password. If you and I are the only ones who know the secret password, than you can e-mail the password to me in order to convince me that you are you. But what's the catch? Anybody on any computer this e-mail passes through might be snooping in on our message. Thus, he or she could easily discover the password. From this moment on, he or she could masquerade as either of us. This is exactly why many people (including me) are reluctant to use their credit card to order anything over the Internet. The bad guys may be watching.

More important even than safeguarding my credit card number, user authentication problems can be a matter of life and death. Consider the friend-or-foe identification systems in fighter aircraft used in the military. Combat among fighter aircraft is a high-speed, high-stakes business. Imagine I'm a pilot. Radar reports an unknown craft rapidly closing in on my tail. Friend or foe? If I'm wrong, I'll shoot down my buddy, or even worse, someone will shoot me down.

Friend or foe? Passwords won't work well for this application. The opposing side certainly has radio receivers and can listen in on everything we transmit to each other. As soon as I broadcast the password, the other side could discover it and teach its aircraft the magic word to sneak up on us. We could change the password often, but that is a dangerous game. If my buddy's password ever gets slightly out of date, he's toast – I'm liable to shoot him down for his carelessness.

Real military friend-or-foe systems work by conducting a question-and-answer session between the two parties. Both parties have stored up a large series of questions and answers. I'll send you a random stream of numbers corresponding to the questions I want to ask you. You send me back the given answers. Someone listening can't immediately use this information, because the next time I want to check somebody out I'll ask him or her a different set of questions. Properly employed, such randomization enables us to protect our secrets while facilitating authentication.

So, how does Gene's e-mail-handling software safeguard my money by processing messages only from me? I'm not telling. Any information I give here will only help young hackers (the future Lukes of America) figure out how to break into my system. And I'm not interested in making any 6–8–7 trifecta bets, thank you.

Internet Gambling

Various sectors of the so-called gaming industry are excited about the prospects for widespread Internet gambling, and chafing at the regulatory constraints that are delaying its widespread introduction.

I've seen the volume of legal gambling in the United States estimated as high as $500 billion per year. This works out to almost $2000 per person per year. Even a small fraction of this total is a healthy chunk of change. I hate to think what the amount of *illegal* gambling is! The Interactive Gaming Council reports that more than $1.2 billion were bet in its member's 700 cyber casino sites in 1999. This is an amazing number comparable to the $1.6 billion dollars in sales that Amazon.com had in the same year. This gives new perspective on who really runs the Internet. The United States Justice Department and Senator Jon Kyle estimate that this annual total could grow to $10 billion within a few years.

Internet gambling differs in many important ways from conventional gambling. Whether these changes are positive or negative depends upon your perspective:

- *Loss of community control* – Today, for better or worse, state, local, or tribal government regulates the opportunities for legal gambling. If the people of a given region believe that casino gambling is harmful, it will be forbidden. If the people of a given region believe that casino gambling is good for economic development, they can pass a law and must live with the consequences.

    But Internet gambling has no such geographic limitations. Anyone with a computer is a potential player, even in the most righteous community on earth. The problems of compulsive gambling won't go away, and indeed their effects will stay local. All the benefits, such as potential profits, taxes, and jobs won't stay local but instead get sucked off into cyberspace.

■ *Lack of regulation* – You are playing virtual roulette in a virtual casino. After 10 straight blacks you just *know* the next ball will be red. You swallow hard as you put down a $10,000 wager on red. It is more than you ever dreamed of betting, and frankly more than you can afford. It comes up black, again. You lose.

But how do you know that the game was fair? Perhaps the programmer decided to make the ball fall in the slot which minimizes the amount returned to bettors, instead of fairly picking a random number. The WWW site you have been sending your money to is on an uninhabited island in the Bahamas. If the game wasn't fair, who could you complain to, anyway?

■ *Lack of infrastructure* – Expanding casino gambling from an enclave in Las Vegas into a nationwide "gaming" industry required a considerable investment in infrastructure and personnel. Massive hotels and powerful politicians had to be bought, the latter to help steer reluctant legislatures towards legalizing their business.

Interestingly, it is the established gaming industry that has the most to lose if Internet gambling gains a foothold in the hearts and minds of gamblers. Operating an Internet gambling site does not require a 3000-room hotel in Vegas. Indeed, well-known establishments like Caesar's Palace have no particular edge in building a virtual casino. Instead, they face the prospect of their customers' sitting home glued to their computer screens. Why lose money in Atlantic City when you can do so from the comfort of your living room?

The Internet Gambling Prohibition Act of 1997 was passed by the Senate on July 23, 1998, by a vote of 90–10. This act amends the Federal criminal code to prohibit and set penalties for: (1) placing, receiving, or otherwise making a bet or wager via the Internet or any other interactive computer service in any State, and (2) engaging in the business of betting or wagering through the Internet or any such service. There are exceptions for state lotteries, horse racing, and (yes) jai alai.

As of this writing, the House of Representatives has failed to vote this bill into law. Special interests line up for or against it in interesting ways.

Liquor store owners and religious groups are for the legislation, but perhaps from different motives. The liquor dealers fear a reduction in their lottery ticket sales owing to competition with on-line lotteries. A surprising collection of state governors stand quietly against it, with their eyes open to losing revenue from these same lotteries.

Internet gambling is currently legal in 50 countries, including Liechtenstein, Gibraltar, Australia, and certain Caribbean countries – more than enough to cause trouble. A California woman who lost $70,000 to an overseas virtual casino sued her credit card company, asserting that she should get their cut of this action.

The Internet Gambling Prohibition Act is broad enough potentially to threaten full deployment of our jai alai system to frontons beyond those supported by *On the Wire*. In particular, we could imagine e-mailing our picks to a local agent, who would place our bets for us in Newport or Miami. As I read the act, this might be a Federal crime, even though it would be perfectly legal to have our same program spewing out the predictions on the agent's own personal computer.

This act works by extending the current prohibitions against using telephones for interstate gambling. There are serious consequences for those who violate it:

> Whoever, being engaged in the business of betting or wagering knowingly uses a communication facility for the transmission or receipt in interstate or foreign commerce of bets or wagers, information assisting in the placing of bets or wagers, or a communication that entitles the transmitter or receiver to the opportunity to receive money or credit as a result of bets or wagers, shall be fined not more than $10,000, imprisoned not more than 2 years, or both.

The prohibition against using telephones for interstate gambling has proven to be a powerful legal tool against organized crime. It presumably does not apply to my use of *On the Wire* because the statute provides exemptions as regulated by state law. As a prerequisite to opening my account, I had to assert that I live in one of the states that permits off-track wagering; fortunately, New York is one of these states. Still, it was disconcerting to learn how close my system came to violating Federal law. If caught, I feel pretty sure it would have been me doing the time, not Maven.

PUTTING MY MONEY WHERE MY MOUTH IS

It was time to put my money where my mouth was. The system was running well, more or less. Roger was busy with his summer job and then his fall classes, and thus the program wasn't destined to improve in the foreseeable future. The longer we waited, the more likely it was that some external event – maybe a hardware problem, maybe Milford changing its WWW site – would put us out of business for good. My *On the Wire* account was stocked with $250. It was time to put the system to the test.

A Gambler's Diary

On July 29, 1998, Maven made its first six bets for $3 each. I bided my time until late that night when I could call in to see how I did.

```
Your account balance is $263.50.
```

I was a winner! I could stop now and forever be ahead. But I was a winner! And I wanted to keep on winning.

The first few days I kept the bet amounts small as we ironed out timing problems with the autodialer. Still, risking even $20 gave me some pause.

```
Your account balance is $242.50.
```

This gave me a sinking feeling. I'd lost my winnings, and more. Was there a bug with my program? Would I ever go ahead again?

174

```
Your account balance is $264.40.
Your account balance is $261.40.
Your account balance is $258.40.
Your account balance is $272.80.
```

The autodialer was clearly working. The program seemed to be making money. At least it wasn't giving it away. I lowered the profitability threshold to convince Maven to make more bets, and on August 26 it put $99 at risk. I was more nervous than usual when I listened that night:

```
Your account balance is $408.70.
```

Big win! In the news, the Russian government had defaulted on its debt, setting off a sharp stock market decline. Because my pension funds are invested in stocks, it meant I was probably several thousand dollars poorer for the day. But what did that matter! I was winning at jai alai. Flushed with success, the phone call to get the day's results became a favorite evening ritual...

```
Your account balance is $350.20.
Your account balance is $384.10.
Your account balance is $302.80.
```

A little loss didn't bother me. After all, I was playing now with the house's money. I was ahead of the game...

```
Your account balance is $284.80.
```

I came to see that wins always came in spurts. The program liked long shots, and they only came in every few days.

```
Your account balance is $300.10.
Your account balance is $223.30.
```

It was September 9, and suddenly I was behind. And on this day of all days, Maven decided to bet nearly twice as much as it ever had before, $169.00. If I got wiped out for the day, my account would nearly be dry. Certainly I would have to throttle back my bets if I was going to make this money last. It was with more than the usual trepidation that I called my electronic bookie that night:

```
Your account balance is $499.75.
```

Dynamite! I had now almost doubled my money! The system worked! When I was winning, this nightly phone call was a source of immense pleasure to me. It was less thrilling to my wife Renee, who started questioning what kind of man she had married.

```
Your account balance is $409.75.
Your account balance is $367.15.
```

I felt like I was participating in a modern type of pushbutton warfare. You hit a switch to send off thousands of missiles, reach for a beer, and then check the videos to see how much you scored. I felt a similar bloodless disconnect between the simulations we were doing and the actual sporting events that were generating my new balance each night. Back at the fronton, two dozen Basques played their guts out in every match, laboring in blissful ignorance of the fact that this game had been played 500,000 times the night before. The likelihood of each possible outcome had already been foretold. All the Basques were doing (in physics jargon) was collapsing this probabilistic wave function down to its ground state.

Similarly, each night I checked my phone to find out how much money I had won without knowing or caring who had won it for me and how well they had played. The e-mail report I received each morning told me which bets had paid off the previous night, but this report didn't include player names or identification numbers – just their post position in the match. The only hint of humanity in this entire process, and it was just a hint, came on the right-hand side of the list of proposed bets. For each bet, we reported the expected probability of its winning that given match. The discerning eye could tell that player 3 in game three was deemed more skillful than player 3 in game four and was hence a better investment.

For this reason, I'm aware that this recital of my bet outcomes suffers from a fundamental flaw. The stories of winning a jai alai match would be infinitely more interesting if the matches were about people. My tales would be about the chic-chac shot Enrique made to win game seven or the way the crowd cried "Fix!" when Laxhi muffed an easy catch in game nine. War movies were infinitely more interesting when people shot people, instead of people shooting missiles.

```
Your account balance is $349.15.
```

It was September 23, 1998. Maven got ambitious again, making $156 worth of bets.

```
Your account balance is $505.75.
```

Maven was on a roll. I got a feeling of confidence whenever it wanted to make a large amount of bets. The system always looked for values, and when the right players sat in the right position it was ready to move in full throttle.

```
Your account balance is $765.40.
Your account balance is $795.70.
```

Maven seemed invincible. Only it really wasn't. Over the next several days I noticed that it seemed only to want to make win, place, and show bets and didn't do so well with them.

```
Your account balance is $778.00.
Your account balance is $768.40.
Your account balance is $756.40.
Your account balance is $750.40.
```

In search of the quiniela and boxes that had done so well before, I looked carefully at the various program activity logs. It became clear that for some reason the 4:30 A.M. run of the program (with $\alpha = 0.4$) was crashing instead of completing, and thus the more adventurous bets were never being found.

Roger wasn't quite sure what caused the problem, but he rummaged around and restarted everything. And it seemed to help. The next day Maven made $117 in bets. I relaxed; the program always did well when it made a lot of bets. Except this time:

```
Your account balance is $687.70.
Your account balance is $646.00.
Your account balance is $577.00.
Your account balance is $544.60.
```

I started taking the losses personally and Renee grew even less happy with the project. "Do you have to call every night?" she asked. "Yes, I'm doing *research*, dammit!," I insisted.

```
Your account balance is $536.50.
Your account balance is $497.50.
```

Throughout October my balance continued to plunge. There was an occasional winning day, but it didn't take long for me to give that money back to the fronton.

Although the downhill trend was evident, the cause for it was not. Perhaps the bug in the program from before hadn't gone away and was lurking in a corrupted data file. Or perhaps there was no bug. The system lived and died by the laws of probability. One had to expect cold streaks as well as hot streaks.

The problem was that it was impossible to tell which of these two possibilities was reality. You could go crazy hunting for a bug that wasn't there. Or you could go broke waiting for your luck to turn when your luck wasn't what was broken.

Similar issues arise in properly interpreting apparent concentrations of diseases. "Cancer clusters" have been discovered on Long Island, regions where the incidence of breast cancer appears to be two to three times higher than the national average. However such concentrations are likely to occur *somewhere* by random chance, and thus it is very unclear whether this is a real phenomenon or a phantom. Breast cancer has become an important political issue here, even though I haven't seen a single elected representative take a pro-breast cancer position. Still, voters demand that they do something about it. There seems to be no obvious environmental culprit to pin it on except the opposing candidate.

Throughout this gloomy period, the autodialer worked faithfully, rising early in the morning to place my worthless bets. On October 29, for whatever reason, my bets were not logged. Needless to say, those bets would have won $120. Maven was playing head games with me, and all I could do was watch my account diminish.

```
Your account balance is $497.50.
Your account balance is $440.50.
Your account balance is $408.40.
```

On November 1, as it did at the beginning of each month, the program recalculated its statistical models of player skills. This provided an intellectually honest reason to hope that the $351 hit that I took in October would be exorcized.

On the morning of November 4, Maven tried to make a $72 investment that the autodialer didn't seem to approve of. It was still early enough to phone them in again, but I was somewhat gun-shy after tabulating the previous month's losses. I took a deep breath and executed the command to tell Otto to try again.

```
Your account balance is $705.10.
```

We were back in business! One big night and we recouped almost all of the month's losses! Maybe it was our stats that had been corrupted, and all was in order now. Maybe not. But it was time to go with the flow and see where it took us.

```
Your account balance is $689.80.
Your account balance is $637.00.
Your account balance is $574.60.
Your account balance is $768.70.
```

Another big night! Again, the bets had not taken that morning. But I was keeping an eye on things and making sure that as much of Maven's intended bets as possible were going to get made. It was a bumpy ride, but I was convinced that we were on the upswing.

```
Your account balance is $723.70.
Your account balance is $679.00.
```

Today, Maven only wanted to make one $3 win bet. It seemed that the bug from last month had returned. But I checked through the logs, and everything looked OK. It was as if Maven held up its nose at the offerings in the marketplace.

```
Your account balance is $695.50.
```

Such taste! Such refinement! The next day, Maven bet $129. Anything over $80 seemed destined to lead to a big day. It was with great confidence that I checked the machine that night:

```
Your account balance is $950.95.
```

It was a new high-water mark! I had now almost quadrupled my original stake. The appearance of the lonely nickel at the end of my total meant that I had hit a trifecta box. Recall that frontons round each payoff to the nearest dime, and so such a payoff would normally be impossible. But we are allowed to invest half the minimum bet per outcome on trifecta boxes; thus, the payoffs could round out to a nickel.

```
Your account balance is $895.95.
Your account balance is $853.15.
Your account balance is $893.65.
Your account balance is $863.65.
Your account balance is $868.75.
Your account balance is $914.95.
```

I ended November up by $506.55. It certainly had not been the cruelest month. Indeed, I was not happy to see it go, for it meant recomputing statistics again.

```
Your account balance is $892.15.
Your account balance is $909.25.
Your account balance is $885.85.
Your account balance is $858.85.
Your account balance is $828.85.
Your account balance is $818.35.
```

The program started breaking in mid-December again, or so it seemed. It attempted no bets on December 13, nor on December 15 or 16. An investigation revealed that Milford closed its fronton each year for 2 weeks before Christmas. Maven refused to bet on games that weren't played.

I too decided to call it quits for the year. It was time to write up this tale of our experiences and plan for the future.

I made a graph summarizing all of the bets we made over this 4½-month time period and what the results were. The upper line shows the growth in the value of my account, starting from the initial deposit of $250. The lower line plots the amount that the system bet each session, as best as I can tell. I tried to call *On the Wire* each morning to confirm how many of our intended bets actually registered with the system, and each night to find out whether we won that day. I may well have misaccounted a little on each day's actual bet amount, but my numbers are fairly accurate.

However, there can be no doubt about the bottom line. On July 29, 1998, the account had $250.00 in it. On December 31, 1998, the account had $818.35 in it. And the difference was entirely the fronton's money.

You could say that we increased our capital by 227% over this period. You could even say that the increase projects to an annual growth

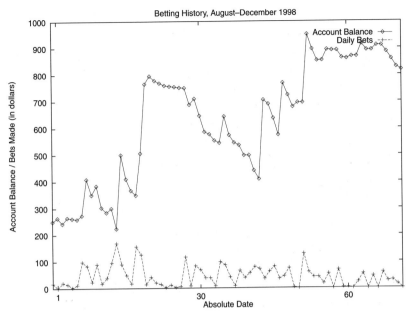

How did we do? Bets and payoffs from August–December 1998.

rate of 605% because all these bets were made in a 4½-month period. By making a profit of $568.35 on $3018.00 worth of bets, we made an 18% return on invested capital, and our capital was compounded daily. Any way you say it, Maven proved to be more than just a self-proclaimed expert.

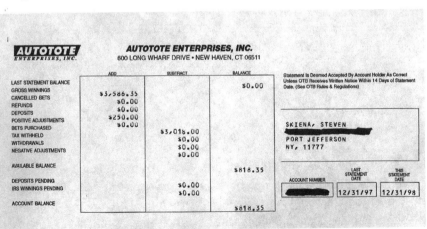

Proof of our winnings – our annual financial statement from Autotote.

Epilogue

Our initial experiments demonstrated that, with jai alai at least, we know what we are doing. We clearly predict the outcome of jai alai matches better than the general public and well enough to make small but nontrivial amounts of money.

So, what would be next for Maven? In order to make much more money off the deal, we had to greatly increase the volume of profitable bets. But we didn't dare bet on Dania for fear of certain insidious parser bugs. And we didn't dare bet on Miami or Newport for fear of the Internet Gambling Act. We didn't even dare bet too much on Milford games, because relatively few games had bets that showed a clear positive return. Finally, even when we were brave enough to go for it, Otto the Auto-dialer often disagreed and did not phone in all the bets. We had much work to do if were were to increase our number of transactions significantly.

Roger came back to work on Maven in the spring of 1999, his last semester at Stony Brook before starting Ph.D. studies in computer science at the University of Massachusetts. We beat on the system, improving it, making it stronger.

I continued letting the original Maven run while we worked on its successor. I throttled back the number of bets it made so that I didn't have to pay much attention to it on a daily basis. Also, in case of disaster I wanted to preserve capital for an improved version to play with.

```
Your account balance is $818.35.
Your account balance is $940.30.
Your account balance is $1037.80.
Your account balance is $793.60.
Your account balance is $865.45.
```

But we had to finish our changes in a rush, with the semester ending before we could complete a real validation phase or as much robustness testing as we would have liked to.

Now Roger was finished with the project. At this point, the account contained $865.45. It was now or never for Maven because the robustness of the program would only deteriorate with time. I gave the new program phone privileges and hoped for the best. The first day, it liked 11 trifecta boxes, but they didn't like us back:

```
Your account balance is $766.45.
Your account balance is $712.45.
Your account balance is $1072.60.
```

Now that was more like it! A new record high!

```
Your account balance is $1051.60.
Your account balance is $952.60.
```

To complicate matters, Renee and I were set to spend the entire month of June 1999 visiting the Polytechnic University (UPC) in Barcelona, Spain. It is hard to imagine a more wonderful place to be than Barcelona, which is perhaps the most graceful and civilized city on earth. But the distance and time difference made it difficult to keep up with what Maven was doing. My last phone call before we boarded the plane was to *On the Wire*.

```
Your account balance is $1105.30.
```

Olé! Maven had hit a new high total again.

Shortly after my arrival, I gave the first public lecture on our jai alai prediction system at the university. The Spaniards were somewhat baffled by my interest in this regional game of theirs (imagine a European scholar writing a treatise on the Pro Bowlers Tour) but were scholars and sportsmen enough to get the drift.

Reading my mail from Barcelona proved difficult. Through the magic of a program called *telnet*, I could sit at a computer in Spain and have complete access to my desktop computer in Stony Brook. Thus, I could read e-mail. But there were network delays on the order of seconds sending bits around the world even when network traffic was light. And as soon as the rest of Spain got to work in the morning, forget about it. It would have been more efficient to hop on a plane and read it from my office.

But the news that arrived was very good. It was clear that Maven was winning. It seemed that every other day for the second week of June, it hit another box. The reported winnings were clearly several hundred dollars. I broke down and checked my balance with *On the Wire*:

```
Your account balance is $1009.30.
```

Huh? Where was my money? I could tell that the calls had been placed by the autodialer, but it seems *On the Wire* decided this wasn't the week to listen – at least to my winning bets.

Renee and I took advantage of our location and visited the Basque region in Spain, watching *remonte* action and gazing at the spectacular scenery. Maven stayed on a roll that third week of June. Again, my e-mail showed me winning. And again, *On the Wire* said.

```
Your account balance is $1009.30.
```

It was impossible to debug the phone calls by long distance. The fourth week of June Maven kept picking winners. But I knew what kind of balance I had waiting for me when I got back.

```
Your account balance is $1009.30.
```

After I returned, it became clear why none of our bets were taking. Autotote had changed its hours, refusing to accept bets until 10 A.M. so my 7:30 A.M. phone calls hadn't taken. With Gene keeping summer hours, however, there was no real barrier to letting Otto call the bets in later. I reset the timing of the program and crossed my fingers that the results I'd been seeing hadn't been fiction.

```
Your account balance is $1401.40.
```

Maven hits two boxes!

```
Your account balance is $1430.35.
```

Maven hits another little box. The program was winning just as it had been that month in Spain.

```
Your account balance is $1385.35.
Your account balance is $1367.35.
```

Maven makes $117 in bets – a record for the new version.

```
Your account balance is $1630.60.
```

Maven hits a 1–4–8 box!

```
Your account balance is $1567.60.
Your account balance is $1513.60.
```

Maven bets $126 – another new version record.

```
Your account balance is $1796.80.
```

Hits 1–2–4 and 2–4–6 boxes! Another new high!

```
Your account balance is $1851.70.
```

Hits a cheap 1–3–6 box! Yet another new high!

Maven had just cleared almost $1000 in only 2 weeks. The program was making money fast enough that it was threatening to become a revenue source instead of just a research project. And that presented me with a fresh set of problems.

University professors are not supposed to use research computing facilities to run book-making operations. This project was a harmless eccentricity when it was playing for peanuts. But at this scale money would very quickly become an issue. I made plans to contact the university's legal counsel, which was a step I feared because it is always easier to beg forgiveness than get permission. Further, if Maven really started making money, the students who built it certainly deserved a cut of the action. But how much?

Maven decided to spare me these problems. Its taste in bets suddenly regressed to 1–2–4 and 1–2–5 trifectas, losing interest in anything else. Something had broken deep inside the program. Professors often complain that student-built software works until the day after graduation. What this really means is that the professors don't have the skills or the gumption to maintain it. At least this professor didn't.

Software rot is a sad but real phenomenon. In principle, software lasts forever because it is just a stream of bits, and these bits are easily maintained on disk with perfect fidelity. Software may be immutable, but the rest of the world changes around it. Suddenly a new data format arrives from Milford, or the operating system of our host computer is upgraded. Software rot is why people must eventually junk Windows 95 – not that it has changed but because the rest of the world has decayed around it.

Maven's betting run was over. With a heavy heart and slightly lighter bank roll, I unplugged Maven from *On the Wire*. Each night, the program continues to scan the net for details of the next day's jai alai action. It continues to play each game half a million times before dawn. It continues to identify the best bets and mail me the results. But the bets have become as virtual as the simulated games themselves.

I write this book almost one year after our last wager. I wrote a check for the amount of my winnings and sent it to a charity associated with the university, to purge my soul and cover my butt. Indeed, a plaque on display at the Stony Brook Hillel acknowledges the generous support of the "Jai-Alai Maven."

Maven still sends me e-mail every morning, and of late it seems our simulated bets have been winning somewhat more steadily than before. Maybe the difficulties we had encountered were due simply to a corrupted data file. If so, after a year it will slip from the Maven's consciousness and profitability will be restored.

Retelling this tale has whet my appetite for another round of jai alai action. If the university lets me, maybe the time has come to bring another student on board to wrestle with the program anew and bring Maven back on line. Check http://www.jai-tech.com for the latest on how we are doing.

Hail the Maven evermore!

CHAPTER NINE

HOW SHOULD YOU BET?

The system described in this book retrieves and analyzes data each night and employs a substantial amount of computational sophistication to determine the most profitable bets to make. It isn't something you are going to try at home, kiddies.

However, in this section I'll provide some hints on how you can make your trip to the fronton as profitable as possible. By combing the results of our Monte Carlo simulations and expected payoff model, I've constructed tables giving the expected payoff for each bet, under the assumption that all players are equally skillful. This is very useful information to have if you are not equipped to make your own judgments as to who is the best player, although we also provide tips as to how to assess player skills. By following my advice, you will avoid criminally stupid bets like the 6–8–7 trifecta.

But first a word of caution is in order. There are three primary types of gamblers:

■ (A) *Those who gamble to make money* – If you are in this category, you are likely a sick individual and need help. My recommendation instead would be that you take your money and invest in a good mutual fund. In particular, the Vanguard Primecap fund has done right well for me over the past few years.

One theme running through this book is how hard we had to work in order to make even a small profit. As the saying goes, "gambling is a hard way to make easy money." You can't expect to make a lot of money without considerably more insight and effort than we expended, and there are far more profitable places to devote this effort to than a track, casino, or fronton.

■ (B) *Those who gamble to lose money* – If you are in this category, you are likely a *very* sick individual and *really* need help. I recommend that you contact Gambler's Anonymous (1-213-386-8789, or www.gamblersanonymous.org) immediately and get to work on your problem.

My Grandfather was a problem gambler and almost destroyed himself and his family. Don't let this happen to you or the ones you love.

■ (C) *Those who gamble to have fun* – If you are in this category, I pronounce you perfectly healthy. Modest amounts of wagering can make any sporting event (including jai alai) more exciting by turning you into one of the players.

Having Fun Betting on Jai Alai

Damon Runyon once quoted a bettor as saying "I hope to break even today. I really need the money." It is more fun to win than to lose, or even to break even. The rest of this chapter is intended to show you how to maximize the amount-of-fun-per-dollar-invested ratio when you go to watch jai alai.

To maximize your chances of having fun, I start with the following recommendations:

■ *Go to the fronton* – Jai alai is a fantastic sport to watch. You get to see great professional athletes making amazing plays, and there is nothing like the sound of a pelota clicking off the granite frontcourt. Figuring out the machinations of the Spectacular Seven scoring system is excellent exercise for the mind. These charms are completely lost when you invest via off-track betting (OTB) or a phone betting scheme. The kids will love a day or an evening at the fronton. I greatly recommend the experience.

■ *Buy a Pepe's Green Card* – We always do. To be honest, there is no reason to believe in any of the picks you see there. In fact, a truly savvy bettor will *avoid* all of Pepe's recommendations, not necessarily because they are bad but because too many other people will put their trust in Pepe. Enough copies of the card are sold that the odds on any suggested bet will likely be seriously depressed and unable to pay off big even if Pepe is right.

■ *Always make the minimum bet* – The betting pools in jai alai are small enough that they get saturated by making the minimum bet. Betting more than the minimum likely means that you are betting against yourself. Certainly anyone making more than the minimum bet on any trifecta ought to have his or her head examined.

If you find it much more exciting to have $6 riding on a match than $3, then you might fall into problem gambler categories (A) or (B) above. But if you *are* determined to invest more than the minimum, you should bet on two separate outcomes. First, you increase the chance that you will have a winner or at least be close. Second, such a tactic is justified by the laws of probability. The expected value $E(A + B)$ of two random variables A and B satisfies the formula

$$E(A + B) = E(A) + E(B)$$

regardless of whether the random variables are independent. This means that whenever you can find two bets, both of which (you perceive) have an expectation of a positive return, the sum of the two bets will also have an expectation of positive return. Thus, don't bother worrying whether your 4–1–2 trifecta contradicts your 5–7 quiniela. If both of these bets are individually good, then they are good in combination.

■ *Bet quinielas to maximize your action* – In my humble opinion (IMHO), quiniela bets offer the most entertainment value for your dollar. Under the Spectacular Seven scoring system, the quiniela offers you enough possible ways to win that you are likely to be able to identify at least one relatively promising victory scenario in almost every match. Further, the payoff is such that if you win once you pay for the evening and maybe even dinner afterwards.

■ *Bet show to maximize your chances of cashing a ticket* – If you want to maximize your chances of sauntering up to the cashier and getting money back, bet on 2 to show. You have a 49% chance of making an insignificant amount of money, but at least it means that you won't be a total loser for the night.

■ *Check your tickets carefully before discarding them* – Make sure your tickets are official losers before throwing any of them away. Because of the Spectacular Seven scoring system, the complexion of a game can change instantly from defeat to victory. Wait until the scoreboard declares the results official, because there is always some chance of disqualification or other surprise until then.

Within every gambling establishment lurk a few "stoopers," people who rummage around trying to find discarded but winning tickets. Don't feed the stoopers. If you have to leave the fronton early, don't worry. You typically have up to one year to cash winning tickets, and the WWW makes it easy to check the results from a distance.

The Best Bets in Jai Alai

Several bets in jai alai offer spectacularly bad value because they are almost impossible to win, and even if they were to win couldn't pay off high enough to justify the effort. I provide tables in this section to help you steer clear of trouble.

Table 9.1 presents what I think are the 30 best and worst trifectas to bet on. The value column in all of these tables estimates the expected return for the given bet. A value of 1.0 signifies that the bet is neutral, meaning that on average you should break even with these bets. Ratios of above 1.0 are predicted moneymakers, but don't take these numbers too seriously. The act of placing a real minimum bet on a given combination will decrease this ratio; recall that our betting system uses trifecta boxes instead of individual trifectas so we can make a smaller minimum bet. See Table 9.2 for our ranking of the merits of various trifecta boxes.

If you see other people at the fronton with a copy of this book, it probably pays to move a few notches down on the list of best values to avoid sharing the pool with them if you win. If you don't see other people with my book, please recommend it to your neighbors, because it means I really could use the advertising.

Bets with ratios significantly below 1.0 are not worth your investment. And please, please lay off that 5–8–7 trifecta. You can expect to lose at least 99.7 cents of each dollar you bet. Tables 9.3–9.6 present the expected values of all trifectas if you want to check how your license plate, social security number or birthdate stack up.

Tables 9.7, 9.8, and 9.9 present expected values for the various win, place, and show bets. Be aware that the pools for these bets are typically very small; placing anything more than the minimum bet means that you

TABLE 9.1. The 30 Best and Worst Trifectas to Bet on According to Expected Return

	Best Trifectas			Worst Trifectas	
Rank	Trifecta	Value	Rank	Trifecta	Value
1	1–4–2	1.7857	307	3–5–6	0.1849
2	1–2–5	1.6170	308	8–7–6	0.1842
3	2–4–1	1.5984	309	7–5–6	0.1832
4	1–3–2	1.5924	310	6–8–2	0.1813
5	2–1–7	1.5644	311	1–8–2	0.1798
6	3–2–8	1.5021	312	7–8–1	0.1539
7	4–2–1	1.5007	313	4–5–8	0.1531
8	4–1–2	1.4855	314	6–5–7	0.1471
9	1–5–2	1.4743	315	3–6–7	0.1427
10	2–3–7	1.4519	316	5–8–6	0.1408
11	2–1–5	1.4514	317	3–4–5	0.1376
12	2–1–6	1.4466	318	3–5–4	0.1338
13	3–1–2	1.4384	319	4–5–7	0.1061
14	1–3–8	1.4027	320	4–8–6	0.0856
15	3–2–1	1.4009	321	4–6–8	0.0794
16	2–3–1	1.3952	322	7–6–8	0.0655
17	3–1–8	1.3887	323	4–6–5	0.0549
18	4–3–2	1.3670	324	4–5–6	0.0547
19	1–2–7	1.3655	325	4–7–8	0.0530
20	1–2–6	1.3525	326	4–7–6	0.0529
21	4–3–1	1.3492	327	8–6–7	0.0507
22	2–5–3	1.3369	328	5–6–8	0.0451
23	1–5–3	1.3257	329	4–6–7	0.0381
24	3–1–6	1.3249	330	5–7–6	0.0235
25	1–3–6	1.2948	331	5–6–7	0.0172
26	1–2–4	1.2946	332	4–8–7	0.0147
27	3–2–7	1.2896	333	5–7–8	0.0117
28	8–3–1	1.2714	334	6–7–8	0.0041
29	1–7–4	1.2704	335	6–8–7	0.0037
30	3–2–5	1.2360	336	5–8–7	0.0034

start betting against yourself, whereas placing the minimum bet means you make only peanuts even if you do win. You can decide which option is best for you.

Table 9.10 presents the expected values for quiniela bets. Here your best options seem to be the outcomes that occur most frequently. This is a happy circumstance and more evidence to support my claim that quinielas are the most fun to bet on.

TABLE 9.2. Trifecta Boxes Ranked by Probability, Expected Payoff, and Value

Bet	Frequency Win %	Rank	Payoff Payoff/$	Rank	Value Value/$	Rank
1–2–3	3.3053	5	213.27	50	1.1748	3
1–2–4	4.4966	1	195.29	54	1.4635	1
1–2–5	4.0122	2	186.76	56	1.2488	2
1–2–6	3.1057	6	217.81	46	1.1274	4
1–2–7	2.1727	22	239.58	42	0.8675	22
1–2–8	0.8489	45	361.22	9	0.5111	43
1–3–4	2.9196	9	214.11	49	1.0418	10
1–3–5	3.4641	3	193.67	55	1.1182	6
1–3–6	3.0561	7	219.12	45	1.1160	7
1–3–7	2.5106	11	231.73	43	0.9696	16
1–3–8	2.2299	21	276.46	28	1.0274	11
1–4–5	2.3172	17	203.49	51	0.7859	26
1–4–6	2.4524	13	230.64	44	0.9427	18
1–4–7	2.3301	16	258.44	34	1.0036	13
1–4–8	2.3759	15	256.73	36	1.0166	12
1–5–6	1.4584	31	280.58	26	0.6820	36
1–5–7	1.6655	29	260.50	31	0.7231	33
1–5–8	1.9529	25	273.93	29	0.8915	21
1–6–7	0.9698	39	357.43	12	0.5777	38
1–6–8	1.4311	33	321.85	19	0.7676	29
1–7–8	0.7016	48	354.01	13	0.4140	48
2–3–4	2.8950	10	202.32	52	0.9762	15
2–3–5	3.4162	4	197.18	53	1.1226	5
2–3–6	3.0036	8	216.78	47	1.0852	8
2–3–7	2.4673	12	259.38	32	1.0666	9
2–3–8	2.1589	23	258.42	35	0.9298	20
2–4–5	2.2775	20	215.94	48	0.8196	25
2–4–6	2.4034	14	245.25	41	0.9823	14
2–4–7	2.2819	19	247.78	40	0.9423	19
2–4–8	2.3090	18	251.32	38	0.9671	17
2–5–6	1.4228	34	283.61	25	0.6725	37
2–5–7	1.6267	30	269.35	30	0.7302	31
2–5–8	1.8885	26	248.14	39	0.7810	27
2–6–7	0.9444	40	357.81	11	0.5631	40
2–6–8	1.3796	37	298.95	21	0.6874	35
2–7–8	0.6754	50	366.46	7	0.4125	49
3–4–5	0.9154	42	344.77	16	0.5260	42
3–4–6	1.3816	36	331.41	18	0.7631	30
3–4–7	1.7386	28	287.89	24	0.8342	24
3–4–8	1.9653	24	259.34	33	0.8494	23
3–5–6	1.1771	38	292.48	23	0.5737	39
3–5–7	1.4039	35	296.85	22	0.6945	34
3–5–8	1.8136	27	256.62	37	0.7756	28
3–6–7	0.9057	43	338.04	17	0.5102	44
3–6–8	1.4506	32	300.59	20	0.7267	32
3–7–8	0.7819	47	361.20	10	0.4707	46
4–5–6	0.4319	52	465.40	4	0.3350	53
4–5–7	0.8286	46	361.95	8	0.4998	45
4–5–8	0.9050	44	348.87	14	0.5262	41
4–6–7	0.6203	51	380.71	6	0.3935	51
4–6–8	0.9420	41	279.04	27	0.4380	47
4–7–8	0.6985	49	346.64	15	0.4035	50
5–6–7	0.2017	55	540.41	2	0.1817	55
5–6–8	0.4136	53	511.42	3	0.3525	52
5–7–8	0.4071	54	443.26	5	0.3008	54
6–7–8	0.0889	56	582.24	1	0.0862	56

TABLE 9.3. Trifecta Bets (1/2 to win) Ranked by Probability, Expected Payoff, and Value

Bet	Frequency		Payoff		Value	
	Win %	Rank	Payoff/$	Rank	Value/$	Rank
1-2-3	0.206%	188	278.63	188	0.575	229
1-2-4	0.567%	45	228.23	240	1.295	26
1-2-5	0.792%	8	204.14	290	1.617	2
1-2-6	0.790%	10	171.20	326	1.353	20
1-2-7	0.708%	18	192.83	310	1.365	19
1-2-8	0.282%	159	359.30	134	1.014	88
1-3-2	0.810%	7	196.54	304	1.592	4
1-3-4	0.112%	255	530.90	35	0.594	221
1-3-5	0.355%	126	259.88	202	0.922	120
1-3-6	0.495%	70	261.70	198	1.295	25
1-3-7	0.566%	48	198.03	302	1.121	57
1-3-8	0.567%	46	247.38	216	1.403	14
1-4-2	0.919%	1	194.31	306	1.786	1
1-4-3	0.334%	133	323.04	157	1.079	70
1-4-5	0.078%	280	405.58	101	0.317	294
1-4-6	0.200%	193	376.50	123	0.752	175
1-4-7	0.344%	131	282.62	186	0.973	98
1-4-8	0.387%	110	260.01	201	1.006	90
1-5-2	0.818%	5	180.25	317	1.474	9
1-5-3	0.660%	24	200.88	299	1.326	23
1-5-4	0.252%	170	367.23	129	0.924	119
1-5-6	0.087%	269	599.28	20	0.520	249
1-5-7	0.183%	206	358.65	135	0.657	204
1-5-8	0.274%	160	304.58	172	0.835	152
1-6-2	0.541%	58	227.92	243	1.233	31
1-6-3	0.606%	37	201.07	298	1.218	35
1-6-4	0.434%	88	219.32	264	0.953	107
1-6-5	0.149%	220	460.44	75	0.687	194
1-6-7	0.074%	283	502.43	44	0.372	277
1-6-8	0.113%	254	430.31	92	0.485	257
1-7-2	0.264%	164	283.67	182	0.749	176
1-7-3	0.538%	59	194.27	307	1.046	79
1-7-4	0.574%	43	221.50	255	1.270	29
1-7-5	0.384%	111	233.94	231	0.898	128
1-7-6	0.130%	235	398.32	107	0.518	250
1-7-8	0.056%	296	582.27	27	0.328	291
1-8-2	0.055%	298	325.75	155	0.180	311
1-8-3	0.375%	117	244.39	218	0.915	124
1-8-4	0.504%	67	222.07	253	1.118	58
1-8-5	0.455%	83	227.95	242	1.037	82
1-8-6	0.312%	142	372.65	125	1.163	47
1-8-7	0.061%	290	530.23	36	0.323	292

(continued)

TABLE 9.3, continued

Bet	Frequency Win %	Rank	Payoff Payoff/$	Rank	Value Value/$	Rank
2–1–3	0.201%	192	321.67	160	0.647	209
2–1–4	0.548%	56	203.75	293	1.116	59
2–1–5	0.774%	14	187.61	314	1.451	11
2–1–6	0.782%	12	184.94	316	1.447	12
2–1–7	0.709%	17	220.70	259	1.564	5
2–1–8	0.285%	158	301.83	173	0.861	142
2–3–1	0.792%	9	176.14	323	1.395	16
2–3–4	0.109%	257	396.78	108	0.434	266
2–3–5	0.348%	130	239.93	222	0.835	151
2–3–6	0.484%	74	236.10	229	1.143	52
2–3–7	0.566%	49	256.71	203	1.452	10
2–3–8	0.550%	54	215.72	270	1.186	39
2–4–1	0.916%	2	174.57	325	1.598	3
2–4–3	0.327%	138	283.66	183	0.927	117
2–4–5	0.078%	281	454.01	78	0.353	286
2–4–6	0.197%	195	374.12	124	0.736	181
2–4–7	0.351%	128	264.49	195	0.928	116
2–4–8	0.380%	113	224.37	249	0.853	144
2–5–1	0.816%	6	142.47	333	1.163	46
2–5–3	0.651%	28	205.31	289	1.337	22
2–5–4	0.248%	171	351.55	139	0.871	139
2–5–6	0.087%	268	599.28	19	0.523	247
2–5–7	0.185%	204	382.52	118	0.707	186
2–5–8	0.270%	161	242.69	219	0.655	206
2–6–1	0.542%	57	211.15	279	1.145	51
2–6–3	0.595%	40	180.24	318	1.072	71
2–6–4	0.430%	90	268.44	194	1.155	49
2–6–5	0.147%	222	462.45	72	0.680	195
2–6–7	0.074%	285	605.55	7	0.445	264
2–6–8	0.113%	253	534.09	33	0.602	219
2–7–1	0.265%	163	228.00	241	0.604	217
2–7–3	0.522%	65	221.44	256	1.155	50
2–7–4	0.555%	51	215.45	274	1.196	37
2–7–5	0.381%	112	256.05	204	0.974	97
2–7–6	0.129%	238	445.50	86	0.573	230
2–7–8	0.054%	300	491.09	46	0.266	298
2–8–1	0.057%	295	445.50	85	0.253	300
2–8–3	0.360%	123	263.81	196	0.949	110
2–8–4	0.486%	72	241.92	220	1.177	41
2–8–5	0.437%	87	215.66	272	0.942	113
2–8–6	0.300%	147	293.19	178	0.880	136
2–8–7	0.058%	294	599.28	18	0.349	287

TABLE 9.4. Trifecta Bets (3/4 to win) Ranked by Probability, Expected Payoff, and Value

Bet	Frequency		Payoff		Value	
	Win %	Rank	Payoff/$	Rank	Value/$	Rank
3–1–2	0.658%	25	218.45	267	1.438	13
3–1–4	0.460%	82	208.14	287	0.957	105
3–1–5	0.606%	36	202.59	296	1.228	32
3–1–6	0.591%	41	224.09	250	1.325	24
3–1–7	0.479%	76	230.29	238	1.103	63
3–1–8	0.566%	47	245.35	217	1.389	17
3–2–1	0.637%	32	219.97	262	1.401	15
3–2–4	0.465%	80	220.54	260	1.026	84
3–2–5	0.609%	35	203.03	294	1.236	30
3–2–6	0.591%	42	200.49	300	1.185	40
3–2–7	0.472%	78	273.45	189	1.290	27
3–2–8	0.552%	52	272.16	192	1.502	6
3–4–1	0.525%	64	233.52	232	1.227	33
3–4–2	0.518%	66	210.85	281	1.092	66
3–4–5	0.030%	316	462.59	70	0.138	317
3–4–6	0.080%	278	428.36	93	0.344	288
3–4–7	0.122%	242	504.82	41	0.618	213
3–4–8	0.263%	165	321.09	162	0.843	148
3–5–1	0.502%	68	209.49	282	1.051	78
3–5–2	0.485%	73	203.90	292	0.989	93
3–5–4	0.043%	304	308.73	169	0.134	318
3–5–6	0.031%	314	599.28	17	0.185	307
3–5–7	0.053%	301	599.28	16	0.321	293
3–5–8	0.143%	225	377.77	122	0.540	240
3–6–1	0.428%	92	237.92	226	1.019	86
3–6–2	0.418%	94	202.78	295	0.848	146
3–6–4	0.145%	224	598.39	22	0.867	141
3–6–5	0.031%	315	616.30	6	0.190	305
3–6–7	0.024%	319	604.96	9	0.143	315
3–6–8	0.059%	293	616.30	5	0.363	281
3–7–1	0.415%	95	236.20	227	0.981	96
3–7–2	0.404%	104	291.38	180	1.176	42
3–7–4	0.430%	91	223.40	251	0.960	104
3–7–5	0.187%	202	412.60	98	0.773	168
3–7–6	0.056%	297	474.51	50	0.266	299
3–7–8	0.046%	303	445.50	84	0.205	304
3–8–1	0.311%	143	263.02	197	0.819	155
3–8–2	0.297%	150	254.09	207	0.755	173
3–8–4	0.465%	79	238.96	225	1.112	62
3–8–5	0.317%	140	260.89	199	0.828	154
3–8–6	0.210%	186	361.02	133	0.757	172
3–8–7	0.037%	307	599.28	15	0.219	302

(continued)

195

TABLE 9.4, continued

Bet	Frequency		Payoff		Value	
	Win %	Rank	Payoff/$	Rank	Value/$	Rank
4–1–2	0.778%	13	190.85	312	1.486	8
4–1–3	0.838%	3	124.59	334	1.044	80
4–1–5	0.526%	62	201.95	297	1.063	74
4–1–6	0.406%	101	232.57	235	0.945	112
4–1–7	0.328%	137	233.22	234	0.765	170
4–1–8	0.425%	93	223.05	252	0.949	111
4–2–1	0.768%	16	195.29	305	1.501	7
4–2–3	0.835%	4	121.02	335	1.011	89
4–2–5	0.526%	63	215.63	273	1.133	54
4–2–6	0.407%	100	233.39	233	0.949	109
4–2–7	0.328%	136	283.01	185	0.929	115
4–2–8	0.407%	98	204.01	291	0.830	153
4–3–1	0.650%	29	207.54	288	1.349	21
4–3–2	0.640%	31	213.48	276	1.367	18
4–3–5	0.177%	208	377.92	121	0.670	198
4–3–6	0.225%	180	388.68	114	0.875	138
4–3–7	0.210%	187	318.49	164	0.667	200
4–3–8	0.366%	118	251.79	208	0.922	121
4–5–1	0.296%	152	229.28	239	0.678	196
4–5–2	0.290%	154	241.81	221	0.701	189
4–5–3	0.200%	194	370.66	128	0.740	178
4–5–6	0.012%	323	462.59	69	0.055	324
4–5–7	0.034%	309	308.73	168	0.106	319
4–5–8	0.050%	302	308.73	167	0.153	313
4–6–1	0.193%	199	458.26	77	0.883	135
4–6–2	0.189%	200	409.52	99	0.775	167
4–6–3	0.159%	214	351.42	141	0.558	235
4–6–5	0.012%	322	462.59	68	0.055	323
4–6–7	0.008%	329	462.59	67	0.038	329
4–6–8	0.017%	321	462.59	66	0.079	321
4–7–1	0.298%	149	322.52	158	0.960	103
4–7–2	0.288%	155	341.00	145	0.983	94
4–7–3	0.366%	120	280.13	187	1.025	85
4–7–5	0.068%	288	416.93	97	0.283	297
4–7–6	0.011%	325	462.59	65	0.053	326
4–7–8	0.011%	324	462.59	64	0.053	325
4–8–1	0.256%	167	365.92	130	0.936	114
4–8–2	0.254%	169	320.01	163	0.813	156
4–8–3	0.351%	129	225.62	245	0.792	162
4–8–5	0.116%	248	464.21	52	0.537	243
4–8–6	0.026%	318	325.75	154	0.086	320
4–8–7	0.003%	332	462.59	63	0.015	332

TABLE 9.5. Trifecta Bets (5/6 to win) Ranked by Probability, Expected Payoff, and Value

	Frequency		Payoff		Value	
Bet	Win %	Rank	Payoff /$	Rank	Value /$	Rank
5–1–2	0.407%	99	219.50	263	0.893	132
5–1–3	0.664%	23	160.54	330	1.066	73
5–1–4	0.788%	11	112.41	336	0.886	134
5–1–6	0.244%	174	321.67	159	0.786	164
5–1–7	0.184%	205	347.56	143	0.639	211
5–1–8	0.227%	178	379.02	120	0.860	143
5–2–1	0.405%	102	220.70	258	0.894	131
5–2–3	0.658%	26	178.60	322	1.175	43
5–2–4	0.773%	15	142.52	332	1.102	65
5–2–6	0.242%	175	272.44	191	0.659	203
5–2–7	0.177%	207	295.77	176	0.525	245
5–2–8	0.216%	185	305.58	171	0.661	202
5–3–1	0.678%	19	164.74	327	1.116	60
5–3–2	0.665%	22	174.97	324	1.164	45
5–3–4	0.261%	166	298.27	175	0.778	166
5–3–6	0.223%	183	393.05	111	0.878	137
5–3–7	0.188%	201	387.11	116	0.728	182
5–3–8	0.265%	162	300.55	174	0.797	158
5–4–1	0.377%	114	224.65	247	0.847	147
5–4–2	0.364%	121	208.58	286	0.759	171
5–4–3	0.204%	190	340.60	146	0.696	191
5–4–6	0.063%	289	582.27	26	0.369	278
5–4–7	0.115%	250	602.87	13	0.691	192
5–4–8	0.138%	230	399.16	106	0.553	237
5–6–1	0.117%	247	306.44	170	0.359	283
5–6–2	0.113%	252	462.45	71	0.524	246
5–6–3	0.151%	218	391.68	113	0.591	223
5–6–4	0.093%	263	504.82	40	0.472	261
5–6–7	0.004%	331	462.59	62	0.017	331
5–6–8	0.010%	328	462.59	61	0.045	328
5–7–1	0.125%	240	339.73	147	0.423	269
5–7–2	0.119%	245	445.35	87	0.532	244
5–7–3	0.219%	184	337.40	150	0.737	180
5–7–4	0.162%	211	339.39	148	0.550	238
5–7–6	0.005%	330	462.59	60	0.024	330
5–7–8	0.003%	333	462.59	59	0.012	333
5–8–1	0.093%	265	582.27	25	0.540	241
5–8–2	0.090%	267	616.30	4	0.553	236
5–8–3	0.194%	197	334.61	152	0.648	208
5–8–4	0.162%	212	485.77	47	0.785	165
5–8–6	0.023%	320	602.87	12	0.141	316
5–8–7	0.001%	336	462.59	58	0.003	336

(continued)

TABLE 9.5, continued

Bet	Frequency Win %	Rank	Payoff Payoff/$	Rank	Value Value/$	Rank
6–1–2	0.226%	179	351.77	138	0.795	159
6–1–3	0.309%	144	230.97	236	0.714	185
6–1–4	0.670%	20	159.55	331	1.069	72
6–1–5	0.665%	21	162.85	328	1.084	68
6–1–7	0.162%	210	380.10	119	0.617	214
6–1–8	0.138%	231	458.97	76	0.632	212
6–2–1	0.224%	182	353.31	137	0.792	161
6–2–3	0.307%	145	343.76	144	1.054	77
6–2–4	0.652%	27	178.63	321	1.165	44
6–2–5	0.641%	30	162.25	329	1.039	81
6–2–7	0.154%	216	338.15	149	0.520	248
6–2–8	0.133%	233	506.42	39	0.672	197
6–3–1	0.627%	33	179.59	319	1.127	55
6–3–2	0.609%	34	198.60	301	1.209	36
6–3–4	0.359%	124	273.39	190	0.982	95
6–3–5	0.500%	69	178.87	320	0.895	130
6–3–7	0.175%	209	325.08	156	0.570	231
6–3–8	0.150%	219	384.59	117	0.576	227
6–4–1	0.549%	55	192.03	311	1.055	75
6–4–2	0.528%	61	210.93	280	1.114	61
6–4–3	0.414%	96	230.60	237	0.954	106
6–4–5	0.122%	243	407.02	100	0.496	254
6–4–7	0.140%	227	421.99	96	0.590	224
6–4–8	0.128%	239	396.65	109	0.507	252
6–5–1	0.196%	196	335.63	151	0.656	205
6–5–2	0.193%	198	316.56	166	0.611	216
6–5–3	0.241%	176	292.40	179	0.705	187
6–5–4	0.130%	236	435.23	90	0.564	233
6–5–7	0.032%	312	462.59	57	0.147	314
6–5–8	0.061%	291	604.96	8	0.369	279
6–7–1	0.090%	266	427.69	94	0.385	274
6–7–2	0.086%	270	550.53	29	0.475	259
6–7–3	0.160%	213	399.81	105	0.639	210
6–7–4	0.156%	215	394.95	110	0.616	215
6–7–5	0.072%	286	501.58	45	0.362	282
6–7–8	0.001%	334	462.59	56	0.004	334
6–8–1	0.042%	305	582.27	24	0.242	301
6–8–2	0.039%	306	462.59	55	0.181	310
6–8–3	0.096%	262	599.28	14	0.576	226
6–8–4	0.101%	259	371.44	127	0.377	275
6–8–5	0.055%	299	602.87	11	0.331	289
6–8–7	0.001%	335	462.59	54	0.004	335

TABLE 9.6. Trifecta Bets Ranked by Probability, Expected Payoff, and Value

	Frequency		Payoff		Value	
Bet	Win %	Rank	Payoff/$	Rank	Value/$	Rank
7–1–2	0.115%	249	371.44	126	0.427	268
7–1–3	0.135%	232	446.28	80	0.603	218
7–1–4	0.305%	146	361.85	131	1.102	64
7–1–5	0.494%	71	213.36	277	1.055	76
7–1–6	0.413%	97	249.43	213	1.029	83
7–1–8	0.086%	272	502.43	43	0.430	267
7–2–1	0.112%	256	443.40	88	0.495	255
7–2–3	0.139%	229	293.91	177	0.407	271
7–2–4	0.298%	148	218.95	266	0.653	207
7–2–5	0.478%	77	187.85	313	0.898	129
7–2–6	0.402%	105	221.32	257	0.890	133
7–2–8	0.082%	276	502.43	42	0.411	270
7–3–1	0.377%	115	255.82	205	0.964	102
7–3–2	0.366%	119	251.05	209	0.919	123
7–3–4	0.206%	189	349.41	142	0.721	183
7–3–5	0.401%	106	209.48	283	0.839	150
7–3–6	0.360%	122	236.15	228	0.850	145
7–3–8	0.114%	251	506.42	38	0.575	228
7–4–1	0.482%	75	197.32	303	0.950	108
7–4–2	0.461%	81	209.31	284	0.966	100
7–4–3	0.405%	103	250.59	212	1.015	87
7–4–5	0.203%	191	330.30	153	0.670	199
7–4–6	0.186%	203	321.47	161	0.598	220
7–4–8	0.140%	228	351.45	140	0.491	256
7–5–1	0.296%	151	225.50	246	0.667	201
7–5–2	0.286%	157	260.23	200	0.745	177
7–5–3	0.356%	125	216.15	269	0.769	169
7–5–4	0.247%	173	283.13	184	0.699	190
7–5–6	0.030%	317	616.30	3	0.183	309
7–5–8	0.085%	273	598.39	21	0.507	251
7–6–1	0.101%	260	541.17	30	0.545	239
7–6–2	0.100%	261	475.27	49	0.476	258
7–6–3	0.131%	234	453.55	79	0.594	222
7–6–4	0.119%	246	392.67	112	0.466	262
7–6–5	0.059%	292	602.87	10	0.358	285
7–6–8	0.011%	327	616.30	2	0.066	322
7–8–1	0.035%	308	445.50	83	0.154	312
7–8–2	0.034%	310	550.53	28	0.189	306
7–8–3	0.074%	282	536.53	32	0.399	272
7–8–4	0.104%	258	425.00	95	0.443	265
7–8–5	0.078%	279	400.71	104	0.313	295
7–8–6	0.034%	311	616.30	1	0.209	303

(continued)

TABLE 9.6, continued

Bet	Frequency		Payoff		Value	
	Win %	Rank	Payoff/$	Rank	Value/$	Rank
8–1–2	0.086%	271	530.90	34	0.458	263
8–1–3	0.082%	275	445.50	82	0.367	280
8–1–4	0.254%	168	355.76	136	0.904	125
8–1–5	0.452%	85	220.23	261	0.995	92
8–1–6	0.597%	39	193.81	308	1.158	48
8–1–7	0.390%	108	235.63	230	0.920	122
8–2–1	0.083%	274	361.26	132	0.301	296
8–2–3	0.082%	277	460.44	74	0.375	276
8–2–4	0.247%	172	403.06	103	0.995	91
8–2–5	0.432%	89	208.86	285	0.903	126
8–2–6	0.570%	44	214.96	275	1.225	34
8–2–7	0.376%	116	239.47	223	0.901	127
8–3–1	0.328%	135	387.13	115	1.271	28
8–3–2	0.319%	139	254.56	206	0.812	157
8–3–4	0.129%	237	434.27	91	0.560	234
8–3–5	0.331%	134	227.34	244	0.753	174
8–3–6	0.601%	38	186.82	315	1.123	56
8–3–7	0.387%	109	217.53	268	0.842	149
8–4–1	0.550%	53	215.66	271	1.186	38
8–4–2	0.535%	60	212.34	278	1.135	53
8–4–3	0.391%	107	221.86	254	0.868	140
8–4–5	0.145%	223	269.19	193	0.390	273
8–4–6	0.353%	127	224.59	248	0.794	160
8–4–7	0.287%	156	249.41	214	0.716	184
8–5–1	0.453%	84	239.32	224	1.083	69
8–5–2	0.443%	86	219.19	265	0.972	99
8–5–3	0.563%	50	193.15	309	1.087	67
8–5–4	0.295%	153	250.79	210	0.739	179
8–5–6	0.122%	244	442.32	89	0.539	242
8–5–7	0.148%	221	318.31	165	0.472	260
8–6–1	0.230%	177	403.19	102	0.927	118
8–6–2	0.225%	181	250.63	211	0.564	232
8–6–3	0.335%	132	288.17	181	0.965	101
8–6–4	0.316%	141	248.85	215	0.786	163
8–6–5	0.143%	226	483.64	48	0.691	193
8–6–7	0.011%	326	462.59	53	0.051	327
8–7–1	0.074%	284	445.50	81	0.328	290
8–7–2	0.071%	287	508.11	37	0.359	284
8–7–3	0.124%	241	469.84	51	0.585	225
8–7–4	0.153%	217	460.44	73	0.703	188
8–7–5	0.093%	264	536.53	31	0.497	253
8–7–6	0.032%	313	582.27	23	0.184	308

TABLE 9.11. Exacta Bets Ranked by Probability, Expected Payoff, and Value

	Frequency		Payoff		Value	
Bet	Win %	Rank	Payoff/$	Rank	Value/$	Rank
1–2	3.346%	2	38.50	44	1.288	1
1–3	2.905%	7	40.63	41	1.180	9
1–4	2.262%	15	47.92	33	1.084	19
1–5	2.274%	13	49.25	31	1.120	15.
1–6	1.917%	24	59.39	17	1.138	12
1–7	1.947%	23	57.77	20	1.125	13
1–8	1.761%	32	68.75	8	1.211	6
2–1	3.299%	5	38.78	43	1.279	2
2–3	2.849%	8	44.20	39	1.259	3
2–4	2.248%	18	49.32	30	1.109	16
2–5	2.257%	17	46.45	36	1.048	25
2–6	1.901%	26	52.59	24	0.999	34
2–7	1.905%	25	57.74	21	1.100	17
2–8	1.698%	33	60.97	16	1.035	28
3–1	3.361%	1	35.79	48	1.203	8
3–2	3.326%	3	36.97	45	1.229	4
3–4	1.538%	36	67.56	10	1.039	27
3–5	1.257%	42	64.03	12	0.805	45
3–6	1.105%	43	68.20	9	0.753	47
3–7	1.538%	37	61.99	13	0.953	37
3–8	1.637%	34	61.56	14	1.008	32
4–1	3.303%	4	36.75	47	1.214	5
4–2	3.271%	6	36.90	46	1.207	7
4–3	2.268%	14	51.18	29	1.161	10
4–5	0.881%	46	99.82	1	0.879	41
4–6	0.578%	49	93.39	2	0.540	53
4–7	1.043%	44	83.17	4	0.867	42
4–8	1.006%	45	80.18	6	0.807	44
5–1	2.514%	9	42.33	40	1.064	21
5–2	2.472%	10	39.17	42	0.968	36
5–3	2.281%	12	44.91	38	1.024	30
5–4	1.262%	40	73.80	7	0.931	38
5–6	0.488%	54	135.19	49	0.660	49
5–7	0.632%	48	101.34	56	0.641	50
5–8	0.562%	51	81.65	5	0.459	54
6–1	2.170%	19	51.70	28	1.122	14
6–2	2.110%	20	47.66	34	1.006	33
6–3	2.420%	11	45.21	37	1.094	18
6–4	1.881%	27	56.07	22	1.055	24

(continued)

TABLE 9.11, continued					
	Frequency		Payoff		Value
Bet	Win %	Rank	Payoff /$	Rank	Value /$	Rank
6–5	0.852%	47	105.23	55	0.896	40
6–7	0.565%	50	111.05	54	0.628	51
6–8	0.334%	56	111.21	53	0.372	56
7–1	1.547%	35	58.15	19	0.900	39
7–2	1.510%	38	52.43	25	0.792	46
7–3	1.823%	30	55.59	23	1.013	31
7–4	1.877%	28	51.92	26	0.974	35
7–5	1.299%	39	65.73	11	0.854	43
7–6	0.520%	53	116.66	52	0.607	52
7–8	0.360%	55	126.70	51	0.455	55
8–1	1.862%	29	61.45	15	1.144	11
8–2	1.790%	31	59.30	18	1.062	23
8–3	2.096%	21	49.10	32	1.029	29
8–4	2.262%	16	47.10	35	1.065	20
8–5	2.024%	22	51.78	27	1.048	26
8–6	1.259%	41	84.41	3	1.063	22
8–7	0.546%	52	130.75	50	0.714	48

all legal gambling winnings are properly reported. In response to this problem, the IRS withholds taxes from all sufficiently profitable bets, meaning those that pay off at greater than 300–to–1 odds or return a total of at least $1000.

This withholding system represents a compromise between the legal requirements of performing withholding and the difficulty in providing a 1099 form for every single bet. A bettor who wins a significant amount of money on many little bets (like me) will not trigger withholding, which might be deemed unfair, but I feel that the system is quite reasonable.[1] Bottom line – if you are religiously opposed to paying taxes, avoid trifectas and other exotic bets that might rise above this threshold. On the other hand, I am unaware of any religion that prohibits taxes but encourages pari-mutuel wagering, so give Uncle Sam his due.

If you do win a sufficiently large payoff to be subject to withholding, be sure to save all of your betting tickets, especially the losers. You can deduct your gambling losses from your winnings. Of course, you must

---

[1] I am proud to report that I have paid taxes on all of Maven's winnings.

have winnings to defray it; you can't use losses at the fronton to reduce your taxable income.

■ *Employ smart money management* – Money management is considered to be a key to successful gambling as it is in any financial venture. If you are putting nontrivial amounts of money at risk, do so for sound reasons, not hunches.

Rating the Players

Betting the players, instead of just post positions, can make for a more profitable and entertaining evening. The single best measure of player skill is probably the in-the-money percentage. Any player or team that has a 0.400 win–place–show average is a good player and quite possibly worth an investment. Only 8 of the 48 players on Milford's 1998 roster achieved this level of performance.

I have prepared a pair of charts to make it easier for you to evaluate the performance of a given player or team. First, I provide a scatter plot of all the regular players (more than 400 games) at Milford in 1998 and 1999. Each player is represented by his game-win and in-the-money averages. These two ratios are typically provided in each night's program. If not, they can be easily computed by dividing their number of wins (or the number of wins + places + shows) by the number of games played.

Using this plot, you can eyeball how your player or team stacks up to other players. Suppose that Mediocre won 12.5% of his games and was in the money 38% of the time. That performance puts him in the middle of the cloud of players, suggesting that he is of average skill. Suppose that Magnifico won 14% of his games and finished in the money 41% of the time. This point is to the upper right of the cloud, showing that he is a very successful pelotari.

I also provide contour lines to make it easier to compare the performance of two players or teams. Which is better, Julio, who won 12% of his games and finished in the money 40% of the time, or Iglacias, who won 18% of the time but didn't place or show as much and so paid off only 34% of the time? Contour lines link performances our program thinks are equivalent.

Thus, to identify the more successful player, find which of the lines the two players are closest to and pick the player with the higher line. For example, Julio's performance puts him on the fourth line from the top,

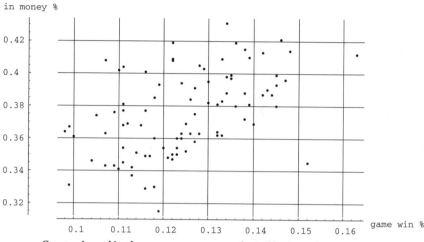

Game-win and in-the-money percentages for Milford Jai-Alai, 1998–1999.

whereas Iglacias is on the sixth line. This means that Maven and I would put my money on Julio, and I urge you to do the same.

Using the Odds Board

If you are really on the ball, you might want to try to scan the odds board for undervalued combinations. The odds on win, quiniela, and exacta bets are typically updated every 90 seconds or so during the betting period. Be

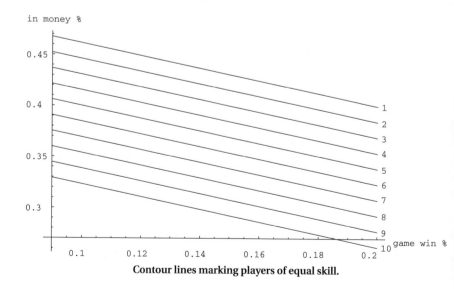

Contour lines marking players of equal skill.

aware that these odds can change very rapidly as more money is bet. Odds on place and show are not posted because the payoffs depend upon the other winning entrants as well. However, frontons may post the place and show pools telling you how much money is currently invested on each post position. Pool sizes are also typically posted instead of odds for trifectas, presumably because they are easier to read.

Making sense of an odds board means being able to convert the posted numbers to the payoff you would get if you won. Posted odds are presented as a ratio of your return to your investment. To be precise, odds of $a - b$ pay off at your investment times $(a + b)/b$. For example, odds of $1 - 1$ pay you off at double your investment, for $(1 + 1)/1 = 2$. The greater the ratio between a and b, the more your bet returns. Odds of 9–2 multiply your investment by $11/2 = 5.5$ times. Less desirable is when $a < b$. The gambler's axiom that "all life is 6–5 against" implies that you will get paid back $11/6$ times your wager on an even money proposition (such as a football game against the spread) because 6–5 against is the same as conventional 5–6 odds. Finally, I provide a table of dollar payoffs for given investment–odds pairs (Table 9.12).

TABLE 9.12. Payoffs for Common Odds for $2 and $3 Bets

Odds	Investment multiplier	Payoff for $2 Bet	Payoff for $3 Bet
1–3	1.33	$2.67	$4.00
1–2	1.50	$3.00	$4.50
2–3	1.67	$3.33	$5.00
3–4	1.75	$3.50	$5.25
1–1	2.00	$4.00	$6.00
6–5	2.20	$4.40	$6.60
3–2	2.50	$5.00	$7.50
8–5	2.60	$5.20	$7.80
9–5	2.80	$5.60	$8.40
2–1	3.00	$6.00	$9.00
5–2	3.50	$7.00	$10.50
3–1	4.00	$8.00	$12.00
7–2	4.50	$9.00	$13.50
4–1	5.00	$10.00	$15.00
9–2	5.50	$11.00	$16.50
5–1	6.00	$12.00	$18.00
7–1	8.00	$16.00	$24.00
10–1	11.00	$22.00	$33.00

All this data can easily get overwhelming; consequently, I recommend that you initially limit your attention to two or three combinations you have prescreened using other criteria. Then bet on the one that shows the best current odds. The trick is to bet as late as possible while still getting to the betting window in time. The art lies in gauging the length of the lines and the speed of the clerks.

Let the buyer beware, and good luck!

PROJECTS TO PONDER

Mathematical modeling is a subject best appreciated by doing. The trick is finding an interesting type of prediction to make or question to study, and then identifying sufficient data to build a reasonable model upon. Even if you are not a computer programmer, spread-sheet programs such as Microsoft Excel can provide an excellent environment in which to experiment with mathematical models.

In this section, I pose several interesting questions to which the modeling techniques presented in this book may be applicable. To provide starting points, I include links to existing studies and data sets on the WWW. Web links are extremely perishable, so treat these only as an introduction. Any good search engine like www.google.com should help you find better sources after a few minutes' toil. Happy modeling!

Gambling

■ *Lottery numbers* – How random are lottery numbers? Do certain numbers in certain states come up more often than would be expected by chance? Can you predict which lotto combinations are typically underbet, meaning that they minimize the likelihood that you must share the pot with someone else if you win?. How large must pool size grow in a given progressive lottery to yield a positive expected value for each ticket bought?

Plenty of lottery records are available on the WWW if you look hard enough. Log on to http://www.lottonet.com/ for several year's historical data from several state lotteries. Minnesota does a particularly good job, making its historical numbers available at http://www.lottery.state.mn.us.

■ *Horse racing* – Many of the ideas employed in our jai alai system are directly applicable to horse racing. How can you take a horse's record and compute a measure of how fast it will run on a particular track in the given weather conditions? How will the other bettors price the respective horses in a race? Is there a betting strategy that will offer you positive returns?

The *Daily Racing Form*, available at http://racingform.com, has the schedules and results for every track in the country. Schedules and results from New York tracks, including Aqueduct and Belmont Park, are available from http://www.nyra.com/.

■ *Blackjack* – Write a Monte Carlo simulation of a card-counting strategy in Blackjack. Thorp's book is the granddaddy of all such schemes, but dozens of other strategies are available in books or on the WWW. Which one is best? For each strategy, what are the expected winnings per hand as a function of the number of decks employed by the casino?

Develop and simulate card-counting strategies for other card games such as gin rummy or poker variations in which cards are publicly discarded. What impact does memorizing the discards have on your ability to predict the odds of getting the card that you want?

■ *Bidding strategies on Ebay* – Ebay (www.ebay.com) is an Internet phenomenon, a giant on-line auction house that lets just about anybody auction just about anything (it draws the line at organs and other body parts). Successful bidding requires considerable strategy. When do you raise a bid, and by how much?

Ebay is an excellent resource to study auction strategies because the bidding history is available, giving the name, bid amount, and time for each bid on every completed auction. How often does making a big presumptive bid knock everyone else out of the game? Does it pay to be the first one to make a bid? Are the rules different for expensive and inexpensive items? How much variance in bids is there, among different auctions, for exactly the same item?

Sports and Games

■ *Baseball* – Can you define a single ranking function that accurately assigns value to hitters, pitchers, or both on the basis of their statistics, ranking them from best to worst? Can you predict, on the basis of statistics, whether a player will be elected to the Hall of Fame? Can you find the best batting order for a given team or the ordering of its hitters that maximizes the expected number of runs the team scores? How does this total compare with the worst possible order?

Batting averages give many children their first inkling of the power of mathematics. Complete team-by-team baseball statistics can be found at http://www.baseball-reference.com. Check http://www.usatoday.com/sports/baseball/sbstats.htm for player statistics since 1992.

■ *Football* – Can you write an improved Clyde-like program for predicting the outcome of football games? What fraction of the games can you pick correctly, and how do you do against the spread? Are college football games easier or harder to predict than professional games?

Last season's NFL statistics are available at http://www.sporting-news.com/nfl/statistics/. The official NFL site is www.nfl.com. Complete college football records are harder to find, but http://www.washingtonpost.com/ offers standings for all teams at all levels of play.

■ *Basketball* – Being a game of individual player matchups and discrete shot attempts, basketball lends itself to Monte Carlo simulation in addition to Clyde-type prediction programs. Can you write a good basketball simulation?

What about predicting the outcome of the NCAA college basketball tournament, by assigning a probability of who wins each game based on statistics and rerunning the entire tourney many times?

Last season's NBA statistics are available at http://www.sporting-news.com/nba/statistics/. The official NBA site is www.nba.com. Complete college basketball records are available from http://www.washingtonpost.com/.

■ *Board games* – Many interesting board games are controlled by dice, implying that an accurate knowledge of the probabilities of certain events is essential for optimal play. Monte Carlo simulations can be used to gain insight into these events.

Take Monopoly as an example. Which properties are worth the most? This is a function of how often people land there as well as what the rents and costs are. Such probabilities can easily be studied by simulation. The results of one such study appear at http://www. tkcs-collins.com/truman/monopoly/monopoly.shtml

What about the simpler board game of Chutes and Ladders or the card game War? What is the expected number of rolls or turns you will be committed to when your 5-year old nephew demands just one more game?

People Prediction

■ *Election Prediction* – Mathematical models abound in politics. And the results matter – just ask Al Gore. Incorrect television projections based on partial returns and exit polls may well have cost him the U.S. presidential election in 2000.

Properly interpreting the results of a scientific poll involves serious statistical analysis to remove polling biases. For example, telephone polls will oversample retired and unemployed people because they are more likely to be there to pick up the phone.

A famous model to predict the outcome of U.S. presidential elections was "As Maine goes, so goes the nation." This became "As Maine goes, so goes Vermont" after the 1936 election, when those two New England states accounted for all of Alf Landon's 8 electoral votes against Franklin Roosevelt. Developing a more accurate predictor is an interesting project. Check out Fair's economic model http://fairmodel.econ.yale.edu/, which has missed only two presidential elections between 1916 and 1992. This site also contains information on economic models to predict the stock market and other things.

■ *Distribution of first names* – First names fall in and out of fashion owing to the strange combination of forces affecting popular culture. Steven was the 10th most popular boy's name in 1961, but we dropped to 47th by 1999. Jacob was the 35th most popular boy's name in the 1980s, but was on top by 1999. Can you predict the 10 most popular boy's and girl's first names for next year using previous years statistics? Extensive data on the popularity of yesteryear's names are available from the Social Security Administration WWW site, at http://www.ssa.gov/OACT/NOTES/note139/note139.html.

■ *Distribution of last names* – Traditionally, children are given the last name of the father. Last names can and do become extinct when families do not produce sufficient numbers of male heirs. The Skiena line in the United States, which started with my grandfather Sol Skiena in 1911, has expanded to 19 as of this writing. But our ultimate survival cannot be guaranteed.

What is the expected number of generations until a last name with n people out of a population of m becomes extinct? How should the number of distinct last names in a population decrease as a function of time? Similar issues arise in biodiversity studies with respect to animal species. What explains the nonuniform popularity of certain last names? Is it a phenomenon due largely to chance, or is it due to other factors such as immigration?

The U.S. Census Bureau posts the frequencies of the 88,800 most popular last names, according to the 1990 census, at http://www.census.gov/genealogy/names/. These account for only 90.483% of the population, and the Skienas are nowhere to be found. From this data, can you estimate how many distinct last names there are in the United States?

Financial Modeling

■ *Stock market investing* – Predicting the stock market is without question the most financially rewarding mathematical modeling opportunity. There is no shortage of people who have studied the question, and plenty of people believe that stock prices are a random walk and inherently unpredictable. But that shouldn't stop you from hunting for market inefficiencies by evaluating different investment strategies.

Although there is a plethora of sites that will tell you today's closing prices, it is surprisingly difficult to find good historical stock data on the WWW in a format suitable for downloading. Long-term daily price data on selected stocks are available from R & C Research at www.grainmarketresearch.com. One year's worth of historical stock market data is available from http://biz.swcp.com/stocks/.

■ *Economic forecasting* – There is much more to modeling the economy than stock prices. How are interest rates tied to the dollar against foreign currencies? The U.S. Federal Reserve (http://www.federalreserve.gov/releases/) provides extensive historical economic data, including well over 10 years of international exchange and interest rates.

Scientific Forecasting

■ *Weather prediction* – Predicting tomorrow's weather today is one of the most important and challenging problems in mathematical modeling. Today's weather prediction codes are extremely sophisticated, so don't expect to be able to beat the TV weatherman. But it is interesting and healthy to see how well or badly simple predictors can do, just from knowing what the weather was like for the past few days.

The National Climatic Data Center (NCDC) of the National Oceanic and Atmospheric Administration (NOAA) http://www.ncdc.noaa.gov/ has a variety of weather data sets and makes a good starting point. Historical weather data is available from climates as disparate as Los Angeles (http://www.losangelesalmanac.com/topics/Weather) and Omaha (http://www.crh.noaa.gov/oax).

The *Old Farmer's Almanac* boldly makes weather predictions a full year in advance and puts them on-line at http://www.almanac.com/. Compare their predictions with current and historical weather data to see how well they do!

■ *Population demographics* – What will the population of the world be in 2050? An accurate answer depends largely upon predicting two different issues: human life expectancy and human fertility rates.

The U.S. Census Bureau maintains a world population clock projection service at http://www.census.gov/cgi-bin/ipc/popclockw, which reports that there are exactly 6,083,935,136 potential buyers for this book at the moment I am writing this. This site explains their model and points to on-line sources of demographic information. The details of your model can have huge impacts on the size of your predicted population. The Census Bureau and the United Nations differed by more than 3 months as to the date when the human population first crossed the 6 billion mark. The two counts differed by roughly 18 million people. Projecting such disparities forward for 50 years can lead to vastly different conclusions.

GLOSSARY

Basques   The ethnic group from the Pyrenees Mountains that invented jai alai.

causal relationship   Two events A and B such that event A actually triggers B as opposed to their merely occurring simultaneously.

cesta   The reed basket jai alai players use to catch and throw the ball.

computer simulation   Replicating the behavior of an aspect of the physical world through the execution of a computer program.

correlation   Two events A and B that tend to occur in synchrony with each other and that may or may not imply a causal relationship.

correlation coefficient   A measure (from -1 to 1) of the extent to which two events tend to occur in synchrony with each other.

curve fitting   The art of best matching a standard mathematical shape to a given numerical data set.

efficiency of markets   The extent to which information on prices is fairly distributed to all potential customers.

expected value   The mean or average of a given set of numbers; a measure of the most likely value of a sampled function.

fronton   A stadium specially constructed to hold jai alai matches.

gambling systems   Betting strategies designed (usually unsuccessfully) to ensure positive returns in a specific game of chance.

jai alai   A Basque variation on the sport of handball in which players alternate throwing and catching a goatskin ball (pelota) with a reed basket (cesta). It is legal to bet on jai alai in Connecticut, Florida, and Rhode Island.

martingale system   A gambling system in which losing wagers are repeatedly doubled to ensure a positive return, given an infinite bankroll and unrestricted betting limits. An excellent way to go broke in the absence of such assumptions.

mathematical model   A formula or algorithm to obtain additional insights from observations of the physical world.

Monte Carlo analysis   A computer simulation technique using repeated runs and random numbers to model a complex system.

overfitting   The danger, inherent to all mathematical models, of simulating the training data so faithfully as to model the real world unreliably.

pari-mutuel wagering   The method of setting payoffs employed in horse racing and jai alai that dispenses with a central odds maker in favor of dividing the betting pool among the holders of winning tickets.

parsing   The computer science term for interpreting the gross structure of a given input file; it is necessary for any further processing.

pelota   The hard rubber, goatskin-covered ball used in jai alai matches.

Pepe's Green Card   A tout sheet purporting to predict the winners of a given collection of jai alai matches.

Perl   A computer programming language well suited to parsing and other essential housekeeping tasks.

post positions   The order of play for all jai alai players involved in a given match; an order critical to predicting the outcome of a match under the Spectacular Seven scoring system.

probability   The branch of mathematics devoted to calculating the likelihood of events given a well-defined set of assumptions; a number from 0 to 1 measuring the likelihood of a given event.

regression analysis   A mathematical technique for determining the best curve (usually a straight line) matching a given collection of data.

Spectacular Seven   The scoring system employed in professional jai alai matches in the United States that imposes inherent biases on the probability of the possible outcomes.

statistics   The branch of mathematics devoted to analyzing the significance of real-world data, often with an eye towards defining or improving a given mathematical model.

trifecta   The pari-mutuel wager that requires correctly identifying the top three performers of a given match in the right order of finish.

Worldwide Web   A distributed collection of text and data files located on computers all over the world that is made accessible through a system of links, indices, and addresses; an amazing resource for most anything you can think of, including jai alai.

FOR FURTHER READING

BOOKS ON JAI ALAI

1. E. Blazy. *La Pelote Basque.* Librairie Pailloux, Bayonne, France, 1929.
2. K. H. Herrington. *Jai Alai: The First Inside Look at America's Newest Sports Craze.* WICC Books, 1977.
3. Z. Hollander and D. Schultz. *The Jai Alai Handbook.* Pinnacle Books, Los Angeles, 1978.
4. W. R. Keevers. *The Gambling Times Guide to Jai Alai.* Gambling Times, Hollywood, 1984.
5. M. C. Leal. *El Juego de Pelota: The Ball Game.* Museo Nacional de Anthropologica, Mexico, 1973.
6. D. Lostritto. *Jai Alai Wagering to Win: The Complete Book for Jai Alai Wagering.* Fair Haven Press, Fair Haven, CT, 1985.
7. The President. *How to Win at Jai-Alai.* President Books, Los Angeles, 1964.
8. R. Taylor. *Jai Alai.* Doubleday, New York, NY, 1987.
9. Carmelo Urza, editor. *Historia de la Pelota Vasca en Las Americas.* University of Nevada Press, Reno, 1994.

ARTICLES ON JAI ALAI

1. Milford jai-alai – festive building for the merry festival. *Architectural Record,* 163–4:119–124, 1978.

2. P. Axthelm. The $500,000 sure thing: Pick 6 bet at jai-alai fronton. *Newsweek*, 101, March 21, 1983.
3. A. Balfour. The longest strike in U.S. professional sports history: Jai alai – part I (?). *Labor Law Journal*, 41:394–409, July 1990.
4. J. Charnes and H. Gitlow. Using control charts to corroborate bribery in jai alai. *American Statistician*, 49:386–389, November 1995.
5. M. J. Goodfriend and J. H. Friedman. Monte Carlo analysis of jai-alai. Presented at the Fall Joint National Meeting of the Operations Research Society of America and the Institute of Management Science, 1975.
6. B. Grofman and N. Noviello. Jai-alai outcomes as a function of player position and skill level. *Simulation and Games*, 16:211–223, June 1985.
7. L. Moser. A mathematical analysis of the game of jai alai. *American Mathematical Monthly*, 89:292–300, 1982.
8. S. Skiena. A fairer scoring system for jai-alai. *Interfaces*, 18–6:35–41, November/December 1988.

MATHEMATICS, MODELING, AND DATA ANALYSIS

1. F. Brooks. *The Mythical Man-Month: Essays on Software Engineering*. Addison–Wesley, Reading, MA, 1975.
2. D. E. Knuth. *The Art of Computer Programming, Volume 2: Seminumerical Algorithms*. Addison–Wesley, Reading, MA, second edition, 1981.
3. F. Roberts. *Discrete Mathematical Models*. Prentice–Hall, Englewood Cliffs, NJ, 1976.
4. L. Steen, editor. *For All Practical Purposes*. W. H. Freeman, New York, NY, 1993.
5. E. Tufte. *The Visual Display of Quantitative Information*. Graphics Press, Cheshire, CT, 1983.
6. S. Wagon. *Mathematica in Action*. W. H. Freeman, New York, 1991.
7. W. Weaver. *Lady Luck*. Dover Publications, Mineola, NY, 1982.

SPORTS, GAMBLING, AND PREDICTION

1. R. M. Adams. Momentum in the performance of professional pocket billiards players. *International Journal of Sport Psychology*, 26:580–587, 1996.
2. P. Asch and R. E. Quandt. *Racetrack Betting: The Professors' Guide to Strategies*. Auburn House Publishing, Dover, MA, 1986.
3. T. Bass. *The Eudaemonic Pie*. Houghton Mifflin Company, Boston, 1985.
4. T. Bass. *The Predictors*. Henry Holt and Company, New York, 1999.
5. M. Drosnin. *The Bible Codes*. Simon and Schuster, New York, 1997.
6. B. Freeman, B. Freeman, and J. McKinley. *Wanta Bet? A Study of the*

Pari-Mutuels System in the United States. Freeman Mutuels Management, USA, 1982.

7. D. L. Gilden and S. G. Wilson. Streaks in skilled performance. *Psychonomic Bulletin and Review,* 21:260–265, 1995.

8. T. Gilovich, R. Vallone, and A. Tversky. The hot hand in basketball: On the misperception of random sequences. *Cognitive Psychology,* 17:295–314, 1985.

9. B. James. *The Bill James Historical Baseball Abstract.* Willard Books, New York, 1988.

10. B. Malkiel. *A Random Walk Down Wall Street.* W. W. Norton, New York, 1999.

11. B. D. McKay, D. Bar-Natan, M. Bar-Hillel, and G. Kalai, Solving the Bible code puzzle, *Statistical Science,* 14:150–173, May 1999. Also: http://cs.anu.edu.au/~bdm/dilugim/torah.html.

12. E. Thorp. *Beat the Dealer: A Winning Strategy for the Game of Twenty-One.* Random House, NY, 1966.

INDEX